Data Strategies
to Uncover and Eliminate
Hidden Inequities

This book is dedicated to all the current and future educators and other adults whose mission and work lead them to make schools places where all young people, regardless of background, can learn the knowledge and skills necessary to have limitless opportunities in the twenty-first century. We hope this book will assist them to use data to open eyes; reveal blind spots; give guidance; stimulate dialogue and reflection; challenge inequitable systems; alter policies and practices; and not remain silent in the face of wrongs done to young people.

Data Strategies
to Uncover and Eliminate
Hidden Inequities

Ruth S. Johnson
Robin Avelar La Salle

CORWIN
A SAGE Company

For information:

Corwin
A SAGE Company
2455 Teller Road
Thousand Oaks, California 91320
(800) 233-9936
Fax: (800) 417-2466
www.corwinpress.com

SAGE Ltd.
1 Oliver's Yard
55 City Road
London EC1Y 1SP
United Kingdom

SAGE Pvt. Ltd.
B 1/I 1 Mohan Cooperative
   Industrial Area
Mathura Road, New Delhi 110 044
India

SAGE Asia-Pacific Pte. Ltd.
33 Pekin Street #02-01
Far East Square
Singapore 048763

Printed in the United States of America

Library of Congress Cataloging-in-Publication Data

Johnson, Ruth S.
Data strategies to uncover and eliminate hidden inequities: the wallpaper effect / Ruth S. Johnson, Robin Avelar La Salle.
        p. cm.
Includes bibliographical references and index.
ISBN 978-1-4129-1493-2 (pbk.)

   1. Educational evaluation—Data processing. 2. Educational equalization. 3. School improvement programs. I. La Salle, Robin Avelar. II. Title.

LB2822.75.J64 2010
379.2'60285—dc22   2010014059

This book is printed on acid-free paper.

10   11   12   13   14   10   9   8   7   6   5   4   3   2   1

Acquisitions Editor:	Dan Alpert
Associate Editor:	Megan Bedell
Editorial Assistant:	Sarah Bartlett
Production Editor:	Veronica Stapleton
Copy Editor:	Nancy Conger
Typesetter:	C&M Digitals (P) Ltd.
Proofreader:	Gretchen Treadwell
Indexer:	Sheila Bodell
Cover Designer:	Michael Dubowe

Contents

Additional materials and resources related to *Data Strategies to Uncover and Eliminate Hidden Inequities* can be found at www.corwin.com/wallpapereffect

Acknowledgments

We deeply appreciate the many colleagues, family, and friends who inspired us and contributed their comments during the writing of this book. Much of the text evolved from our opportunities to engage with those who have a passion to educate children who have been historically underserved in our schools.

We thank our Corwin editors Rachel Livsey and Dan Alpert. Rachel was the initial editor who embraced the concept of exploring other data and the link to equity. After her departure from Corwin, Dan Alpert provided us with the needed guidance and unwavering support to make this book a reality. We deeply appreciate his patience, constant encouragement, and his belief in the importance of our work. Sarah Bartlett, Dan's editorial assistant, provided guidance on a myriad of items connected with publication.

During the writing of the manuscript, many contributed comments and ideas and we give them our heartfelt thanks. We thank Shan Boggs, Tonia Bush, Denise Collier, Jennifer Frentress, and Diane Treadway for taking time to listen to our ideas for the manuscript and for their thoughtful contributions. Laura Flenoury and Brandon Smith assisted with locating pertinent research and creating many of the tables and charts. Glenn Payne assisted with graphics and Helen Quon helped when we had formatting problems. Martha Avelar made major contributions, and her insights and on-the-ground knowledge from inside schools was invaluable. Many examples in this book are from her experiences as a parent, teacher, assistant principal, and principal. Her input on Chapters 4 and 5 (special education and English learners) was especially appreciated. We deeply appreciate Shawn Johnson-Witt, who spent many hours reading the text and providing us with valuable ideas and insights on how to improve it. We are thankful for the insights shared by Goldie Buchanan related to her work with parent and community involvement. Many of the charts and graphs and examples came from the real world of our work in schools and districts. We especially thank the PRINCIPAL's Exchange for the contribution of many tables and charts.

RUTH'S SPECIAL ACKNOWLEDGEMENTS

My loved ones—family and friends—have been neglected as we dedicated time to bringing this book to life. I thank them for their patience and understanding. Special acknowledgements go to my daughters Catherine and Shawn and my grandchildren Glenn and Lil Shawn. They have given me many insights on a personal level about their schooling journeys and have been the inspiration for much of my writing.

I thank all of those who have used my book *Using Data to Close the Achievement Gap*. As a result of this publication, I have traveled nationally and had the opportunity to meet and work with hundreds of hard-working educators who are passionate about making a difference in the lives of children. I have learned much from them, and they are a source of hope and inspiration. Many have contacted me by phone and e-mail about how the book has helped them in their work. They have been very encouraging and are very excited about this new book. I deeply appreciate their continuing support of my work.

Finally, I thank Robin for joining me in this venture. She has expanded my horizons. The partnership exceeded my expectations about what was possible in our collaborative writing journey. Her intellect, insights, intuitiveness, and pragmatism resulted in rich contributions to the document. It was a truly wonderful experience.

ROBIN'S SPECIAL ACKNOWLEDGEMENTS

My family is always my greatest source of strength, encouragement, and learning. Since our early days at Stanford, my husband, David, has been my rock. He is an expert in computers, integrated technology, marriage, and parenting—an invaluable skill set for a life partner of twenty-five years. Without even a hint of complaint, David accepts whatever responsibilities I cannot fulfill at home—most recently so that I could join Ruth in our quest to ensure that other people's children have the same educational opportunities that our own children had. Thank you, mi amor. To my children, Coco, Tati, Bobby, and David—thanks to each of you for challenging everything I thought I knew about education by being your unique, amazing selves. Seeing learning and schooling through your eyes has opened my mind and heart to a world I would never otherwise have known. Every aspect of my work is affected by the lessons you teach me every day. I love you, babies.

My sister, Martha Avelar, a consummate educator in her own right, has been my best friend, my cheerleader, and my spirit, our entire lives Also, thank you Sofi, Nini, and Leila, for understanding when I could not meet for our traditional Sunday morning family breakfasts because I had to write. Just know that sometimes, *tía* was writing about you too! Prima Idalia is not only my cousin, but also my mentor. Thank you for your wisdom and counsel during life events that occurred through the writing of this book. Finally, though they are here only in my heart and memory now, thank you mom and daddy. Linda and Robert Avelar, both educators, were my first and best teachers. From them I learned that the best antidote to poverty is a good education. Be assured—my sister and I have the baton now and we are in the race to help other families experience the transformation that ours did as a result of a good education. We are working to make you proud.

Estella Ramirez, cofounder and executive director of PRINCIPAL's Exchange, has partnered with me for almost two decades in our joint quest for educational excellence for all students. She is the driving force behind the work of PRINCIPAL's Exchange in the hundreds of struggling schools and districts we have supported for the past thirteen years. She is our Charlie of "Charlie's Angels," quietly directing us and ensuring that we stay focused on our mission to change the world, one school and district at a time. To Estella and all our amazing associates, thank you for courageously and adeptly facilitating profound changes in schools and districts every day, and also for continuously informing and improving our work by bringing back the lessons you learn from the field. I am proud to be affiliated with each of you.

Ricardo Stanton-Salazar, your expertise in social networking theory and its application to Latino students was invaluable. More than that, your willingness to share your scholarship as well as your passion for historically underperforming students fortified my foundation at key points in the process.

To Professor Bob Calfee: From the day you accepted me into the doctoral program at Stanford over two decades ago, until today, I am and always will be proud to be your student. Thank you for your support on this and every other major academic endeavor throughout my career.

Many, many thanks to the hundreds of school and district administrators and teachers who over the years have opened themselves up to true partnerships with us on behalf of students in their charge. Your struggles have become our best lessons, and your successes, our greatest joy. Keep the faith.

Finally, Ruth Johnson: Thank you for giving me the opportunity to share this unbelievable experience with you. Together, we have laughed, cried, stomped, and danced. You are a rare and wonderful educator who has devoted a lifetime to promoting equity in schools, even before it was popular. Your have influenced the thinking of the thousands of educators across the country who have heard you speak, attended your professional development sessions, or used the lessons from your book, *Using Data to Close the Achievement Gap: How to Measure Equity in Our Schools*. You have influenced me by serving as a model of unwavering commitment to the cause of educational equity, while always radiating hope and grace. Thank you for everything, dear friend.

PUBLISHER'S ACKNOWLEDGMENTS

Corwin gratefully acknowledges the contributions of the following reviewers:

Gary Anderson, Professor, Steinhardt School of Culture, Education and
    Human Development
New York University
NY

Tonia Causey-Bush, Director of Research, Evaluation, and Elementary
    Assessments
Rialto Unified School District
Rialto, CA

Reyna Corral, Categorical Coordinator
Los Angeles Unified School District
Commerce, CA

John L. Hosp, Assistant Professor and Research Faculty
Florida State University/Florida Center for Reading Research
Tallahassee, FL

Vinetta C. Jones, Professor, Secondary Education Program Coordinator
Howard University
Mitchelville, MD

Scott McLeod, Assistant Professor
University of Minnesota
Minneapolis, MN

About the Authors

Ruth S. Johnson is a professor emeritus at California State University, Los Angeles. She has served in a variety of educational settings in New Jersey and California. Ruth received her EdD in 1985 from Rutgers, The State University of New Jersey. Her dissertation was titled *An Exploratory Study of Academic Labeling, Student Achievement and Student Ethnographic Characteristics.* At the K–12 level, she served as a classroom teacher, an instructional consultant, a director of elementary education, an analyst, an assistant superintendent of schools in the areas of curriculum and business, and superintendent of schools. She initiated efforts that resulted in raising academic standards and student achievement in low-performing school districts. She served as an education consultant for the New Jersey Department of Education and as a director for two nonprofit organizations in California that focused on raising student achievement in underserved student populations. Her major scholarly interests and publications focus on processes related to changing the academic culture of urban schools, with an emphasis on access and equity. In addition to her four published books, she has written numerous book chapters, articles, editorials, research reports, and manuscript reviews. As a recognized speaker, she has presented nationally to scholarly and professional audiences and serves as a consultant to schools and districts.

Robin Avelar La Salle grew up in Echo Park, near downtown Los Angeles. Avelar La Salle holds a PhD in education from Stanford University, with emphasis on language, literacy, and culture. She taught elementary, middle, high school, and university students in Southern and Northern California. Avelar La Salle spent years as the administrator for curriculum, staff development, and assessment at a school district outside of Los Angeles. She has held numerous positions in research and consulting focused on advancing academic success for historically underperforming students. Currently, Avelar La Salle is cofounder and chief program officer for PRINCIPAL's Exchange, a California state-approved external evaluation firm dedicated to improving schools and districts serving high-poverty, high-minority communities.

Introduction

*D*ata Strategies to Uncover and Eliminate Hidden Inequities: The Wallpaper Effect* is an outgrowth of Ruth's book *Using Data to Close the Achievement Gap* (2002). Shortly after its publication in 2002, Rachel Livsey, a former acquisition editor for Corwin, asked Ruth to explore the possibility of expanding on some of the book's topics to create another book. This proposed book would offer deeper treatment of how to expand data use in schools and districts. These data would be of the type that would allow educators to go beyond test scores to delve into more complex issues related to equity and outcomes. Ruth agreed to write another book and invited Robin Avelar La Salle to become a second author for this new endeavor. Robin was a natural choice, based on her extensive and successful work in skillfully using data to create models for equitable achievement in underperforming schools, through PRINCIPAL's Exchange, an organization she cofounded with Estella Ramirez and David La Salle.

Our national work in K–12 schools and districts, higher education, and other educational venues influenced our approach to writing. The intent of this book is to demonstrate ways for schools and districts to realize the possibilities for changing the status quo and to propel action. We know that schools and districts can significantly impact inequitable practices. And we shed light on the positive and negative long-term life consequences that are connected to levels of educational attainment. These consequences are both economic and social. Research shows that lower levels of educational attainment are linked to substantially lower lifetime earnings, quality of life, and possibilities for spending time in the criminal justice system. The groups that are currently underperforming in our nation's schools are African Americans, Latinos, Native Americans, English learners (EL) those receiving special education services, and low-income students. As educators, we believe that it is imperative to address the current schooling disparities that these groups are experiencing and whenever possible engage in the coordination of those efforts with community and social sectors.

THE WALLPAPER EFFECT AND THE OTHER DATA

Data Strategies to Uncover and Eliminate Hidden Inequities: The Wallpaper Effect presents more and different types of performance indicators than those required by No Child Left Behind (NCLB). For example, we explore non-academic issues such as an analysis of the use of existing time, disciplinary practices, and the connection to academics and equity. Equity issues in areas such as special education placement, gifted and talented, and achievement of English learners are examples of topics that receive closer attention. We present the types of data that will offer a larger window into these areas that are seldom considered in conversations about achievement.

After building a context for this work in the first chapter, each subsequent chapter presents issues that are fertile ground for exercising "equity muscle." Data stories, cases, and background literature are used to explain aspects of an achievement condition. The research is used to guide and inform the types of indicators that influence school achievement. For instance, we discuss indicators as early as elementary school that have been linked to high school outcomes. Too often, this type of information remains in research, policy, and higher education circles and does not penetrate the places where teachers and principals work. If they do have the information, the implications for practice are rarely discussed in meaningful ways.

We demonstrate not only what "other data" need to be uncovered but how to peel off the layers of "wallpaper" to uncover fundamental inequities that perpetuate poor performance. Once those systemic inequities are uncovered, we discuss some appropriate strategies and policies that need to be changed or created in order to transform current conditions. We acknowledge societal conditions but reject them as the sole reason for the failure of some students. We focus on those areas that are under school, central administration, and board of education control.

By using actual school cases, we analyze commonly misinterpreted school issues, and apply the strategic use of *other data* to challenge inequities that have been accepted as normal patterns of achievement. Throughout the text we use the voices of students and others to tell the stories from their on-the-ground perspective. A feature of this book includes exercises and activities for data teams and other student advocates to use as they look at their schools or districts. We provide an extensive list of resources to support follow-up efforts. An active website for those who purchase this book provides access to activities, templates, resources, and more.

ORGANIZATION OF THE BOOK

Chapters 1 and 2 (Part I) provide the equity framework that is applied to specific populations (African Americans, Latinos, Native Americans, English learners, those receiving special education services, and low-income students) and issues throughout the book. Chapter 1, "The Wallpaper Effect: Uncovering Inequities Using the Other Data," orients readers to the national equity picture. The chapter introduces the recurring metaphor that is used throughout the book: the "wallpaper effect." The *wallpaper effect* is the process of peeling off layers of data to reveal hidden inequities. Chapter 2, "Peeling the Wallpaper: Uncovering Inequities," opens with a discussion and definitions about the achievement gap. Traditional outcome data sets are presented and interpreted as they most commonly are in schools today. We present the need for deeper-level data to surface the gaps. Real-world applications of how this can happen in a school and district are presented.

Chapters 3–7 (Part II) highlight issues that are fertile ground for exercising *equity muscle*. The chapters provide a framework for each topic and review literature sources. Each chapter integrates the literature with actual school and district examples as a way of exploring first-level understandings most commonly discussed, and then the "true stories" that emerge from strategic analysis of *other data.*

In Chapter 3, "The Journey Through School: Starting With the End in Mind," our focus is on looking at end of K–12 school outcomes—graduation, dropping out, and university readiness—and the indicators that are associated with the student's journey through school. We present information on the devastating losses to society when options for students are limited and make the case for why data should be more accurately and longitudinally collected.

Chapter 4, "Special Education and Gifted and Talented," and Chapter 5, "English Learners," highlight data complexities related to three major student populations: students who receive special education services, students who are underrepresented in gifted and talented, and English learners. Discussions are presented around the need to peel back the data to look at how certain populations are disproportionately over- or underrepresented. We illustrate how some school practices may exacerbate inequities in these areas of schooling.

Chapter 6, "Nonacademic Indicators Associated With Achievement Outcomes," discusses those indicators that appear nonacademic, but, nevertheless, have an influence on academic achievement. Areas that are highlighted include use of time, discipline, student and teacher attendance, teacher and student mobility, and extracurricular activities.

Chapter 7, "Systemic Inequities: Structures, Policies, and Procedures," focuses on how structures and policies have the potential to influence positive or negative academic climates for students. Some structures may benefit some students to the detriment of others. Indicators related to policies and practices found to exacerbate inequities are highlighted.

Part III includes the concluding chapter. Chapter 8, "Increasing Equity Muscle," focuses on issues often uncomfortable to discuss and promotes the need for dialogue. The chapter offers some ways to approach these issues with a concentration on culturally responsive strategies. The chapter describes evidence in the literature and organizational resources that can assist those ready to create equitable schools and districts. Conclusions and implications for further actions are presented. The chapter concludes with a call for schools and districts to become relentless advocates for all students and to surface hidden inequities and eliminate them.

In the end, this is a storybook about conditions of achievement in our schools and how to apply strategies to reveal *other data* that uncover "the real story," and in doing so, lead schools and districts to greater achievement levels for all children. It would be impossible for us to address all of the conditions in schools and districts that may be creating inequitable outcomes. However, we hope our approach will provide some tools and an impetus to reverse current patterns of low achievement for certain groups. It is important for those who care about underperforming students, no matter what their background, to carefully analyze their own institutions for hidden data. It helps to have the disposition, will, and passion for changing inequitable practices and to have a commitment to do something about it, but no one needs to be excluded from making the journey to eliminate inequities. Our children deserve no less than our very best.

Part I

The Need
for the Other
Data

1 The Wallpaper Effect

Uncovering Inequities
Using the Other Data

SCENARIO: STUDENT COURT CASE TESTIMONY

I have just finished my sophomore year at City High School, and I am about to begin my junior year. The lack of textbooks and lack of textbooks in good condition is a serious problem in my school. It makes learning much more difficult than it should be. For example, we did not have any textbooks in my tenth grade U.S. History class. Not only did we not have textbooks to bring home, but we also did not have any textbooks in my classroom. Therefore, the teacher lectured all the time and put notes on the board at the front of the room. This was a real problem, because the teacher lectured very fast, and we did not have books to keep track of the information she was lecturing about. After five weeks without books, our teacher borrowed books from another class. However, we did not have enough to take home, so we could not do homework with them. Then, our teacher needed to return the books to the class from which she got them, and we again had no books. Finally, the teacher borrowed books from another class, but again we did not have enough to take home with us. It was a real problem that we were using this second set of borrowed books, because they were really old—maybe ten years old or older. Also, the tests we took were based on material that was not in the second set of borrowed books. Therefore, we had open-book tests, but the textbooks were useless because the subjects of the tests were not in the books we had. I could have done better on these tests if I had a book to take home and study from and if the books we used in class covered the material on the tests.

We read only one novel, The Lord of the Flies, in my English class this year. We did not read more because there were no other books for us to take home. The teacher had to bring in some of his own books to class and read to us in class because there were not enough books for us to have in class or to take home. The rest of the time we copied vocabulary words and watched a lot of movies. This does not seem fair. I also cannot learn as much as I should because my teachers sometimes come late to class. Usually this is because I have a substitute teacher who says that she could not find the classroom. About once every two weeks, one of my teachers or substitute teachers is up to fifteen minutes late to class. We are forced to stand outside of the classroom until the teacher comes.

The bathrooms are also in really bad shape. Students sometimes cannot flush the toilets because the plumbing is broken. It takes too long for the school to send someone to fix it. The school used to lock the bathrooms because they are in such bad condition. They have since opened up all of them, but I still cannot use them. This caused a big problem for me last year. Even if I have to go to the bathroom as soon as I get to school in the morning, I hold it in until the end of the day. This is the reason that I got a kidney infection. My doctor told me not being able to use the bathroom during the day was a cause of the infection. It was very painful, and it also then caused my back to hurt. I had to go to the hospital to get treated, which was expensive, and I missed almost a whole week of school because of it.

It is really hard to study when the school and the state do not seem concerned about my education. How do they expect us to get good grades when we do not have the equipment that the rich schools have? I care less if the school and the state care little about me. The conditions in the school make the school look really bad. It makes me want to go to another school. I want to go to a school that does not look so cheap and that looks like the school and the state really care about their students.

I want to be proud of my school. However I deserve a better education. I should have all the resources that students in richer school have. I deserve it.

High School Student
Unified School District
Williams v. State of California
Deposition Testimony, June 30, 2001

OVERVIEW

The student in the scenario represents thousands of pages of testimony that were submitted as part of *Eliezer Williams et al. v. State of California et al.*, filed as a class action lawsuit in 2000. Settled after four years of litigation, the basis of the lawsuit was that the state failed to provide public school students with equal access to instructional materials, safe and decent school facilities, and qualified teachers.

This chapter establishes the critical context and the need for digging deeper into data to uncover fundamental inequities that limit educational opportunity for many students. Our aim in this book is to provide readers with a framework for becoming clear about on-the-ground conditions in schools and districts that negatively affect academic success for millions of students. This book provides readers with specific tools for effectively peeling off the layers of complexity that anchor so many students in failure. We provide readers with effective strategies for mobilizing an offensive against plaguing inequities in schools. Ultimately, we hope to promote a collective disposition of intolerance for the normalization of academic failure for large groups of students. The student's words in the scenario echo the frustration of thousands of students from mostly poor neighborhoods and communities of color who can only imagine experiencing a quality education.

> Ultimately, we hope to promote a collective disposition of intolerance for the normalization of academic failure for large groups of students.

We begin this chapter by describing the five potential roles that data can play in schools and districts in promoting educational equity. Next, we discuss the national data context with a caveat about focusing only on high-stakes data when addressing underachievement in schools and districts. The chapter then provides a brief overview of current achievement patterns. Next we introduce our concept of the *wallpaper effect*, stressing the need for adeptly peeling off layers of data to uncover practices, programs, and policies that contribute to and exacerbate educational inequities. We emphasize the short- and long-term harm that comes to students when probing questions and other data sources are neglected or not properly used to improve student outcomes. Throughout this chapter and the entire book, we provide information that, in the end, should create a sense of urgency for us to rally around our children and create a better future for them and our nation.

KEY ROLES FOR DATA: TRADITIONAL AND OTHER DATA

This book's central focus is on the critical roles that data can play to expose information that can and should compel schools and districts to rectify fundamental equity issues for students. *Data* refers to information that can be used to describe conditions in schools and districts that affect students' school experiences in either positive or negative ways. For many, data implies test scores. However, even when disaggregated, the common uses of such data offer limited change power. In contrast, the *other data* we illustrate in this book, when used adeptly by educators working together in collegial groups, can help build *equity muscle.* These *other data* can uncover insightful information about the academic culture of a school (see Johnson, 2002; Johnson & Bush, 2005) and how students are faring in the system. These data give clues to what needs to change in the culture and practices of schools and districts (Johnson, 2002; Johnson & Bush, 2005; McKinsey & Company, 2009; Noguera & Wing, 2006).

We offer five major ways to use data to build *equity muscle.* These categories overlap and are not exhaustive of all of the possible ways to use data. However, they represent methods of using data to assertively advocate rich educational opportunity for all students.

Role 1. Getting Real: Telling the Whole Story

A driving question for every decision in every educational institution should be: Is this in the best interest of our students . . . *all* of them? "This" can be anything, including instructional practices, materials, schedules, district systems, school policies, common routines, decisions about personnel, budgets, or facilities. Schools, districts, and communities need to understand with crystal clarity what happens to diverse groups of students and determine whether inequities exist in their schooling. Rather than engaging in rhetoric about slow or fast students, caring or uncaring parents, capable or incapable teachers and administrators, well-grounded information can help pinpoint specific areas of concern in order to arrive at appropriate solutions and resource allocation. Careful analysis of data helps us dig deeper into our understanding of conditions affecting student success. Traditionally, high-stakes tests are the sole measures used to describe school improvement. High-stakes tests are those that have life-altering consequences, such as students not getting promoted or graduating. Schools with high testing results get positive public attention. Schools that score poorly may be candidates for drastic sanctions such as school reconstitution or takeovers. If high-stakes tests scores go up, schools are deemed improved. In many low-performing schools, a seesaw effect occurs with scores going up one year and down the next. Regardless, annual test scores typically offer minimal clues about whether a school has changed its normative culture so that higher achievement for all children becomes institutionalized.

> Schools, districts, and communities need to understand with crystal clarity what happens to diverse groups of students and determine whether inequities exist in their schooling.

Data can play a powerful role when indicators of school improvement are connected to short- and long-term higher-learning outcomes for all students. In schools engaged in real change—by, for example, guaranteeing access to higher-level curriculum for all students—educators document and respond to baseline information and incremental progress checks. Similarly, if teachers encourage students to develop higher-order thinking skills, administrators should document progress on how this is implemented in classrooms, along with the impact on student achievement. Educators often describe changes or perceived changes in processes and practices as evidence of school improvement. Yet, a true picture of school or district conditions requires the analyses of multiple data points, from various sources, specifically inquiring about and answering student-related issues.

Example: A working team of high school teachers, administrators, and counselors wanted to find out about the college-going rates of different groups in their school. They suspected that the rate was low for African Americans and Latinos. The principal observed that while doing classroom walkthroughs, he could identify the levels of classes by the ethnic and racial makeup of the students, even without consulting official course lists. The principal and school team had many hunches; however, they had not systematically studied the issue. They generated a list of questions, including the following:

- What is the ethnic/racial/language proficiency composition of courses, by level (remedial, advanced)?
- What is the college-readiness rate of seniors, by subgroup?
- How many students take college-entrance exams (PSAT, SAT, ACT) and Advanced Placement courses, by subgroup?
- How are placement procedures made? Who is involved? What role do parents and students play in the final placements?

The team identified indicators, collected and then reviewed the data on course enrollments and college-going rates, and disaggregated the data by student groups. The analysis revealed an alarming gap in college-going rates by race/ethnicity, language groups, and gender. They also collected data from middle school feeders demonstrating the same patterns. Few African American, Latino, and English learners (EL) took algebra.

Peeling back further, the group also examined the roles of the administrators, counselors, and teachers and how their policies and practices influenced students' aspirations, placements, and outcomes. Results from student and parent surveys combined with achievement indicators provided startling information. These data jolted the perceived reality of the teachers, counselors, and administrative leadership teams. They also studied the literature and visited schools to learn about others' successes in educating African American, Latino, English learners, and low-income students. They needed to grasp what was possible.

The inquiries led to uncovering institutional biases in policies and everyday conditions such as sorting students into leveled classes and misperceptions about students' college-going aspirations. The team also found that many students and parents were not informed or were misinformed about educational opportunities. Many team members were troubled about what the data exposed. As a result, the school leadership and many teachers and counselors took ownership of the data and worked in collegial teams to transform practices. Counselors stepped up efforts to increase numbers of African American, Latino, English learners, female, and low-income students taking college preparatory courses. Administrators used baseline indicators and progress indicators to closely monitor implementation and results. Teachers received training on how to teach more rigorous courses to historically underachieving groups of students. Parents received information about the options and opportunities for their children. Practices and expectations changed. The school offered fewer remedial courses and eventually eliminated them altogether. Over a three-year span, enrollments in college preparatory classes dramatically increased, as did college acceptance rates for all students. Counselors and teachers received time and support to learn to work in different ways. They kept their baseline data and continued to use data indicators to track student progress. This courageous team used data to uncover a hidden story at their school and did something about it.

Role 2. Examining Institutional Heart

Data can help expose how certain educational practices reflect our institutional belief systems. Because historical legacies and practices create institutional norms, many educators do not regularly engage in self-reflection about personal beliefs or their assumptions about student potential and ability. Skillful use of data can stimulate personal and systemic examination in ways that completely alter the type and quality of opportunities provided to students. Devoting time to highlight and do something about institutional biases must take place on an unremitting basis with all of those involved in the educational enterprise.

Example: Many schools believe that they place students in high- or low-level courses based on academic merit. Schools often cite test scores or grades as placement criteria. However, upon reviewing test scores and course placement by race, ethnicity, or language proficiency, we often

> Devoting time to highlight and do something about institutional biases must take place on an unremitting basis with all of those involved in the educational enterprise.

find student placement based on assumptions about their abilities. Not uncommonly, African American and Latino students who score in the top quartiles on standardized tests are not programmed into higher-level courses at the same rate as comparably scoring Asian and White students. Confronted with this information, educators must reflect on why they made those decisions that so dramatically affect students' lives. Similarly, data comparing disproportionality of who gets placed in gifted courses versus special education or low-level courses show conclusively how access to knowledge is unequally rationed on a daily basis. Such patterns frequently misplace and lock students into inappropriate programs for their entire academic careers, thereby squandering talent, which can result in long-lasting negative consequences. In subsequent chapters we present ways to highlight, use, and combine multiple data sources to shed light on these practices.

Role 3. Mobilizing for Action

When strategically used, data have the power to mobilize parents, students, educators, and the community at large. Schools should create opportunities for these groups to help collect, analyze, and represent data. This process builds ownership and understanding of the power and credibility of data. It also helps create a sense of urgency to engage in appropriate reforms for young people. We must not assume that parents and young people cannot collect, analyze, and represent data. Their voices are critical and compelling. Data presentations by a collective of stakeholders lead to a richer dialogue about factors that contribute to outcomes, as well as the roles of different stakeholders to improve the future for children and communities.

Example: The New York Association of Community Organizations for Reform issued a report called *Secret Apartheid* (1996). The members of the organization had a hunch that African American and Latino parents did not receive comprehensive information about academic opportunities in their neighborhood schools, thereby limiting their ability to make informed decisions about their children's education. They decided to find out if there was evidence of this type of discrimination in the schools. They suspected that parents received different types of information based on their race and ethnicity, so they gathered data to answer whether there was bias in the treatment of different parent groups.

This group conducted a study and gathered data from one hundred school visits. Parents who represented different racial and ethnic groups but lived in the same neighborhood visited their neighborhood schools. Examples of the findings include the following:

- School personnel granted African American and Latino parent requests to speak with an educator *less* than half as often as White parents.
- School personnel gave school tours to White parents two and a half times *more* often than African American or Latino parents.
- Access to information about gifted programs varied by the race of the parent making the inquiry (New York Association of Community Organizations for Reform Schools Office, 1996, p. 1).

Role 4. Stop, Look, and Listen: Caring Enough to Check Up

The excitement about a new endeavor can cause schools and districts to rush to implement well-intentioned reforms with no forethought as to how they will measure the impact of those reforms. We must resist this quick implementation temptation and devote time to determining how to measure the results of planned reforms, prior to their implementation. A data-informed monitoring process allows for midcourse corrections, the reinforcement of positive directions, and the celebration of success. Monitoring students longitudinally as they progress through the system tells us about their progress and about what teachers, curriculum, and programs they have experienced. From this information, schools can describe conditions and patterns for individuals or groups of students. Practices and policies can then be critically examined to determine whether they enhance or inhibit student progress. Data can uncover how some policies have differential impacts on different populations.

> Data can uncover how some policies have differential impacts on different populations.

Example: California policy makers implemented class-size reduction starting with first through third grade, hoping to give students a stronger foundation early in their educational careers. However, some unintended consequences materialized, negatively affecting students in poorer neighborhoods. This policy portrays a real-life example of the old adage, "Sometimes the cure is worse than the disease."

Ross (1999) examined the impact of the class-size reduction policy on the Los Angeles Unified School District, the second largest school district in the nation. He found that there was an unexpected redistribution of teaching talent. What occurred is what we describe as a massive *teacher flight* from lower- to higher-income districts. Ross states of the wealthier districts, "They had no inexperienced teachers before the introduction of the program, and they had none after it" (p. 1). Those districts received stacks of applications from experienced teachers. Districts in lower-income areas had to scramble for warm bodies, mostly hiring inexperienced teachers and long-term substitutes to fill their many vacancies.

Ross states, "The precipitous rise in the number of inexperienced teachers is but one part of the dark side of the story of how class-size reduction lowers the quality of teaching in poor, inner-city neighborhoods" (p. 3). For example, the initiative created facilities challenges. The schools in poorer neighborhoods were older, had higher enrollments, and often did not have enough unused classrooms to house the new classes required by class-size reduction. So they had to resort to placing two teachers in one room or other less desirable spaces, such as libraries or cafeterias. We visited several schools where classes met on the stage of the auditorium because that was the only space available.

This example is not about pro or con issues regarding class size, but instead underscores the need to plan for the use of data, from an equity perspective, at every stage of the educational process. Failure to do so prior to, during, and at the conclusion of an initiative may actually exacerbate existing gaps.

Role 5. Expect It and Inspect It

Nationally, the public is demanding greater accountability from schools. At the local level, parents and educators require information regarding the plans and progress made by educational institutions. Internal and external accountability systems require data. A school or district needs a plan for collecting, analyzing, and representing data that will answer key questions. No Child Left Behind (NCLB, 2002) launched a major accountability effort linked to funding and sanctions. While the politics surrounding NCLB are complex, the notion that schools and districts should be accountable for student performance is straightforward and generally accepted. Individuals and organizations perform best when expectations are clear and progress is frequently monitored. Data are central to this effort.

> While the politics surrounding NCLB are complex, the notion that schools and districts should be accountable for student performance is straightforward and generally accepted.

Example: A superintendent and the board expected all middle school principals to increase the algebra pass rate of historically underrepresented students in their district, including African American, Latino, English learners, and girls. The principals, teachers, counselors, and key central office staff poured over the data related to algebra enrollments and pass rates.

As part of his usual practice, the superintendent evaluated the principals' performance annually and met with each one to review their evaluations. In 2010, however, he realized that his typical process had a major problem. His evaluations were heavily based on annual test scores instead of indicators related to increasing algebra success for target students.

When he identified this flaw in the system, he said, "I need to inspect what I expect." Subsequently, he asked the school teams to establish other indicators that they would monitor relating to the algebra initiative. Principals embraced this type of evaluation because it was a clear indication of the district priority and their charge as school leaders.

THE DATA CONTEXT: UNFULFILLED PROMISES

No Child Left Behind (NCLB) mandates created a cottage industry for collection and analysis of high-stakes quantitative data. In the past, data collection, analysis, interpretation, and use was not a priority in schools or districts. In our current work, however, we see reams of data in most classrooms and offices. Many educators are overwhelmed by the sheer volume of the information and are at a loss to know how to use it. It seems we have gone from being data deprived to data drenched. The terms "data-driven" and "research-based programs" are abundant in the literature and are espoused by many educators. It is frequently announced with pride that "We are a data-driven school" or "We are a research-based district," and "All of our decisions are based on data." All too often when we probe deeper to find out what types of data are the sources for those data-driven decisions, answers reflect an over reliance on high-stakes tests and district-level assessments to the exclusion of other current academic and nonacademic indicators.

We find that many schools have a love-hate relationship and exhibit contradictory behaviors concerning test-score data. If outcomes are low, test results are "unfair," for various reasons. Yet, those same data are frequently used to sort students into leveled classes or programs, such as gifted and talented or other advanced courses, special education, or leveled classes for English learners (Nichols & Berliner, 2007).

The American Educational Research Association (AERA) published a position statement on high-stakes testing in 2002. This organization is a highly respected and prominent international professional group that encourages scholarly inquiry on education and evaluation with the aim of disseminating practical applications of the research findings. Its 25,000-person membership includes educators, administrators, researchers, testing and evaluation experts, counselors, graduate students, and behavioral scientists in federal, state, and local agencies. AERA cautions that

> [t]hese various high-stakes testing applications are enacted by policy makers with the intention of improving education. For example, it is hoped that setting high standards of achievement will inspire greater effort on the part of students, teachers, and educational administrators. Reporting of test results may also be beneficial in directing

public attention to gross achievement disparities among schools or among student groups. However, if high-stakes testing programs are implemented in circumstances where educational resources are inadequate or where tests lack sufficient reliability and validity for their intended purposes, there is potential for serious harm. Policy makers and the public may be misled by spurious test score increases unrelated to any fundamental educational improvement; students may be placed at increased risk of educational failure and dropping out; teachers may be blamed or punished for inequitable resources over which they have no control; and curriculum and instruction may be severely distorted if high test scores per se, rather than learning, become the overriding goal of classroom instruction. (p. 2)

AERA's full position statement on high-stakes testing and the conditions that must be present for the appropriate implementation of testing programs can be found at http://www.aera.net/policyandprograms/?id=378.

The Association of Supervision and Curriculum Development (ASCD) is another national, highly respected organization that adopted a position on high-stakes testing in 2004. ASCD is an influential educational leadership organization with 175,000 members in 119 countries who are professional educators from all school levels and subject areas. Members include superintendents, supervisors, principals, teachers, and professors of education. An excerpt from their cautionary statement about testing follows:

Decision-makers in education—students, parents, educators, community members, and policy makers—all need timely access to information from many sources. Judgments about student learning and education program success need to be informed by multiple measures. Using a single achievement test to sanction students, educators, school, districts, states/provinces, or countries is an inappropriate use of assessment. ASCD supports the use of multiple measures in assessment systems that are

- fair, balanced, and grounded in the art and science of learning and teaching;
- reflective of curricular and developmental goals and representative of content that students have had an opportunity to learn;
- used to inform and improve instruction;
- designed to accommodate nonnative speakers and special needs students; and
- valid, reliable, and supported by professional, scientific, and ethical standards designed to fairly assess the unique and divers abilities and knowledge base of all students (ASCD, 2005, p. 2).

Making AYP

NCLB requires that progress or lack of progress be reported for groups. The summary data are disaggregated by racial, ethnic, language proficiency, economic, and program (special education) groups. These disaggregated data place a national spotlight on groups making adequate yearly progress (AYP) and those that are not. Consequences exist for schools and districts that do not improve the test performance of groups who are falling behind. It is impossible to compare levels of achievement across states because each state has its own test, different performance cut points, and requirements to define grade-level proficiency. Thus, proficient students in one state may not be considered proficient in another.

The underlying assumptions of NCLB are: (1) tests are reliable, fair, accurate, and reflect what students know; (2) accountability and consequences provide incentives for schools and districts to improve; (3) schools and districts know how to address equity issues, but are choosing not to; and (4) schools and districts bear the accountability burden for student progress. Noguera and Wing (2006) observe, "Public reports that certain subgroups are not making adequate yearly progress have helped to expose race and class disparities in school districts, but it has done little to help them figure out what to do to remedy the problem" (p. 7).

> Noguera and Wing (2006) observe, "Public reports that certain subgroups are not making adequate yearly progress have helped to expose race and class disparities in school districts, but it has done little to help them figure out what to do to remedy the problem" (p. 7).

The pressure to make AYP in order to avoid consequences has created some disturbing practices that cause us to doubt the credibility and accuracy of some test results. Nichols and Berliner (2007) argue that:

> Our nation needs to worry about the environment created by high-stakes testing, since we found hundreds of examples of *adults* who were cheating, costing many of these people their reputations as well as their jobs. The high-stakes testing environment has produced instances of administrators who "pushed" children out of school or did little to keep them in school if their test scores were low, costing too many students the opportunity to receive a high school diploma. (p. xvi)

We are not aware of any comprehensive studies on how widespread these practices are, but there is much anecdotal information and many reports of these activities; this leads us to conclude that there should be some exploratory studies in schools and districts to find out more about the magnitude of these practices and the implications of using high-stakes testing as the primary way to address equity issues in schools.

There is also concern on narrowing the focus on improvement only for students who score slightly below proficient levels (students who are on the cusp). In some cases, these are the only students who are targeted for special help. They are viewed as the ones easiest to move into proficient status. A principal in a school with more than 2,000 students calculated how many students were needed to make AYP and announced, "We just need seven more students to score proficient in order to achieve AYP. Find me those seven students!" Moreover, schools extend the analyses to identify students who are *score increasers* (gifted and talented) and *score suppressors* (students receiving special education services, remedial students, and EL students) (Nichols & Berliner, 2007).

Our observations of accountability lead us to conclude that, all too often, the accountability burden falls on the backs of students and their families. When students do well, schools and districts take the credit. However, when a subgroup does not achieve well, blame is often attributed to the underachieving groups "who brought our test scores down" (score suppressors). The groups most singled out are African American, Latino, English learners, special education students, and lower socioeconomic students. These are the groups that NCLB intended to *not leave behind.* Historically, struggling schools and districts continue for years before any substantive intervention or sanctions are imposed. We hear little public conversation about the relationship between struggling schools or districts and the very real price students pay for attending certain schools. The promise of NCLB has largely gone unfulfilled as the educational system has not used the red flags triggered by NCLB reporting requirements as a springboard for digging deeper and understanding the "real" and "complete" story that explains test results and then motivating substantive change.

As an example, the *Williams* case in California (2000) was settled after four years of intense litigation, including thousands of pages of testimony from students and parents, as well as expert witnesses from among the most highly respected educational authorities in the country. (Refer to www.decentschools.org/ to access deposition testimony.) The settlement required legislation to provide funding to repair low-performing schools, phase out year-round schedules that reduce the number of instructional days in a year, create new standards for instructional materials and facilities, "intervene" in low-performing schools that have teacher qualification and retention problems, and collect compliance data. This settlement created a heightened sense of hope that real change would finally happen and that students in failing and neglected schools would actually receive the attention they so deserved.

Sadly, our extensive work in schools and districts throughout the state before and since the *Williams* settlement leads us to conclude that the intended outcome has not materialized in many schools serving the highest-need students. Although the legislative requirement mandated necessary changes, the requirements were not sufficient to create deep-level changes in the schools' culture.

As is often the case, rules do not change institutional heart. In fact, the operational requirements of *Williams* are reduced to documentation of monitoring visits to count credentialed teachers, and books and facilities checks, including an inspection to ensure that every classroom has posted a notice regarding *Williams's* requirements and complaint procedures. These "data" requirements have become largely routine and clerical. While some monitoring officials sincerely attempt to comply with the *Williams's* requirements, we have found that many persistently failing schools are found *Williams* "compliant." For example, schools are required to issue every student their own textbook for each core subject and to provide a credentialed teacher for every class. We reviewed a large urban high school that opened without books for almost half of the mathematics and English classes and had not hired one-third of the math and science teachers. The *Williams's* review served to document the violations and require that the situation be rectified immediately.

Actually, all issues were resolved by the end of the second month of school and the school received a clean bill of compliance health. Unfortunately, by then hundreds of students had missed the first quarter of algebra, biology, and English, including honors and AP courses. State subject exams at the end of the third quarter verified that students equipped with textbooks and qualified teachers for the entire school year had a distinctive advantage over students who lacked these basic elements when school began. Further, the school was organized in "teams," and due to master schedule constraints, certain groups of students experienced the same lack of resources three years in a row. The achievement profile of those students confirmed that though the school was granted a clean bill of health using one set of data, the *other data* clearly demonstrated that the education of hundreds of students was severely harmed.

Current Patterns of Student Achievement

An April 29, 2009, *New York Times* headline proclaimed, "'No Child' Law Is Not Closing a Racial Gap" (p. 1). Current indicators of achievement based on high-stakes exams and educational attainment show that some groups of students are making better strides than others. The achievement gaps among racial groups appeared to be closing in the 1980s, but in the 1990s, and currently, the gap seems to be widening as students journey through school. Urban and rural schools are generally performing at lower academic levels than suburban schools. Low-income, African American, Latino, American Indian, and some Asian groups are performing at lower levels than White students. The achievement gaps are found in K–12 through postsecondary levels, and these gaps grow larger as students move through the schools (McKinsey & Company, 2009).

Figures 1.1 and 1.2 highlight the public school demographics for race, ethnicity, and income (Education Trust, 2009). African American, Asian, Latino, and Native Americans represent 47% of our nation's public school enrollment. Low-income students (many of whom are students of color) represent 42% of the student population. The projection for biggest changes in the population growth of young people ages 5 to 24 by 2020 are Asian (39%) and Latino (33%). White students are expected to decrease by 6% in population by 2020 (Education Trust, 2009). Data in this chapter and throughout the book illustrate that most students in these groups, particularly African American, Latino, and Native Americans, are the most under-educated and least prepared to compete in the global economy.

These outcomes not only affect students and their families, but our nation as a whole. McKinsey & Company (2009), in their report on the economic impact of the achievement gap in our nation's schools concludes, "Avoidable shortfalls in academic achievement impose heavy and often tragic consequences, via lower earnings, poorer health, and higher rates of incarceration" (p. 5). This underscores the need for everyone to be concerned about this performance picture and the need to work to reverse it.

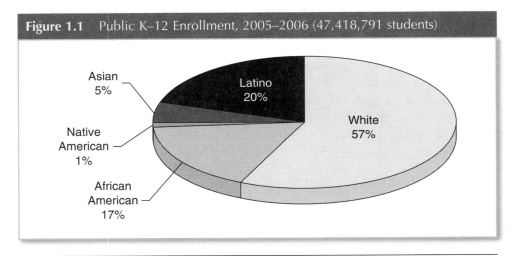

Figure 1.1 Public K–12 Enrollment, 2005–2006 (47,418,791 students)

Asian 5%
Native American 1%
African American 17%
Latino 20%
White 57%

Source: The Education Trust. (2009, April). *Education watch: National report.* Washington, DC: The Education Trust. Page 1.

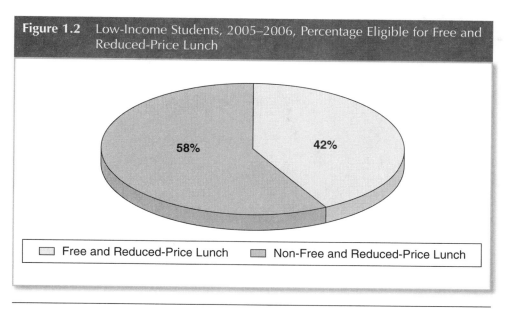

Figure 1.2 Low-Income Students, 2005–2006, Percentage Eligible for Free and Reduced-Price Lunch

Source: The Education Trust. (2009, April). *Education watch: National report.* Washington, DC: The Education Trust. Page 2.

Because of the inconsistencies in comparing measures of progress from state to state, researchers and policy makers use the National Assessment of Education Progress (NAEP) to report on the academic health of our nation's schools. The scores reported are based on a sample population of students from participating states. NAEP reports three achievement levels: basic, proficient, and advanced. NAEP testing began in 1990, and the results provide long-term trend data. Barton and Coley (2009) warn that "*none* of the measures presented consider what individual students, classroom of students, or whole schools of students learned over the course of a year's instruction" (p. 5). However, NAEP does provide an "item map" to identify the types of problems that students can answer. For example, in mathematics at Grade 8, the average White student "can solve problems of square root, while the average African American student can draw the reflection of a figure" (p. 5). For more detailed information, we recommend the NAEP website (http://www .nationsreportcard.gov) as a tool to gain more background information on NAEP achievement in our nation's schools and view available reports and data tools for downloading.

The Education Trust's National Report provides an overview using NAEP and other indicators to highlight achievement patterns. Figure 1.3 shows that only 31% of fourth-grade readers scored at the proficient level and above in reading in 2007.

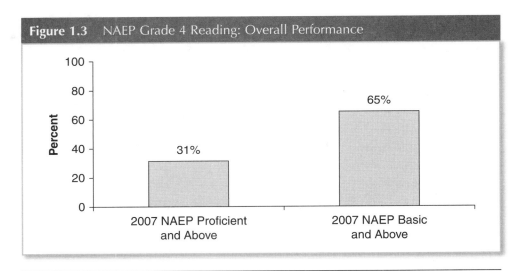

Figure 1.3 NAEP Grade 4 Reading: Overall Performance

Source: The Education Trust. (2009, April). *Education watch: National report.* Washington, DC: The Education Trust. Page 4.

The disaggregated data in Figure 1.4 show how ethnic groups perform. The horizontal line in the middle represents proficient. Groups that appear below the line are not proficient. African American and Latino students are the largest groups scoring below proficient. Though Asians and Whites

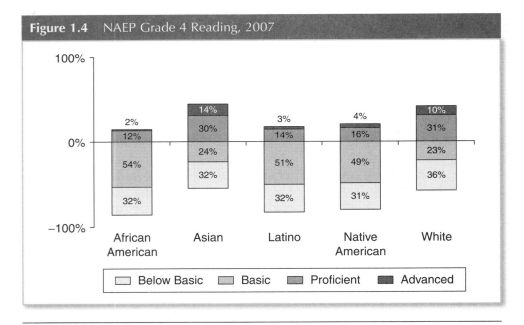

Figure 1.4 NAEP Grade 4 Reading, 2007

Source: The Education Trust. (2009, April). *Education watch: National report.* Washington, DC: The Education Trust. Page 4.

have the highest percent of students at proficient and above, 56% of Asian students and 59% of White fourth graders score below proficient, indicating that all groups have members who are not proficient. Although African American, Latino, and Native Americans have more students at the lower levels, each group contains students that score at advanced levels.

Table 1.1 shows trend data for fourth-grade reading from 1998 to 2007. All groups show improvement, but gaps in performance of groups still exist. The last column indicates the change and the states that demonstrated the biggest gains for different groups of students.

Table 1.1 Is NAEP Performance Improving? Grade 4 Reading				
	NAEP Scale Score		Change From 1998–2007	
	1998	2007	National Change	Biggest Gainers
African American	192	203	11	24 (DE)
Asian	211	231	20	30 (MA)
Latino	192	204	12	42 (DE)
Native American	N/A	206	N/A	17 (NM)
White	223	230	7	15 (DE, FL)
All	213	220	7	18 (DE, DC, FL)

Source: The Education Trust. (2009, April). *Education watch: National report.* Washington, DC: The Education Trust. Page 5.

Figure 1.5 shows NAEP eighth-grade mathematics performance. The majority of the students scored at basic and above, and only 31% scored at proficient and above.

Figure 1.6 and Table 1.2 (see pp. 24 and 25, respectively) show NAEP eighth-grade mathematics levels by race and ethnicity. In Figure 1.6, only 11% of African American students, 15% of Latino students, and 17% of Native American students scored at proficient and advanced. Asian students demonstrated the highest performance, with 49% at proficient and above.

Table 1.2 shows that over time all groups' scores increased. Again, as in reading, some states had large gains for certain groups. For instance, in North Dakota, performance scores show 21 points for Native Americans versus 2 points nationally. This may indicate that some states do a better job

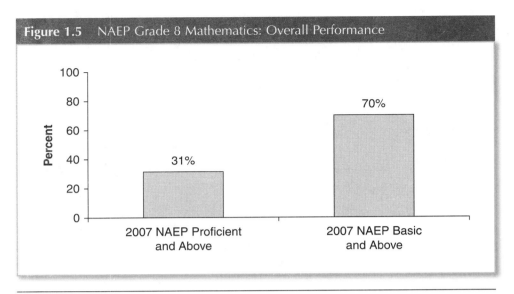

Figure 1.5 NAEP Grade 8 Mathematics: Overall Performance

Source: The Education Trust. (2009, April). *Education watch: National report.* Washington, DC: The Education Trust. Page 5.

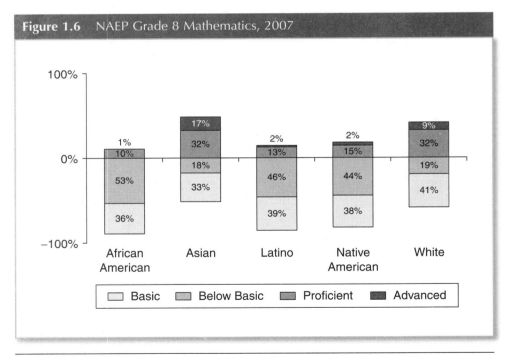

Figure 1.6 NAEP Grade 8 Mathematics, 2007

Source: The Education Trust. (2009, April). *Education watch: National report.* Washington, DC: The Education Trust.

Table 1.2 Is NAEP Performance Improving? Grade 8 Mathematics				
	NAEP Scale Score		**Change From 2000–2007**	
	2000	**2007**	**National Change**	**Biggest Gainers**
African American	243	259	16	27 (AR)
Asian	287	296	9	23 (MA)
Latino	252	264	12	24 (MA)
Native American	263	265	2	21 (ND)
White	283	290	7	21 (MA)
All	272	280	8	19 (MA)

Source: The Education Trust. (2009, April). *Education watch: National report.* Washington, DC: The Education Trust. Page 8.

in increasing performance for different groups of students. If some states have effective strategies, this can possibly guide and encourage others. Of course, there exists a need to look at *other data,* such as graduation and dropout rates, and college enrollments for different groups of students K–12 prior to declaring that one state does a better job than others. The only thing we can say for sure is that according to these data, there are gains in scores.

Unfortunately, the trend data on seventeen-year-olds in reading and mathematics has remained flat from 2004–2008. The bottom scores showed some improvement for White students in mathematics, but not significant changes for African American or Latino students (Barton & Coley, 2009).

Other test score and educational attainment indicators illustrate the same achievement gap patterns throughout the schooling experiences of different groups. There are underrepresentation and overrepresentation of different groups in advanced classes, special education, gifted and talented, suspension, expulsions, dropouts, and graduation rates. Moreover, these and other indicators are traceable to elementary schooling experiences such as retention and placements in special education, gifted and talented, and critical nonacademic indicators, such as suspensions and expulsions (Artiles, Harry, Reschly, & Chinn, 2001; Balfanz & Legters, 2004; Losen & Orfield, 2002; McKinsey & Company, 2009; Orfield, 2004). Subsequent chapters expand on these and other data indicators.

Figures 1.7 and 1.8 show similar achievement patterns to NAEP scores for different groups in on-time graduation rates and public college

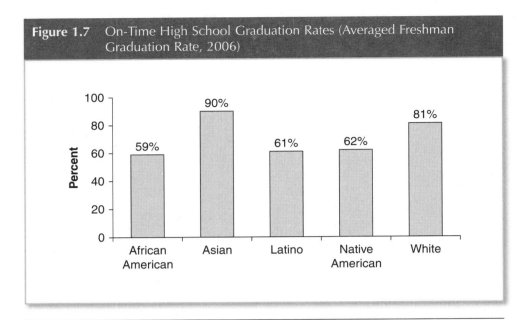

Figure 1.7 On-Time High School Graduation Rates (Averaged Freshman Graduation Rate, 2006)

Source: The Education Trust. (2009, April). *Education watch: National report.* Washington, DC: The Education Trust. Page 21.

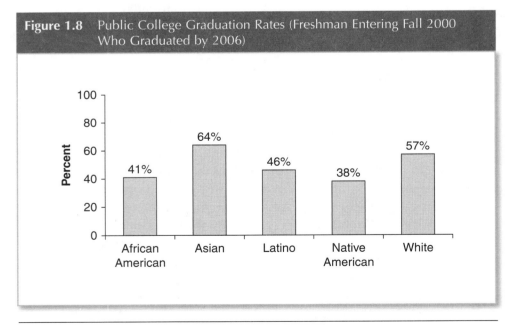

Figure 1.8 Public College Graduation Rates (Freshman Entering Fall 2000 Who Graduated by 2006)

Source: The Education Trust. (2009, April). *Education watch: National report.* Washington, DC: The Education Trust. Page 21.

graduation rates. Unfortunately, Native Americans, African American, and Latino students continue to appear persistently at the lower rungs of the educational attainment ladders.

Research demonstrates that there is still a disparity in achievement by race and ethnicity regardless of income (Ali, 2007; McKinsey & Company, 2009). This is a sobering reality. Children's racial backgrounds, and perceptions about their capacity to learn have the power to trump income levels. Gaps in achievement are found among racial and ethnic groups regardless of socioeconomic level. For example, Ferguson's 2003 research looks at the achievement gap among racial groups whose parents have similar levels of education. He found consistent gaps by racial groups within income levels. Similarly, McKinsey & Company (2009), using data from the National Center for Education Statistics (NCES), reports that at each of the income levels, White students achieve at significantly higher rates than African American and Latino students. When race/ethnicity and family income data are combined, there are achievement gaps within and between racial ethnic groups. Generally, higher-income students perform at higher levels than those in the lower-income groups. However, further analyses of the data show that White students achieve at higher levels than their African American and Latino peers at every income level. For example, poor White students with family incomes of $25,000 or less achieve at similar levels to African American students with family incomes of $75,000 or more. Simply identifying and using income as the sole reason for underperformance is shortsighted, thus reinforcing the need to look at *other data* to unravel outcome data. According to National Assessment of Educational Progress (NAEP) data, poor White students are about three and a half years ahead of poor African American students. Noguera and Wing (2007) point out that besides economic capital, social and cultural capital make a significant contribution in the ways that parents and students negotiate and are treated in the educational enterprise.

> A child's racial background and perceptions about their capacity to learn have the power to trump income levels.

McKinsey & Company (2009) state in their recent report that "avoidable shortfalls in academic achievement impose heavy and often tragic consequences, via lower earnings, poorer health, and higher rates of incarceration" (p. 6). Their findings highlight the enormous cost of these shortfalls for individuals and our nation. Typical data show the familiar gaps in achievement by income and race, but they point out some data that are often not highlighted: the differential achievement that occurs within school districts and schools with populations that have similar demographic racial, ethnicity, language, and income characteristics. This type of evidence suggests that it is possible to close these gaps by changing practices and polices in schools and districts (Checkley, 2004; Hilliard, 1991; Johnson, 2002; Johnson & Bush, 2005; McKinsey & Company, 2009). We will provide a more detailed discussion on the achievement gaps in Chapter 2 and throughout the book.

The ongoing contentious debate about whether schools and districts are able to have a substantial impact on student achievement without changes in social policy remains very much alive. All would agree that social policies that impact jobs and health issues influence the well-being of our young people, their families, and their neighborhoods. Those issues need attention (see Barton & Coley, 2009; Ferguson, 2003).

Children in public schools may come to school hungry, homeless, and without adult support. This is a tough challenge for schools. There are initiatives that are focused on transforming the community and school, such as the Harlem Children's Zone in New York City, a nonprofit organization that has received wide acclaim for its work in improving the lives of the children and adults in the community. To find out more about their work, we refer you to their web address, http://www.hcz.org/home.

Nevertheless, we know from our work and from the research that there are school system factors such as policies, practices, student and teacher assignments, and leadership that have powerful impacts on achievement regardless of student background factors. This book will highlight those factors and conditions over which schools and districts have control. Noguera and Wing (2007) state that " . . . it is possible to address school conditions that contribute to disparities in achievement, such as school size, the student-to-counselor ratio, procedures that are used to track students into higher- and lower-level courses, and processes used to provide academic support to students who are struggling" (p. 31). McKinsey & Company (2009) conclude in their report that "many teachers and schools across the country are proving that race and poverty are not destiny" (p. 6).

THE WALLPAPER EFFECT: MAKING THE INVISIBLE VISIBLE

Outcome data have the potential to produce a misleading picture of actual conditions in schools and districts, thereby creating a *wallpaper effect.* Outcome data, like wallpaper, can cover up cracks or other unwanted blemishes of surfaces. These data may show outcomes in an attractive light, but when the wallpaper is peeled off, problems surface once again, displaying more layers of wallpaper or major cracks. When the wallpaper is partially or fully uncovered, decisions are made about removing the blemishes or recovering with more wallpaper (another reform). It is much easier to choose to cover with new wallpaper than to take the time to repair the cracks. We are not implying bad intentions, but external pressures for quick fixes lead people to take superficial action, often ignoring potentially harmful long-term consequences.

Data used in schools and districts typically answer very narrow sets of questions about student outcomes. Yet, we argue that asking only the most superficial questions about performance outcomes can mislead and mask the organizational and systemic contributing factors (cracks) influencing those outcomes. Failure to probe more deeply leaves a void in the types of data we examine. Pieces of the data puzzle are not apparent. There are invisible *other data* that are not mentioned publicly or are not a part of accountability measures, but are critical pieces of the puzzle nonetheless. These are the powerful data that influence outcomes, have long-term consequences for students, and are critical elements related to issues of equity and social justice. Brought under the microscope, these data have the potential to spotlight institutional behaviors and often paint a very different picture about true conditions that are incongruent with what we say we believe or want for students.

> Yet, we argue that asking only the most superficial questions about performance outcomes can mislead and mask the organizational and systemic contributing factors (cracks) influencing those outcomes.

For example, calculations of dropout and graduation rates have come into question. The publicly reported data are inadequate to inform and reflect on what happens to students as they journey through the educational pipeline. The literature tells us about indicators as early as elementary and middle school that influence student alienation from school, dropping out, and graduation (Quality Data Campaign/Achieve, 2006; Children's Defense Fund, 2007; Editorial Projects in Education, 2009; Flores-Gonzales, 2002; Orfield, 2004). Yet, conversations about these critical issues are absent in most schools and districts. We present more information on these topics in Chapter 3.

Schools, districts, and state departments should examine indicators that influence long-term outcomes longitudinally, with an eye on student and school culture issues that contribute to student success. Barton and Coley (2009) state, " . . . we also need a clear view of the amount of learning that actually occurs during the school year" (p. 42). Schools and districts are closest to the students and must relentlessly inquire, and collect on-the-ground data that can answer deeper questions related to equity, access, opportunity to learn, and culturally responsive school climates. This requires multiple types of data, and may possibly expose some discomforting truths in our schools and systems. We must be courageous enough to peel off the layers of wallpaper and examine what lies beneath.

Appendix A provides a brief overview of the focus areas and types of data that should be collected and analyzed to guide improvements in schools and districts. Many of the indicators for this data table are available but are not used in ways to meaningfully inform classroom teachers, parents, students, or school and district leadership. Subsequent chapters of this book discuss these areas in detail, demonstrate what data need to be collected, and how it can be summarized and analyzed. Research that is linked to the indicators will underscore vital connections to student achievement. Most of the areas show several sources of data. We emphasize the need to combine data sources to tell a complete data story. Triangulation—ensuring that conclusions are drawn from the overlap of multiple sources of data—is critical to the unfolding of an accurate data story. Conclusions, in the absence of triangulation, are mere hunches. Triangulation elevates hunches to "findings" that can then be addressed with equity-minded solutions.

CONCLUSION

We fully understand that collecting, analyzing, and using *other data* to improve student school experiences takes skill, will, and time. Who will want to do this work? This endeavor is reserved for those who are looking to uncover the true story about student achievement, those with the desire to build *equity muscle,* and those whose passion for educating all children drives them to dig deeper to answer hard questions not usually asked. This work also requires us to maintain constant skepticism about whether every student in our charge is receiving optimal educational opportunity. Traditional and single-variable data can often raise suspicion that a blemish may be just behind the wallpaper, helping us to formulate hunches. This book is about developing the capacity to tackle the most sensitive educational issues with the greatest likelihood of impacting the lives of "other people's children" (Delpit, 1988).

2 Peeling the Wallpaper

Uncovering Inequities

SCENARIO: MARTIN LUTHER KING JR. HIGH SCHOOL

Martin Luther King Jr. High School is located in an urban city. It has an enrollment in Grades 9–12 of about 1,300 students. The student population is diverse and includes 9% Asian, 22% African American, 26% Latino, 2% Native American, 40% White, and 1% multiple ethnicities. Seventy-five percent of the students are from low-income families. In statewide assessments, the school's test scores indicated that some racial and ethnic groups were performing better than others. There were large gaps in scores between White and Asian students and their African American, Latino, and Native American peers.

A unique professional development opportunity for administrators on data use became available in the district during summer recess. The principal of the high school encouraged the vice principal to attend the training where the major focus was on how to use multiple types of indicators to find out how different groups of students performed at school. During the workshop, the attendees analyzed their school's data. As a result of this activity, the vice principal gained insight into how different groups performed in academic courses and saw the representation of different groups in college preparatory or general education classes. Although test-score data provided clues to some disparities, the vice principal was alarmed at the magnitude of gaps among different groups in each of the grades.

When the vice principal returned to school she shared with the principal what she had discovered from the data analysis. The principal was alarmed and surprised to find out about the magnitude of the disparities. Clearly identifying the problem created a climate of dissatisfaction with the performance of different student groups in the school, particularly for African American and Latino students. They discussed a strategy for using the data to create the need for change in the academic culture of their school. They decided to focus on one department. The chair of the mathematics department was especially dissatisfied with student performance, so they asked her to meet with them. The mathematics chair liked the idea of using a departmental team approach to use data for change. She convinced her teachers to engage in an improvement process. The department embarked on a journey to build a culture of inquiry.

The strategy involved asking pertinent questions and peeling off traditional data to answer questions that would inform their improvement strategies. The department examined several years of statewide assessment scores, mathematics course enrollments, and grades by teacher and by student racial, ethnic, language, and gender groups. These data revealed that African American, Latino, and EL students were disproportionately enrolled in lower-level mathematics courses, and a majority of them received Ds and Fs in those low-level and remedial courses. These lower-level courses were purportedly designed to give weaker students more success in higher-level and advanced classes. The department also examined grades by individual teachers. They were disturbed to find large disparities in grade distributions for the same course taught by different teachers. Patterns emerged whereby some teachers routinely awarded their students a high percentage of passing grades, while others failed a sizable percentage of students. One of the explanations for this disparity was that some teachers were more rigorous than others. But no data supported this claim. The team realized they needed information. They realized that the ninth-grade class had the greatest number of failures and also the highest retention rates because students lacked credits for promotion to Grade 10. Therefore, the ninth grade included students that had been in the school for one or two years. Examining syllabi, textbooks, and course requirements, the teachers recognized that they used different grading criteria and at times covered different amounts of content for the same course. They identified the need to develop a common curriculum and expectations for each course. After much discussion and some discomfort,

> They were disturbed to find large disparities in grade distributions for the same course taught by different teachers. Patterns emerged whereby some teachers routinely awarded their students a high percent of passing grades, while others failed a sizable percent of students.

the teachers agreed to develop end-of-course assessments. They also faced the reality that in lower-level classes students were failing at higher rates than their peers in higher-level courses. For the first time as a department, they addressed the issue that African American, Latino, and EL students were disproportionately placed in mostly dead-end courses.

The vice principal encouraged them to dig deeper, ask more questions, and get even more data. She suggested that they interview students, so they conducted focus groups. In order to reduce students' feelings of intimidation, teachers interviewed students who were not enrolled in their classes, and counselors and the vice principal participated. Students expressed their feelings about teacher expectations, about instructional inadequacies, and about what they felt were entitlements for some but not other students. Many of the students in lower-level classes felt that the school had low expectations for them and had no idea about their career aspirations. As a result of digging deeper and using multiple sources of data, a three-year math plan emerged. The plan included the following action steps:

- *Redesign math classes replacing the low-level classes with algebra.*
- *Create a numeracy support class as a "double dose" for identified students.*
- *Align curriculum with state and National Council of Teachers of Mathematics (NCTM) standards.*
- *Conduct meetings with middle schools to improve articulation and placement.*
- *Develop common assessments: formative and summative.*
- *Develop exit criteria.*
- *Include alternative and special education students in regular math classes.*
- *Place highly effective teachers with struggling students.*
- *Evaluate student work to inform instruction.*
- *Continue staff development in academic literacy and instructional strategies, including cooperative learning and culturally responsive strategies.*

The short-term results in just one year were striking. In the baseline year, 27.5% of Martin Luther King Jr. freshmen had satisfactory grades in math. After one year of planned implementation, 60.2% of Martin Luther King Jr. freshman earned satisfactory grades in math. All students were enrolled in math college preparatory courses.

OVERVIEW

This chapter serves two primary functions. First, it provides readers with an equity framework to anchor the type of inquiry process we describe throughout the book. Second, it demonstrates the application of a specific line of inquiry, similar to the inquiry conducted at Martin Luther King Jr. High School whereby equity questions are systematically asked and traditional

> The *other data* include:
> (a) data not typically
> analyzed, or (b) typical
> data viewed through an
> equity lens.

and *other data* are used to uncover answers, layer by layer, until the true story affecting students is revealed. The *other data* include: (a) data not typically analyzed, or (b) typical data viewed through an equity lens. We begin by briefly discussing the need to build capacity through organizing to accomplish the work. This is key, but not central to this book. We direct readers to Johnson (2002) for a more complete treatment on capacity building for collaborative work. Next, we delve into the concept of the achievement gap and add a twist to the conventional definition that helps us clarify the purpose of this type of inquiry process. We follow with another example of a how schools can use the inquiry process to better understand their achievement profile. Then, as an antidote to superficial analyses, we describe levels of analysis applicable to data work in schools and districts. The case of Cortez Intermediate School is then presented. This is an example of using data to create schoolwide change. Led by their inquisitive principal, this school staff used a data-based inquiry process to peel back the layers of school complexities to reveal disturbing realities faced by students every day, every year. Similar to the scenario, this process led to fundamental changes in school culture and practices and resulted in significantly improved schoolwide achievement. The chapter closes with exercises aimed at helping the reader practice using *other data* to uncover the "true story" behind the data.

ORGANIZING FOR MEANINGFUL INQUIRY

School and district reform is not an individual odyssey. The scenario on Martin Luther King Jr. High School describes a team approach that a mathematics department used to tackle mathematics achievement and equity issues. Experience suggests that equitable reform requires hard work from a committed core of individuals including educators, parents, students, and community, all working collaboratively to achieve a vision. Quality time and skill are necessary for groups to work with data. At times, contentious issues arise from a group's deliberations. Handing out and presenting data without structuring time for meaningful dialogue can be dangerous and counterproductive. Inevitably, some of the discoveries that schools and districts make regarding their beliefs, practices, and outcomes are painful and require sensitive facilitation. For guidance on how to have productive conversations that make a difference for students, we suggest becoming familiar with the work of Anderson, Herr, and Nihlen (2007), Johnson (2002), and Singleton and Linton (2006). These sources provide rich information on research, frameworks, and implementation strategies for building teams, leading inquiries, and conducting dialogues on sensitive issues such as race and culture. Though effective collaboration is not the focus of this book, we cannot sufficiently emphasize the need for teams to develop sophistication and skill as they work through equity issues.

THE ACHIEVEMENT GAP

As schools and districts examine their data, it is important to look for gap patterns. We suggest two methods for examining gaps. The first one, which is generally discussed in the literature, is the achievement gap in performance among racial, ethnic, language, gender, and socioeconomic groups. We presented some of that information in Chapter 1 and we will provide additional information throughout this book. The second way to examine the achievement gaps is to analyze the gap between a data point and a target goal. We suggest that in addition to comparing gaps between groups, data should be analyzed in relation to an expectation for achievement. In subsequent chapters, we will examine other ways to look at differences in schooling experiences by groups. For instance, we will present over- and underrepresentation of groups in academic and nonacademic areas and program categories.

At every level, we find national evidence of persistent gaps between African American, Latino, and Native American students and their White and some Asian counterparts. These gaps begin in elementary school and continue to expand through the postsecondary levels of education (Barton & Coley, 2009; Education Trust, 2009; Ferguson, 2003; McKinsey & Company, 2009; Noguera & Wing, 2006).

Persistently low-achievement profiles, as reported in Chapter 1, are found for certain racial and ethnic groups, regardless of socioeconomic level (Ferguson, 2003; McKinsey & Company, 2009). For example, Singham's (1998) study found that the gap existed between middle-income African American and White students in a Shaker Heights high school.

Schools and districts usually examine both aggregate and disaggregated data. Aggregate data points represent the average of a collective group. Disaggregated data breaks data into subsets such as demographic groups, grade levels, programs, and class or teacher. Figure 2.1 shows an aggregate data presentation of how all tenth and eleventh graders performed on a high school exit exam. Figure 2.2 shows how three groups—Latino, African American, and White students—performed in Grade 10. These two figures give performance results in very different ways. The disaggregated data clearly show the disparity in achievement among the three groups. It highlights the fact that Latino and African American students perform abysmally, a fact that is not masked in this disaggregated presentation.

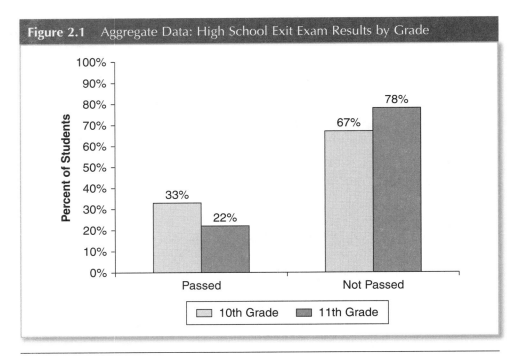

Created by authors based on information from an urban school.

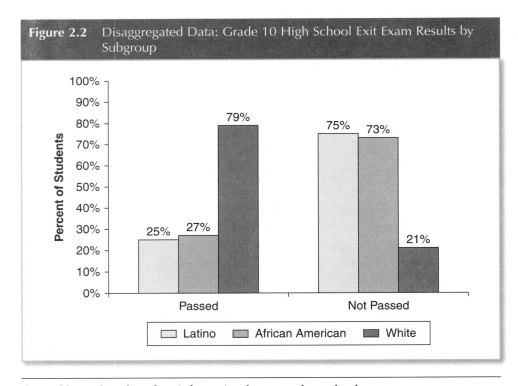

Created by authors based on information from an urban school.

Outcome data need to be examined in relation to what the expectations are for all students. Aggregate scores are only the outer layers of information. If all students are expected to achieve at least on grade level or are expected to be eligible for college enrollment by graduation, the gaps or lack of gaps in achievement need to be noted for each group against that measure. Simply measuring gap information from group to group can shortchange students. We have seen instances in which every group was below the standard. Although some groups were closer to the standard than others, there was an achievement gap for every group rel-

> If all students are expected to achieve at least on grade level or are expected to be eligible for college enrollment by graduation, the gaps or lack of gaps in achievement need to be noted for each group against that measure.

ative to the achievement expectation. In this situation, temptation exists to celebrate the highest-performing group and forget the target goal.

Figure 2.3 illustrates that the district's goal was to have all students graduate prepared for university enrollment. The figure shows two years of data on how far different groups are from the goal. African American and Latino students are far from the goal, and this has implications for more aggressive workable interventions. It also shows only about 50% of White students, the most common comparison group, completed the college prep sequence. What are the implications for these findings?

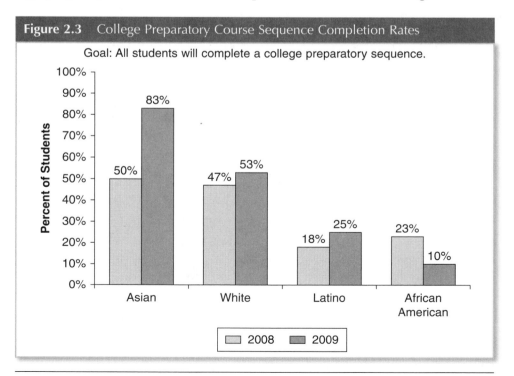

Figure 2.3 College Preparatory Course Sequence Completion Rates

Created by authors based on information from an urban school.

Therefore, rather than discuss a single achievement "gap," we should be analyze multiple achievement "gaps," comparing the highest-performing group with their underachieving counterparts, but also comparing group performance against a predetermined desired academic achievement target for all students. We need to know how far or how near a group is to the desired standard and whether or not the highest-achieving group is falling short of the standard. When thinking of gap data, the *Gap* (capital G) refers to the difference among group and program performance and the desired achievement target, while other achievement gaps (small g) describe differential performance among groups. We suggest that an achievement gap study begin with an analysis of the Gap (the difference between fixed achievement targets and how a group is achieving) and then acquire the different kinds of data to create successful strategies for bringing students to standard. Educators need to collect multiple sources of *other data* to understand why some groups are closer than others and to address ways for groups to attain the goals.

In discussions about closing the gap among different groups, we must examine the direction of the gap reduction. Merely reporting that the gap that might have been 30 points is now 15 points does not describe whether the bottom group went up or the top group went down. In either case, the gap was reduced by 15 points, but the outcomes for students are very different. For example, one school reduced the achievement gap between gifted and talented (GATE) and non-GATE students by half in just one year. While the aggregate result was most impressive, further analysis revealed that the district had opened a GATE magnet school at another site, siphoning off the majority of the neighborhood high-performing GATE students to attend the new site. With only a few GATE students remaining, primarily those who were not as successful, the difference between GATE and non-GATE students appeared to shrink drastically. However, the gap decreased by lowering the ceiling rather than raising the floor.

PEELING OFF LAYERS OF DATA

High-stakes test scores still remain one of the principal measures used by the public to gauge school improvement. Most schools and districts receive mounds of data on test results, but educators rarely have the time, training, or opportunity to analyze or discuss these data in any systematic way. The lack of meaningful data analysis is not the fault of any one group or individual, but rather a systemic flaw that must be addressed in order for deep inquiry to become part of a school or district culture.

Table 2.1 describes peeling data by the levels of data and ways of looking at test information. This is analogous to the *wallpaper effect* described in the Chapter 1. Each level of data provides information for a variety of audiences. At the district levels, the interest is more macro, that is, how the entire system is doing (outcomes). These data give little meaningful information to guide a classroom teacher. As the data get peeled, schools need to focus on the kinds of timely data that can help with instruction. These data include grade-to-grade information and looking at information on how various subgroups of students perform at the program and student levels. Analyzing data at the student level is most useful when identifying specific areas of need related to instruction. Classroom teacher data can reveal strengths as well as areas in need of improvement for teachers and provide useful informa-

Table 2.1	Peeling the Data: Levels of Looking at Types of Data to Access and Use
1. School levels.	
2. Grade level.	
3. Programs and tracks.	
4. Classroom teacher.	
5. Student.	

Source: Johnson, R.S. (2002).

tion for professional development. At all levels of data, analyses must look for patterns in school and district policies and practices and structures. There will be a fuller discussion of these issues in later chapters.

Your Turn: Beginning the Inquiry Process

Using your school or district data, identify your level of analysis (school, grade, and so on), relevant questions, available current data, and *other data* needed for complete answers.

Template 2.1	Beginning the Inquiry Process		
Level	Questions That Need to Be Answered	Current Data	Other Data Needed

Table 2.2 shows a variety of ways to analyze tests or other information. Two major ways are longitudinal cohort data and snapshot noncohort data. Each data collection method is useful for different purposes. We encourage schools and districts to design longitudinal databases that track cohorts to provide more information about students' journeys through school. For example, a question about the rate of progress students make in English language proficiency is best answered by longitudinal data tracking one group of English learners for several years. On the other hand, educators interested in studying the effectiveness of a particular mathematics program might access several years of annual noncohort data by grade level. This type of data report reveals the effect of a program on different students groups. The distinction between the two types of data collection is important especially when a concern arises that one group of students is somehow different from the norm. For instance, when one elementary school's results plummeted one year, the staff noted that the fifth-grade group that moved to the middle school the prior year was extremely strong as a group. Therefore, the scores dropped drastically when they left the school. Longitudinal cohort data shed light on whether the group began strong and simply maintained that position as they moved through the grades or whether this impression was false. Snapshot noncohort data of that group of fifth graders compared with several years of other fifth-grade classes checks for patterns in program effect with different student groups. Skillful data users match the data collection method to their questions to ensure that they can reach accurate interpretations. For example, in Chapter 3, we focus on the need for longitudinal indicators that can pinpoint information on educational attainments and dropping out.

> Skillful data users match the data collection method to their questions to ensure that they can reach accurate interpretations.

Table 2.2   Peeling the Data: Ways of Looking at Test Information
Aggregate data (district, school, and classroom using means and medians).
Quartile data looking at different percentiles and cut sores (levels of proficiency bands).
Cohorts over time (the same group of students as they move through the system).
Disaggregated data.
Individual teacher.
Individual student.
Content cluster strengths and weaknesses (school, grade, class, student).
Content cluster alignment to the curriculum.
Longitudinal and historical.

Source: Johnson, R.S. (2002).

Your Turn: Matching Inquiry Questions to Levels of Data

For several different levels of analysis, use your own school or district data and identify questions that match each level and data that needs to be accessed.

Template 2.2 Matching Inquiry Questions to Levels of Data			
Kind of Data	**Questions That Need to Be Answered**	**Current Data**	**Other Data Needed**

APPLICATION OF THE LEVELS OF ANALYSIS

The following sections demonstrate how to peel back layers of data using different levels of analysis. We explore ways of analyzing standardized test information as a starting point—moving from aggregate data sets to disaggregated and then to combination data that includes *other data* to arrive at deeper understandings.

Imagine that a district had overall increases in the percentage of students passing the high school graduation exit exam one year. One stance is to be pleased with the results and assume that all is well. In contrast, a wallpaper approach does not assume that the results mean all students receive the best educational opportunity. Rather, this approach would extract data from which to test hunches. Using this approach, a school or district team can actively seek data that respond to specific questions or address hunches or suspicions. First, teams collaborate to generate the first layer of wallpaper peeling by asking relevant questions, resulting in being able to determine whether educational equity is occurring.

For example, the district might ask the following questions:

- How far from the desired standard did students score?
- How far from the desired standard did different groups of students score?
- How did various groups of students score relative to each other?

While this first layer responds to accountability concerns, it does not provide any diagnostic information that would help make specific modifications or corrections to current practices.

A second layer of data peeling involves asking questions that yield the type of information that could result in specific changes in practices and real enhancements of opportunities for students. Questions from the second layer include the following:

- How did students perform on the various subparts of the mathematics test?
- How did students representing special populations perform on the test (including special education, pregnant minors, foster children, neglected and delinquent youth, English learners, gifted and talented, migrant students, homeless students)?

A third layer takes the questions to the program and classroom level. Questions in this level require combining typical test-score data with *other data,* including academic and nonacademic indicators. For example:

- What is the relationship between students' mathematics course placement, course content, and their achievement on the exit exam?
- How many times have students taken the exam and what type of support or resources (such as intervention, tutoring) did students receive? How effective was the support? For which students?
- What math courses are students currently taking?
- What are the qualifications, training, and effectiveness of the teachers in each program and course that students experienced in preparation for the exam?
- How many days of intended instruction actually occurred (including issues of substitutes, teachers, and students absences; see Chapter 6 for further discussion).
- What explanations do students and teachers have about the achievement patterns?

The following section describes the case of a school that engaged in the process of peeling back layers of data, being suspicious of superficial data and looking for *other data* to help them exercise *equity muscle.*

PEELING THE DATA AT CORTEZ INTERMEDIATE SCHOOL

Cortez Intermediate is a 900-student school located in a lower socioeconomic urban area in Southern California. Cortez has enjoyed a good reputation as a school with a stable staff and a solid administration who have maintained high academic standards in the face of the demographic changes that occurred over the past seven or eight years. While the neighborhood was once primarily White and middle class, the population of the school became 75% Latino, 70% economically disadvantaged, and 70% English learners.

The direction of achievement for the school was validated when California launched its new accountability program that ranked schools according to their performance on standardized exams. The state provides two rankings reported in deciles from one (lowest) to ten (highest). The first ranking compares schools to *all schools in the state.* Cortez received a three, indicating that their students ranked in the third band from the bottom. This result, while not very high, was not concerning, as the district and school believed it unfair to compare Cortez students to other students in the state with different student populations who historically perform better on standardized exams.

The second ranking compares schools to *other like schools*, that is, schools with similar student characteristics including socioeconomic status, parent education level, and percent of English learners. When compared to like schools, Cortez ranked an eight out of ten, among the highest performance bands, with 40% of all students performing at grade level on the state standardized exam. This result was widely perceived to be an accurate assessment of the strength of the school program for all students. The staff and district felt that the school was meeting the needs of their students and that they were doing the best they could with their student population.

Cortez Intermediate is typical of many schools with diverse populations. Educators worked diligently over years to refine programs and services. As a response to the changing needs of the students, the school decided to use data to help refine their programs to be more responsive. They looked at test scores and found that many students were unsuccessful in the regular classes, so they set up specialized pathways tailored to the needs of each group, including low-, middle-, and high-level courses, depending on students' percentile ranks. The school and district felt confident that their program design was a primary contributor to the perceived positive results in student achievement.

The Real Story: The Other Data

The principal of the school was pleased with the school's direction but had some nagging private concerns. These concerns included

- complacency over low levels of student achievement at Cortez,
- the perception by many that "Cortez students" could not achieve any higher,
- the widespread acceptance that it was normal for some ethnic groups to inevitably perform lower academically than other groups,
- the question of whether the school ranking based on high-stakes test scores told a *complete* story about student achievement at her school.

Simply stated, the principal had a suspicion that her school might not be doing everything it could to promote maximum learning for *all* Cortez students. This is where the real story begins.

The skillful use of data is a powerful tool in directing the work of education. Over the years, educators have become accustomed to receiving a myriad of reports from test publishers and local databases that respond to typical questions including the following:

- How many students are meeting or not meeting grade-level expectation?
- Which groups of students are achieving or not achieving (commonly including ethnic, socioeconomic, language proficiency, and special needs groups)?
- What content areas do students find most challenging?

Typical analyses of test scores will not respond to the types of questions generated by the principal at Cortez Intermediate. The concerns at Cortez stem from an equity and responsibility perspective, posing questions about whether the school is doing all it can to educate every student. In order to address data from this point of view, we must ask different questions:

- What story does the traditional data seem to tell? Could there be more to the story?
- Are the traditional data analyses painting an accurate and complete picture of how all students are performing and whether that performance level is acceptable?

- What are the assumptions or belief systems most likely in place in order to accept the performance levels as normal?
- Have those assumptions or belief systems been tested?
- What types of deeper questions would test those assumptions and complete the story to reveal the complete truth about educational opportunity for every student?
- Bottom line: Is the *wallpaper effect* operating in this situation?

In order to respond, we must look at *other data*. Let's trace the path taken by the principal at Cortez to see how the use of *other data* helps tell the real story at Cortez.

Is Student Achievement the Best It Can Be for All Students at This School?

A widespread belief is that a lower student achievement ceiling exists for schools with particular types of students, especially certain ethnic, cultural, and income groups. The demographic profile of Cortez Intermediate is such that the majority of the school and district staff was comfortable in saying that, for Cortez, student achievement was good enough. Recall that the program structure stratified offerings into three pathways. The prevailing notion is that using data to place students into tailored programs designed for them is a positive move toward promoting achievement. Therefore, once such programmatic decisions are made, the resulting student achievement profile is likely to be the best it can be for that school. However, in order to determine whether a school's achievement profile is the best it can be overall, we must use a variety of data, including the *other data*, to draw accurate conclusions.

Let's trace the study at Cortez Intermediate by posing some "suspicious" questions, identifying the *other data* that relate to the questions, and then answering the questions from an equity perspective.

What is the profile of student placement in the tiered pathway? Is the profile reasonable?

Often, schools continue ineffective practices year after year. Without frequent monitoring, reflection, and evaluation, a danger exists that unintended consequences may result from the evolution of those practices over time. Figure 2.4 displays an example of the typical placement of students in the English program, based on their standardized test scores.

Often, schools continue ineffective practices year after year. Without frequent monitoring, reflection, and evaluation, a danger exists that unintended consequences may result from the evolution of those practices over time.

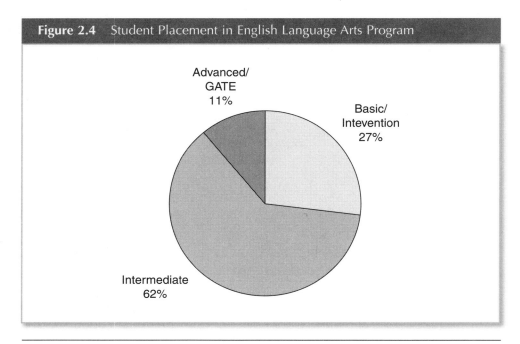

Figure 2.4 Student Placement in English Language Arts Program

Advanced/
GATE
11%

Basic/
Intevention
27%

Intermediate
62%

Source: PRINCIPAL's Exchange, 2008.

The original intent of the pathway design was to have the majority of students in the mid-level classes, the few struggling students in an intervention class, and the identified GATE students in the accelerated classes. Although the demographics shifted over the next five years, teachers and counselors continued to place students based on the same testing criteria. At this point, only 62% of students were placed in the mid-range classes, about 11% in the highest-level classes, and almost one-third of all students were assigned to the lowest level. This was not the intended placement profile when the levels were developed. The staff expected to have the majority of students working at grade level with only a few needing a specialized program.

The school structured their mathematics program following the same assumptions, resulting in the development of various levels of math-course options for students, based on standardized test scores and grades (see Table 2.3). The goal was to have the majority of eighth graders complete a full-year algebra course before they left middle school. Yet, actual student placement had less than 10% of all eighth graders taking the full-year algebra course. The vast majority of students took simplified classes that would result in them leaving middle school without even half a year of algebra.

Table 2.3 Math Course Placement

Math Course	Number of Students
Remedial Math	260
Pre-Algebra	490
Half-Year Algebra	88
Full-Course Algebra	83

Source: PRINCIPAL's Exchange, 2008.

The design of the program had not produced the expected results in student placement. Far too many students were experiencing the lowest, most simplified curricular program.

Sometimes decisions for programs are made because they are intuitively or emotionally appealing, and they are made without the benefit of much study or research. The tiered program design was developed in an effort to better meet the needs of students whom the staff felt were struggling with rigorous, grade-appropriate material. By placing the students in levels according to test scores, the staff expected to make more students successful in school. The principal was uncomfortable with the design and felt the need to test its effectiveness.

In order to evaluate the program, we can begin with typical assessment measures, but we must add an equity lens. For example, the pattern of student achievement at Cortez was associated with student placement levels. Figure 2.5 compares standardized test performance in reading comprehension with the percentage of students in each level of English. Notice that the percentage of students who scored within the intermediate range (between the 30th and 50th percentile) on standardized tests was near the percentage of students who were in "intermediate" courses; the number of students who scored above average (above the 50th percentile) mirrored the percentage of students taking "advanced" courses; the number of students scoring below average (below the 30th percentile) related to the number of students taking "basic" courses. Therefore, the gap between grade-level expectations and student achievement was not closing under the existing program structure. Students placed in the basic classes continued to perform below expected levels, students in intermediate classes performed close to grade level and students in advanced classes continued to perform at above-average levels.

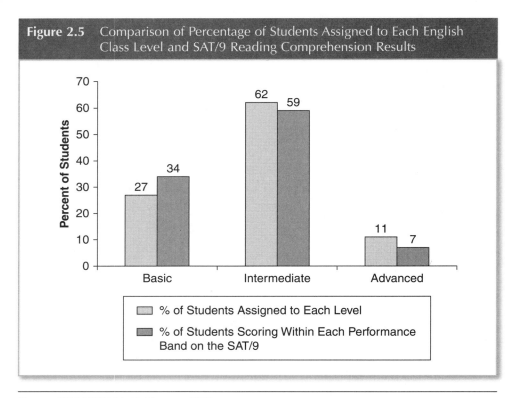

Figure 2.5 Comparison of Percentage of Students Assigned to Each English Class Level and SAT/9 Reading Comprehension Results

Source: PRINCIPAL's Exchange, 2008.

On other measures, such as grades, student performance yields the same profile. Students in the simplified courses experienced the least academic success. For example, Figure 2.6 indicates that 53% of all students in basic classes earned grades of D or F at the end of the first semester. In contrast, only 6% of students who took the advanced course earned a poor grade. Though the easier classes were formed to help students be more successful, in fact, the easiest classes resulted in the greatest failure. We cannot conclude that course assignment in and of itself *caused* the results. However, we can conclude that the current grouping practices did not produce the desired outcomes for the lower-performing students, but resulted instead in the perpetuation of the pattern of achievement that historically existed, and, if left alone, would likely produce similar results in the future.

> Though the easier classes were formed to help students be more successful, in fact, the easiest classes resulted in the greatest failure.

Peeling off wallpaper at Cortez required *other data* from classroom observations that would help find out about the rigor of instruction. Conclusions from the observations indicated that, over time, the lowest level of English classes evolved into instruction that was four to five

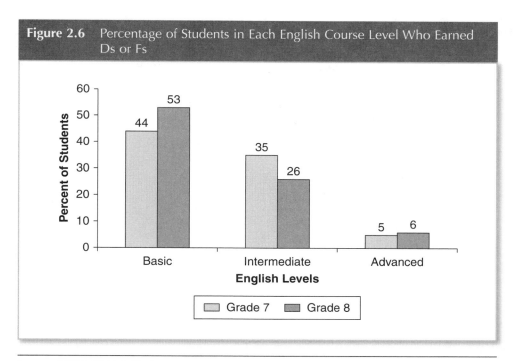

Figure 2.6 Percentage of Students in Each English Course Level Who Earned Ds or Fs

Source: PRINCIPAL's Exchange, 2001.

grades below level. The mid-level classes were about two levels below grade. The advanced group, intended to surpass grade-level standards, was actually only presented with grade-level curriculum. Efforts to tailor the school program to meet the needs of students and accelerate student achievement had, in fact, had the opposite effect by systematically ensuring the underperformance of the majority of Cortez students.

Mathematics instruction at Cortez demonstrated the same profile, with the higher failure rates occurring in the less rigorous classes that were originally created to help struggling students experience more success (see Figure 2.7). Sixty-six percent of all intervention math students earned grades of D or F at the end of the first semester of this year. The percentage of Ds and Fs decreased by one half for algebra classes.

Data from classroom observations suggested that instructional delivery methods did not support student development of advanced mathematical proficiency. Though exceptions existed, math instruction at Cortez tended to consist of lecture/explanation from the board or overhead, followed by individual student practice on solving problems. Students received few opportunities to become actively engaged in cooperative or collaborative learning, or to practice concept application using manipulatives or technology. Students did not often have extended opportunities to communicate, orally or in writing, about their learning, in order to promote metacognition (self-reflection about their depth of understanding).

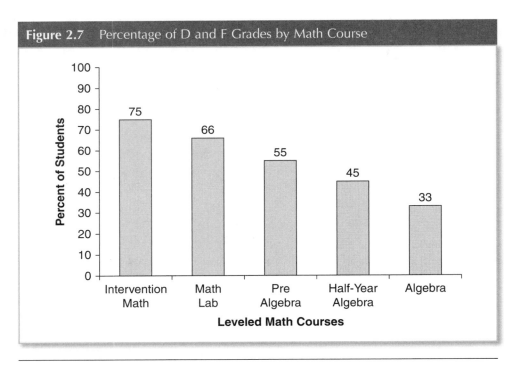

Figure 2.7 Percentage of D and F Grades by Math Course

Source: PRINCIPAL's Exchange, 2008.

Classroom observations also sparked another question. The observation team began to believe they could guess the level of the classes based on the ethnicity of the majority of the students enrolled. *Other data* were then identified to answer the question about the pattern in course level enrollment by ethnicity and confirmed the suspicion. The advanced courses were predominantly White or Asian while the lower-level classes were filled mostly with Latino students.

The design of the program was clearly *not* resulting in improved student achievement. At best, it served to maintain existing levels of performance, and, at worst, it was perpetuating historical patterns of underperformance for certain student groups.

Final Thoughts

The principal of Cortez Intermediate School was courageous in her undertaking of this inquiry of her school. She was motivated not by legal compliance or accountability, but by doing the right thing for students. The community and staff at Cortez were pleased with their progress and comfortable with their student achievement profiles. From all appearances, Cortez was doing fine and as they say, "If it ain't broke . . ."

However, the principal had a gut feeling that more could be done to improve the achievement of all students. Staff accepted as inevitable the achievement story told by traditional test reports for their population of students. By augmenting the school story and uncovering *other data,* the principal was able to tell a very different story about Cortez Intermediate, a story about student placement and instructional factors that was likely creating a ceiling that was stifling learning for the majority of students. Use of the *other data* helped the staff have meaningful discussions, questioning the inevitability of the current achievement profiles and opening up the possibility of doing things differently for students. More importantly, the principal's adept use of the *other data* resulted in the possibility of providing students with high-quality educational opportunities they might otherwise never experience.

The case of Cortez Intermediate School is an excerpt from a full-scale school analysis. It serves to demonstrate a school's initial attempt at using *other data* to peel off layers of historical practices in order to uncover truths about various groups of their students and their achievement patterns. In time, and with more experience, the Cortez faculty became very sophisticated "wallpaper peelers," and in three years the school's achievement results rivaled those of schools in much more affluent neighborhoods.

DATA-BITE EXERCISES

This section presents data tables and graphs targeting key questions that many schools and districts face. Like sound bites, "data bites" are individual, concise data displays that respond to the types of questions, suspicions, and worries that arise when engaging in the process of flexing *equity muscle* in schools and districts. Readers have an opportunity to practice interpreting the data displays and pushing the boundaries of current thinking on each of the topics addressed.

All of the data presented are from actual schools. Refer to the data bites below and see how they inform the posed questions. As mentioned previously, we strongly recommend that this process occur in the context of collegial teams whenever possible. After discussions, review Appendix B to compare your interpretations with the explanations of the data provided.

> ### Your Turn: Engaging With Data Bites
>
> Review the data bites and select the ones that might be relevant to your school or district. Study the questions and examine the findings. Complete the prompts. We encourage use of the literature and other resources to inform the *interpretation, implications,* and *next steps* discussions. The graphs and tables can be projected on screens to engage in full-group discussions or modified using your own data.

Refer to Data Bite 1. Is the school promoting a rigorous course-taking pattern in mathematics for all students? What is the course-taking trajectory for Grades 9–12? (Conduct this same analysis with disaggregated data.)

Data Bite 1	Number of Students at Each Grade Level Taking Each Math Course							
	Pre-Algebra	Half-year Algebra	Alg.*	Geometry*	Algebra 2*	Pre-Calc.*	Calc. AB*	Calc. BC*
9th Graders	220	140	94	57	3	0	0	0
10th Graders	188	62	99	74	66	1	0	0
11th Graders	122	52	29	79	74	26	20	0
12th Graders	48	13	21	30	77	27	36	14
Total	**578**	**267**	**243**	**240**	**220**	**58**	**56**	**14**

*Only these courses are recognized as university prerequisites.

Source: PRINCIPAL's Exchange, 2008.

Findings:

Implications:

Other Data Needed:

Next Steps:

Refer to Data Bite 2. Is the high school promoting a rigorous course-taking pattern in science for all students?

Data Bite 2	Number of Students at Each Grade Level Taking Each Science Course							
	Life Science	General Science	Bio.*	Phys. Sc.*	Bio. AP*	Chem.*	Phys.*	Total
9th Graders	391	1	58	0	0	0	0	450
10th Graders	48	14	87	6	0	40	0	185
11th Graders	25	224	87	15	3	58	31	443
12th Graders	18	14	14	27	21	26	20	140
Total	482	243	246	48	24	124	51	1218

*Note: Only these courses are recognized as university prerequisites.

Source: PRINCIPAL's Exchange, 2004.

Findings:

Implications:

Other Data Needed:

Next Steps:

Refer to Data Bite 3. How do parent and student expectations for college compare to actual college enrollment? The parents and students were surveyed and the school concluded that the students and parents had low expectations for four-year college enrollments based on their perceptions of African American students. How can these data be used to meet the expectations of parents and students?

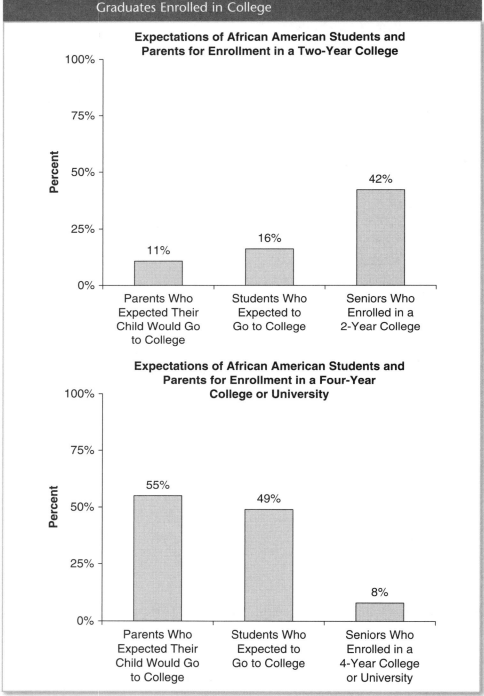

Data Bite 3 Comparison of African American Students' and Parents'
Expectations for College/University Enrollment to Percentage of
Graduates Enrolled in College

**Expectations of African American Students and
Parents for Enrollment in a Two-Year College**

Percent

100%

75%

50%   42%

25%   16%

              11%

0%

Parents Who   Students Who   Seniors Who
Expected Their   Expected to   Enrolled in a
Child Would Go   Go to College   2-Year College
to College

**Expectations of African American Students and
Parents for Enrollment in a Four-Year
College or University**

Percent

100%

75%

              55%
50%   49%

25%

                                                         8%

0%

Parents Who   Students Who   Seniors Who
Expected Their   Expected to   Enrolled in a
Child Would Go   Go to College   4-Year College
to College   or University

Source: Johnson, R.S. (2002).

Findings:

Implications:

Other Data Needed:

Next Steps:

Refer to Data Bite 4. How long have English learners (EL) been labelled EL without meeting the criteria to be considered fluent? Criteria for reclassification to English Fluent include advanced English language proficiency and academic achievement. What are the implications of this profile?

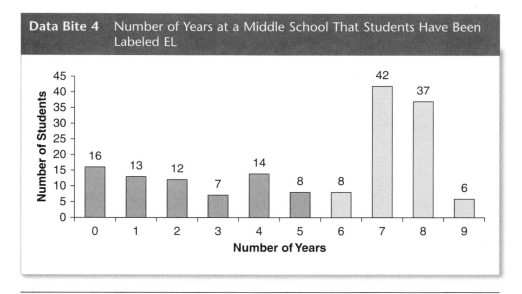

Data Bite 4 Number of Years at a Middle School That Students Have Been Labeled EL

Source: PRINCIPAL's Exchange, 2008.

Findings:

Implications:

Other Data Needed:

Next Steps:

Refer to Data Bite 5. What is the eighth-grade course enrollment in algebra for different racial and ethnic groups over two years? The goal is to enroll all eighth graders by 2010. The graph shows that there are Gaps from the goal and gaps among groups. Analyze the gaps for each group. Is there any good news? Areas of concern?

Data Bite 5 Eighth-Grade Course Enrollment in Algebra: Sample Presentation of a School's Summarized Data

School:

Goal: Enroll all eighth-grade students in algebra by 2010.

AA - African American   A - Asian   W - White
AI - American Indian   L - Latino

Grade 8	AA	AI	A	L	W
2007–2008	37%	20%	80%	31%	67%
2008–2009	54%	36%	92%	58%	74%

Source: Johnson, R.S. (2002).

Findings:

Implications:

Other Data Needed:

Next Steps:

Refer to Data Bite 6. How do second-grade boys and girls score in mathematics at four proficiency levels? What story does it tell about performance for each group and about gaps between the groups? What should be the desired levels of achievement for each group and how far or close is each group to that goal?

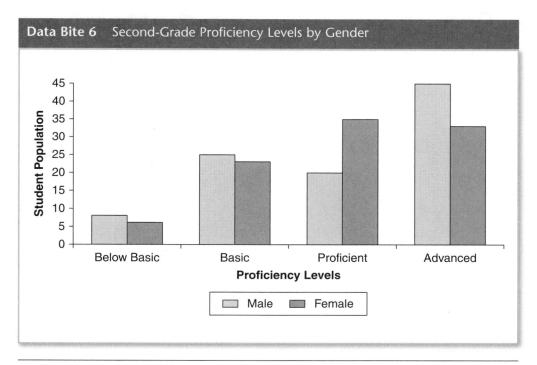

Data Bite 6   Second-Grade Proficiency Levels by Gender

Source: Johnson, R.S. (2002).

Findings:

Implications:

Other Data Needed:

Next Steps:

Refer to Data Bite 7. What is the relationship between the teacher-developed common assessment results (CA) and the annual state assessment results? Grade-level teacher teams create monthly common assessments to check student progress toward mastery of language arts standards. Data Bite 7 displays the result of Unit 5 common assessment, which is administered in April, a month before the annual spring state exams. Note: FBB/BB refers to the lowest performance levels (far below basic/below basic), and Prof/Adv refers to the highest performance levels (proficient/advanced).

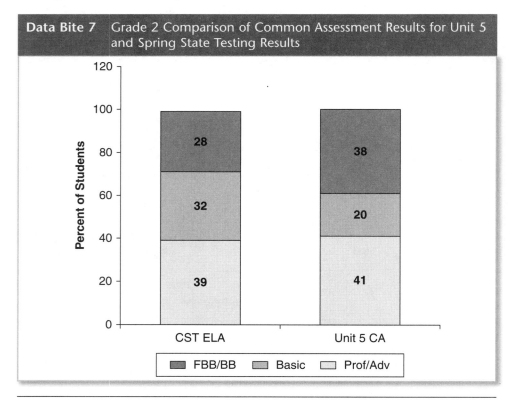

Data Bite 7 Grade 2 Comparison of Common Assessment Results for Unit 5 and Spring State Testing Results

Source: PRINCIPAL's Exchange, 2009.

Findings:

Implications:

Other Data Needed:

Next Steps:

Refer to Data Bite 8. This is the same comparison as Data Bite 7 with very different results for a different teacher team. What is the relationship between these teacher-developed common assessment results (CA) and the annual state assessment results? What might explain the differences? What additional questions come to mind?

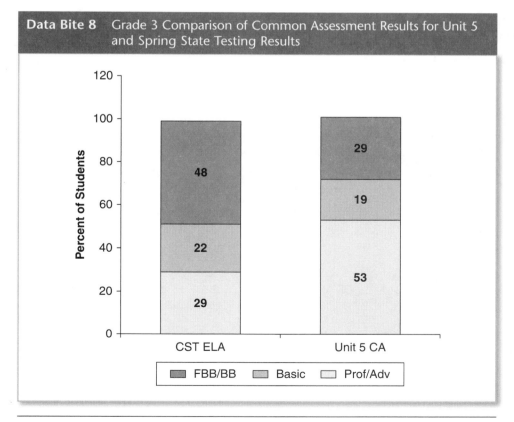

Data Bite 8 Grade 3 Comparison of Common Assessment Results for Unit 5 and Spring State Testing Results

Source: PRINCIPAL's Exchange, 2009.

Findings:

Implications:

Other Data Needed:

Next Steps:

CONCLUSION

This chapter focused on going beyond the use of the traditional data to uncover and address inequities in schools and districts. The scenarios and cases demonstrate the urgent need to peel off the wallpaper when examining traditional data such as high-stakes tests. This deeper layer of information is essential in order to analyze gaps and to reveal patterns of possible inequities among diverse groups of students. Challenging and uncomfortable questions need to be asked and answered. The answers present the opportunities for us to have clearer windows into understanding the complexities of what is occurring with our students in the school environment and to ultimately do something about inequities.

Part II

Peeling the Wallpaper off Everyday Inequities

3 The Journey Through School

Starting With the End in Mind

SCENARIO: KYLE

Kyle was never a star student, but he got by. A quiet and shy boy, he managed to get passed from grade to grade without much notice. He realized early on that if he just stayed out of trouble and turned in assignments, his teachers would be satisfied and he could earn Cs on his report cards. He was the second of three children who lived with their mother in a small rural town. His mom left school early to start working and was pleased that her son was doing fine in school.

When Kyle was in third grade, his teacher told his mother that he would be participating in a morning math program. Kyle did not hate math, he did not hate—or love—any subject, so he dutifully attended. He played some computer games each morning with little interaction with the teacher's aide who opened the door when he and ten other students arrived every day. In the fifth grade, Kyle was assigned to a new teacher and was pleased to see that the ten morning students were in his class. He was not asked to come to school early that year. Instead, the teacher told his mom that she would be using a special math program in class for all of her students. Kyle thought nothing of it since all his classmates had the same book. He noticed that his cousin, who was in another fifth-grade classroom, had a different math book. His was newer.

After a long summer, Kyle started middle school. He reported to the office the first day and received his class schedule. He was pleased to see history listed as his first-period class, as he had secretly very much enjoyed learning about American history in the fifth grade. He was one of the few students to memorize the preamble to the Constitution, though he never let on to his teacher that he had learned it. He was also fascinated whenever he saw replicas of actual historical documents—John Hancock's original signature, old photos. He was especially interested in the government, how the first president came to be, and how people get elected to office.

He got to his first period and was relieved to see many familiar faces of students who were in his fifth-grade class. He sat down next to them and shared their slightly bewildered first-day-of-middle-school looks. As he moved through his day, he noticed that most of his friends were in all of his classes— what a relief! His last period was math. His teacher seemed kind and explained that they were lucky. This class was an "easy A" because they would be reviewing fifth-grade math. She passed out the books and Kyle noticed that it looked a lot like the math book his cousin used the year before, but it was brand new. He would make sure to use a book cover to keep it nice all year.

Kyle's middle school experience was mostly fine. He learned that grades matter to people much more in middle school and that "passing" was any- thing above an F. So, Kyle was "passing" middle school. Still on the shy side, he wanted to play a little sports at school, or maybe join the history club or the future teacher's club (maybe he'd like to teach history one day), but none of his friends were involved in those activities, and he felt uncomfortable around unfamiliar people. So he just went to school every day, turned in homework, and continued to pass his classes. As he crossed the stage at the eighth-grade promotion ceremony, Kyle imagined what high school would be like and decided that it would be different. He decided to tell his high school counselor about his secret interest in history and his idea about becoming a history teacher—maybe he could teach at his own middle school. Maybe he would even run for a student body office. That would be something!

The first day of high school, Kyle reported to the office for his class sched- ule. He was confused to see that he had no history class. He had all the reg- ular subjects, and two electives called Life Skills and High School Success, but no history. While that was disappointing, he was comforted to see so many familiar faces in his classes throughout the day. His sixth-period math class was interesting. The teacher was young and energetic. This was his first teaching job and he was very happy to be at that school. Kyle knew that ninth graders at his high school took algebra. His book was called Readiness for Algebra. *His cousin's book was called* Algebra: College-Prep, *but algebra is algebra, he guessed.*

At the end of the ninth grade, Kyle received a call slip to see his coun- selor. His counselor seemed very nice. As he was passing all of his classes,

Kyle intended to tell her about his interest in history, his plans for a career in teaching, and his hopes of running for school office in the spring. Before he got a chance, the counselor told him that she was meeting with all students who were at risk of not graduating—not graduating! She told him that many students like him in the Title I program . . . what program? . . . with a history of poor test scores . . . huh? . . . often had troubles passing the high school graduation exam . . . you have to pass a test to graduate from high school? She was also worried that he might not complete the required high school courses for graduation, unless he attended summer school each year.

As it turns out, Kyle was on a different track from other students. Though he never realized it (in retrospect, he suspected), Kyle had trouble in math as early as second grade. As a result, he was identified "Title I," which meant the school had to give him extra support. The morning program was supposed to provide that support and close his math gap, but it did not. His elementary school grouped all the fifth-grade Title I students into one class to provide them extra support. That was supposed to close the gap, but it did not. The middle school placed students in pathways based on fifth-grade test scores, so Kyle and the other Title I students were grouped together for math, which by virtue of master scheduling constraints, grouped them together most of the day. Teachers received rosters of their identified Title I students and modified their curriculum and expectations to the level of the class to help students be more successful. Kyle's name was on those lists. That was supposed to close the gap, but actually made it grow, not only in math.

Finally, the high school used test scores and teacher recommendations for placement in ninth-grade courses. Based on his middle school record, Kyle was placed in less rigorous courses. In order to make room for those helper classes, history was deferred that year. That day with the counselor, he learned that biology and chemistry were required courses, but that he could not take them until he took algebra and geometry. It turns out that algebra prep doesn't count for anything but elective credit. He learned that the high school graduation exam was administered to tenth graders and contained middle school and high school material that he never studied in his classes. He saw that his electives and lower-level classes took up the spaces other students were using to graduate on time. For the first time, he felt very out of place and different from other students.

He let the counselor talk, count credits, show him summer school schedules and lists of courses, testing dates, and addresses to local continuation high schools and adult schools. When she finished, she asked if he had any questions. "No. Thank you." As he left the office, he realized he forgot to mention that he loved history. Kyle attended summer school, was transferred to an alternative program and then one day stopped going to school.

A True Story

OVERVIEW

News on graduation and dropout rates in the nation is extremely disturbing, particularly for some populations. In this chapter, we present a national picture on the three major end-of-schooling indicators: graduation, dropping out, and college preparation. We discuss the implications of the current profile regarding K–12 end-of-school attainment levels and raise on-the-ground issues using *other data* looked at through an equity lens. Descriptions of educational endpoints and long-term life consequences for different populations of students are highlighted. We describe the data challenges and limitations and discuss current changes in the NCLB regulations for calculating graduation rates. We draw attention to early warning indicators linked to students' schooling experiences and end-of-school outcomes. The focus is on those factors that schools and districts have the power to influence. We end by arguing for the systematic infusion of the student voice in end-of-school conversations as a means to add a perspective not accessible through other means.

GRADUATING AND DROPPING OUT: THE STATUS OF THE K–12 PIPELINE

Only about seven out of ten students (69.2%) from the 2002–03 ninth-grade class graduated from our nation's public high schools in 2006 (Gewertz, 2009). Editorial Projects in Education (2009) Research Center used the cumulative promotion index (CPI) methodology and data from the U.S. Department of Education to calculate the estimated graduation rates for the class of 2006 using the number of ninth graders that enrolled in 2002–03.

Between 1996 and 2006 the graduation rate increased by an average of 2.8%. There was a steady increase each year until 2005 when there was a drop of almost a percentage point. Figure 3.1 shows that an estimated 1.2 million students had leaked out of the pipeline and failed to

---

Figure 3.1 2005–2006 Graduate and Nongraduates CPI

4 million ninth graders in 2002–03 × 69.6% CPI = **2.8 million graduates** in 2005–06

4 million ninth graders − 2.8 million graduates = **1.2 million nongraduates**

Source: Education Week's Diplomas Count 2006. Reprinted with permission from Editorial Projects in Education.

graduate in 2006. If this trend continues, at the end of ten years there will potentially be 12 million people in our nation who can be categorized as nongraduates.

When disaggregated by racial and ethnic groups, the data show large disparities in 2006 graduation rates, particularly for African American, American Indian, and Latino students. Asian and White students (79% and 76%) graduate a much higher proportion of the their peer group than do African American (51%), Latino (55%), and Native American students (50%) (Swanson, 2009).

> Asian and White students (79% and 76%) graduate a much higher proportion of the their peer group than do African American (51%), Latino (55%), and Native American students (50%) (Swanson, 2009).

In spite of this bleak picture, there is hopeful news. There are districts and states with similar populations that have dissimilar results. Those schools and districts that are making gains can become lighthouses for those that are struggling to improve. (See Editorial Projects in Education publications.)

With the need for students to have a high school diploma at a minimum and with workplace needs requiring postsecondary education past high school, it seems that we should be aiming for a goal of 100% graduation rates. It will be important to measure the gap from that goal for each group to answer the question: How far are African American, Asian, Latino, Native American, and White students from the goal, and how aggressively should graduation rates increase for each group, and over what period of time? The percent of increase for each year needs to be calculated with equity in mind. The same increase by year for each group will continue to leave some groups behind.

Consequences of Not Graduating

There are profound consequences for our nation as well as for individuals when there are high rates of students who don't graduate from high school. We are well aware that societal issues outside of the school heavily influence our young people, but we also know that positive schooling influences matter and that they can override many of the negative external circumstances. Olson (2006a) states "Research has found that while no one factor predicts which students will graduate and which will not, schools play a pivotal role" (p. 10). The students who drop out face the grim prospect of ending up on the bottom of the

> "Research has found that while no one factor predicts which students will graduate and which will not, schools play a pivotal role" (p. 10).

employment ladder, in servitude and minimum wage jobs, unemployed, part of the school-to-prison pipeline, or worse, hopelessly forgotten and disenfranchised (Faircloth & Tippeconnic, 2010). Losen (2006) presents a compelling summarized version of the comprehensive financial and quality-of-life losses stemming from dropout rates, using information from the 2005 Teachers College Columbia University Conference on the social cost of not graduating. The presenters' summarized information is as follows:

- Over a lifetime, an eighteen-year-old who does not complete high school earns about $260,000 less than an individual with a high school diploma, and contributes about $60,000 less in federal and state income taxes. The combined income and tax losses aggregated over one cohort of eighteen-year-olds who do not complete high school is about $192 billion, or 1.6% of the gross domestic product. (*Cecilia Elena Rouse, economist, Princeton University*)

- Individuals with a high school diploma live longer, have better indicators of general health, and are less likely to use publicly financed health insurance programs than high school dropouts. If the 600,000 eighteen-year-olds who failed to graduate in 2004 had advanced only one grade level, it would have saved about $2.3 billion in publicly financed medical care, aggregated over a lifetime. (*Peter Mailman, School of Public Health, Columbia University*)

> Individuals with a high school diploma live longer, have better indicators of general health, and are less likely to use publicly financed health insurance programs than high school dropouts.

- Adults who lack a high school diploma are at greater risk of being on public assistance. If all those receiving assistance who are high school dropouts instead had a high school diploma, the result would be a total cost saving for federal welfare spending, food stamps, and public housing of $7.9 billion to $10.8 billion a year. (*Jane Waldfogel et al., Columbia University School of Social Work*)

- In the 2004 election, college graduates were nearly three times more likely to vote than Americans without a high school diploma. (*Jane Junn, Eagleton Institute of Politics, Rutgers University*)

- High school dropouts are far more likely to commit crimes and be incarcerated than those with more education. A 1% increase in the high school completion rate of men ages 20 to 60 would save the United States as much as $1.4 billion a year in reduced costs from crime incurred by victims and society at large. (*Enrico Moretti, economist, University of California, Berkeley*) (p. 7)

CALCULATION CONFUSION: WHAT IS THE REAL GRADUATION AND DROPOUT PICTURE?

Alarming data on not graduating and dropping out have received some attention but have not triggered a loud enough collective call to action. Typically reporting dropout, graduation, and college preparation data are misleading, with schools, states, and districts reporting inflated rates. For example, some states counted students who receive a General Education Development credential (GED), while others calculate their graduation rates by the percentage of graduates based on the number in the senior class. This method does not account for students who dropped out or those who were retained. We will illustrate examples of this later in the chapter.

NCLB requires states to report high school graduation rates as part of their AYP. Until recently, each state was allowed to use its own methodology in calculating the graduation rates and in setting target goals. Some states only required a 50% graduation rate. There also were major problems with the quality of the data reported. Hall (2007) identified two major problems:

1. State goals for raising graduation rates are far too low to spur needed improvement.

2. Gaps between student groups are allowed to persist by an accountability system that looks only at average graduation rates. (p. 1)

In 2008, the U.S. Department of Education (USDE) modified the NCLB graduation reporting regulations to: permit states to count as part of their graduation rates students who earned diplomas in five or more years, improve the way that graduation rates were calculated and reported, and improve the way in which schools would account for the reported rates. Beginning in the 2009–10 school year, all states must report their rates in the same way by calculating graduation rates as the proportion of the ninth-grade class that graduates with a standard diploma in four years. States can submit proposals to the USDE for permission to include students who graduate within six years as graduating on time. High schools must also disaggregate and report data for racial, ethnic, socioeconomic groups, students with disabilities, and for English learners. Schools will be required to improve graduation rates for all of the subgroups. Though this is good news, Gewertz (2009b) reports that only eighteen states have the required data systems to calculate the rates. Although the

National Governor's Association (NGA) endorsed this method in 2005, it is nevertheless expected that states will be supportive and provide the resources (Hoff, 2008).

Unlike the reporting of graduation rates, there are no NCLB uniform requirements for reporting dropouts. Federal statistics on dropouts are underreported. The most frequently reported national data on dropouts comes form the Census Bureau's Current Population Survey (CPS). Orfield (2004) cites the limitation of these data:

1. Data are self reported.

2. Data exclude the military and institutionalized populations.

3. There is a poor record of accounting for minority males.

Most states do not follow students over time and many simply vanish without a trace from the enrollment counts in schools. There are many ways that states classify students and allow schools to report information about students that are no longer in attendance. Those who are unaware of these factors may believe misleading data reports. For example, if a high school reports a 75% graduation rate, it might be assumed that the school would report a 25% dropout rate and that would account for 100% of the students who entered in ninth grade. However, there is a great deal of underreporting, and the dropout rates for that school would probably be reported as much lower. Schools have a lot of categories to choose from in categorizing whether a student should be reported as a dropout. One incredible example is reported by Orfield (2004). He reports that one state counts and categorizes students who go to jail as transfer students.

Balfanz and Legters (2004) used Common Core Data (CCD) from the National Center of Education Statistics to develop a measure that they term *promoting power*. This measure compares the number of ninth graders to the number of seniors or the number of tenth graders to seniors three years later. Using this measure, they are able to identify schools with high or low promoting power. Schools that graduate only 50 to 60% of their ninth- or tenth-grade cohorts are considered to have low promoting power. They have concluded from their research that one in five public high schools in the nation have weak promoting power, which translates to low graduation and high dropout rates. Those schools tend to be schools with racial and ethnic majorities. They describe these schools as *dropout factories*. These findings indicate a crisis in educational attainment for many of our students and identify major equity issues that must be addressed. This pattern is not inevitable (Balfanz & Legters 2004; Education Week's Diploma's Count, 2009). Balfanz and Legters (2004) identified places where schools that have a majority minority enrollment also have strong promoting power. These high schools have selective admissions and are in large cities such as Newark, NJ; New York City; and Philadelphia. Education Week's Diploma's Count (2009) reports that 2,200 districts throughout the nation exceeded the graduation rate expectations margin by 10 or more percentage points.

We will use an on-the-ground example to more concretely illustrate misleading calculations. At Hope High School, a conversation was occurring regarding the loss of students from Grade 9 to Grade 12. A freshman class of 442 students winnowed to a senior class of 263, of whom only 219 graduated. The school reported a 16% official dropout rate, as defined by this state as the percentage of students who withdraw from school with no intention of enrolling anywhere else, or who never return to school without explanation. In contrast, the Grade 9–12 attrition rate, the comparison between ninth and twelfth grade enrollment, was 60%. This figure defined the percentage of students who began as freshmen and became seniors at Hope High. Finally, the cohort graduation rate was 50%, describing the percentage of ninth graders who eventually graduated from Hope High. The administration decided to gather data and find out more about their lost students. They were able to find records for 104 of the 179 students who did not become seniors. The following list reports the status of those 104 students.

- Sixty-one went to a continuation high school. (Did they graduate and when?)
- Eighteen were transferred to another high school. (Did they graduate and when?)
- Fifteen went to adult education programs. (Did they graduate and when?)
- Five went to juvenile detention. (Did they return? Did they graduate and when?)
- Five were listed as official "dropouts" in twelfth grade.

Although these data provide more in-depth information, the school will need to find out which students left for various reasons and if this attrition was related to policies and practices at the school and/or outside influences. Also, more *other data* are needed about whether these students eventually graduated with their peer group.

Your Turn: Calculating Attrition at Your School

Select your high school or refer to a state department of education website and select a high school. Complete the template to determine the attrition rate between ninth and twelfth grade. Then, compare it to the published dropout rate. Are they the same? If not, what are the implications of the discrepancy?

Template 3.1	Calculating Attrition
Grade	**Enrollment**
9	
10	
11	
12	
Total	
	12th grade enrollment minus 9th grade enrollment _____ divided by _____ (total number of students) equals _____% attrition
	_____% attrition rate versus _____ reported dropout rate

Figure 3.2   The Schooling Journey: What Gets Put in Students' Backpacks?

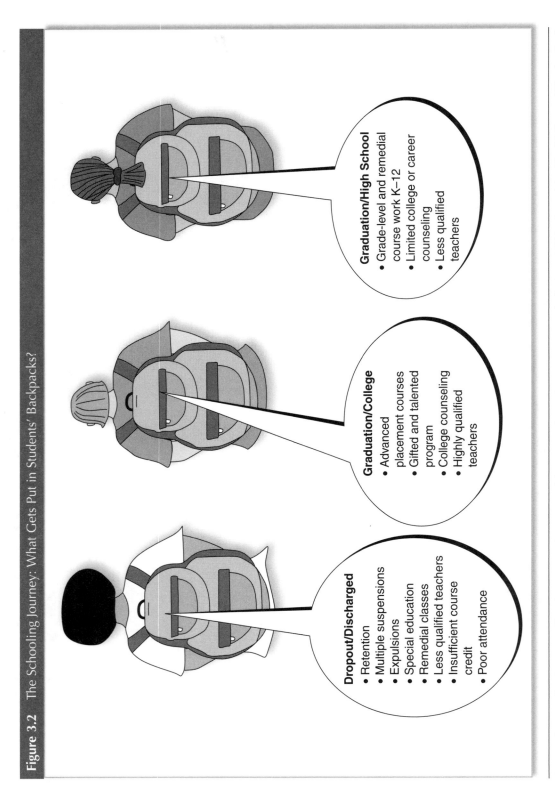

Dropout/Discharged
- Retention
- Multiple suspensions
- Expulsions
- Special education
- Remedial classes
- Less qualified teachers
- Insufficient course credit
- Poor attendance

Graduation/College
- Advanced placement courses
- Gifted and talented program
- College counseling
- Highly qualified teachers

Graduation/High School
- Grade-level and remedial course work K–12
- Limited college or career counseling
- Less qualified teachers

Graduating, dropping out, and being prepared to enter a college or university does not begin when students enter high school. For example, in an evaluation of a large, diverse school district, PRINCIPAL's Exchange found that indicators of whether students would graduate from high school prepared for college were first observable as early as fourth grade, where grouping and sorting practices began (PRINCIPAL's Exchange, 2005). Interestingly, teachers and administrators from the elementary schools had no idea of the impact of those early decisions on the long-term academic trajectory of their students.

Students' experiences as early as elementary school can set forces in motion that impinge on secondary-level outcomes such as graduation from high school, dropping out, and college preparation. Early decisions about grouping and program placements are usually well intended and designed to do no harm. In fact, some of these decisions benefit some students and give them valuable academic and social capital that results in graduation and college or university enrollment. Other decisions, however, can contribute to less favorable outcomes. In Figure 3.2, we use the image of backpacks to illustrate some of the school factors that appear to have a major influence on the student end of school outcomes. The mounting evidence about the effects of early sorting and labeling informs us about the serious implications and consequences of decisions we make on a daily basis about children's lives. The true scenario of Kyle puts a human face on how these decisions look on the ground. We are losing thousands of Kyles every day, and that pattern needs a reversal.

Most schools and districts do not systematically examine the warning signals in the system that put students at risk of not graduating or of dropping out, mostly because they are unaware that this information exists. States and those in leadership positions must call attention to the need to set up data systems with an early warning system that is responsive to the potential for students dropping out and also provides information on preparation for postsecondary education. The purpose of this information is not to feed an *inevitability assumption* to predict that someone will drop out (so why expend any effort), *but as a descriptor* for intervention that will reverse a negative trajectory (see Almeida, Johnson, & Steinberg, 2006; Balfanz & Legters, 2004; Children's Defense Fund, 2007; Flores-Gonzalez, 2002; Haney et al, 2004; Heppen & Therriault, 2008; Holzman, 2006; Orfield, 2004; Olson, 2006b; Viadero, 2006).

The dilemmas and suspicions about the inaccuracy of the graduation and dropout data at first may seem daunting and cause cynicism. To combat this, we need to know the next steps for acquiring an accurate picture of our students as they journey through our schools and, more importantly, what data can lead schools and districts to change existing paradigms that negatively affect students. The looming question asks, do we have clues and data that can help locate and stem the leakage? Yes, we do. Many system indicators for future success or failure in schools are already available. McKinsey & Company (2009) assert, "There is a demonstrable link between early performance in school and subsequent rates of high school graduation, college attendance and completion and ultimately earnings" (p. 17).

EXAMINING THE BOTTLENECK

There is evidence of policies in high schools that result in a ninth-grade *bottleneck* or *bulge.* The bottleneck or bulge refers to ninth-grade numbers that are substantially larger than in subsequent grades. The bulge or bottleneck numbers usually include new freshmen and ninth-grade repeaters who do not have enough credits to move on. In high school, ninth grade is where the greatest loss of students occurs. Many of the students who are ninth-grade repeaters eventually leave school. Haney and colleagues (2004) found that the drop in enrollment between Grades 9 and 10 tripled between 1970 and 2000. They also report that 70% to 80% of those who repeat ninth grade will not graduate. Think about that! They offer possible explanations for the gaping ninth-grade leak:

> . . . when schools are under intense pressure to increase test score averages, and are not given the resources or tools for doing so in an educationally sound manner, the easiest way to make test pass rates (or score averages) appear to increase in the grade at which high stakes tests are administered is to exclude "low achieving" students from being tested. One way to exclude them, at least temporarily, is to flunk them to repeat the grade before the grade tested. Another is to push students out of school altogether. (Haney et al., p. 53)

Table 3.1 depicts the losses in the pipeline nationally by income levels. Noteworthy here is that the highest leakage occurs for Grade 9 for high-poverty districts. While in Grade 10 the losses are similar for both groups, in Grades 11 and 12 the losses are higher in low-poverty districts. What might explain the difference in student losses for ninth graders, with a 40% loss for high-poverty students? What might explain the difference for twelfth graders, with more low-poverty students leaving school? The answers to these questions require a thorough peeling off of layers of *other data* for each school or district. Clearly, we are not graduating enough of our nation's youth, regardless of income levels.

Table 3.1	The High School Pipeline: Student Losses: Low-Poverty Versus High-Poverty Districts	
Grade	**Low-Poverty**	**High-Poverty**
9	27%	40%
10	27%	27%
11	22%	19%
12	24%	14%

Source: 2005–2006 Graduate and non-graduates CPI. *Education Week's Diplomas Count 2006.* Reprinted with permission from Editorial Projects in Education.

Your Turn: Finding Out About Students' Journeys in Your School

Answer and discuss ways to address the following inquiries. Look at the nature of resources, especially at the ninth-grade level, and gather data addressing the following:

- How are students oriented and monitored in the ninth grade?
- How are data about their previous school experiences used to provide safety nets for students whose school experiences include retention, special education, and so on, without labeling?
- Do the students receive appropriate attention from the most qualified teachers and counselors?
- How do students and parents inform the school of concerns? Is there an institutional culture of soliciting, listening to, and using their voices to inform school practice?
- How are expectations communicated to students? How are students' and parents' expectations communicated to staff?
- What resources (human and material) need to redistributed and targeted to ninth-grade students?

Heppen and Therriault (2008) tout the benefits and importance of early warning systems beginning at ninth grade:

Early warning systems use routinely available data housed at the school that are good predictors of whether a student is likely to drop out of high school.

The on-track indicator (based on course performance) is a better predictor of likelihood to graduate than are background characteristics or previous achievement test scores.

First-month, first-quarter, and the first-semester absences are additional strong predictors of drop out; these data are available early in the school year.

Districts and schools can use this information to target interventions that support off-track students while they are still in school before they drop out.

Districts and schools can use the information to look for patterns and identify school climate issues that may contribute to disproportionate rates at a subset of high schools or within subpopulations of students. (p. 2)

Viadero (2006) reports that the Consortium on Chicago School Research at the University of Chicago used *other data* such as course credits and passing courses as predictors of graduation. The Consortium deemed students on track if students earned a least five full course credits and had no more than one F as a semester grade at the end of their freshman year. Figure 3.3 shows the results of information on students that were gathered by the Consortium during their freshman year. We urge schools and districts to set up similar systems to monitor student course credits and passing rates. It is also essential that the rigor of courses be assessed and monitored. Some schools do transcript analyses, but they are used mostly to monitor whether or not students are on track for college. Using a different

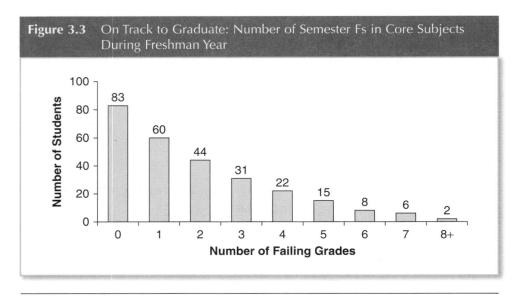

Figure 3.3 On Track to Graduate: Number of Semester Fs in Core Subjects During Freshman Year

Source: Education Week, Vol. 25, Issue 41S, Page 21, June 22, 2006.

lens, transcript analyses can answer a myriad of questions regarding student movement through the educational pipeline and can help identify potential bottlenecks that need to be unblocked.

STEMMING THE LEAKAGES

Schools have the power to play a central role in stemming leakages in the pipeline. Rarely are indicators prior to high school, student course taking, and promotion policies viewed as harbingers that may negatively affect student outcomes. In fact, quite the opposite argument is often posed in euphemistic statements that describe benefits for students that are similar to the arguments for why we track and sort students (Oaks, 1985). For example, typical rationale about retention offers, *The child needs another year so she will succeed in the next grade*. Rationale for placements in remedial, low-level classes, and special education opine, "She will get her needs met." Balfanz (quoted in Viadero, 2006) urges that we focus on school-based indicators, particularly at the elementary level, such as sixth graders who attend school less than 80%, have poor final grades in behavior from teachers, and are not passing in mathematics or English. This information should then be leveraged and lead to, hopefully, appropriate interventions. If we examine the backpack of the students who end up graduating and going to college, the school factors include: a gifted and talented curriculum, quality teachers, and rigorous courses. We are not encouraging another sorting scheme, rather, we are encouraging interventions that are responsive to students and ones that would be carefully monitored and provide them with access to the knowledge, curriculum, and instruction they will need to be prepared for postsecondary education options.

Table 3.2 summarizes key indicators that are links to nongraduation with the supporting research citations. We urge readers to use the references and resources in this book to gain further insights and information that can be used to help empower their particular school community to bring about the necessary scrutiny and conversations about their everyday practices. A research brief by the National High School Center, *Developing Early Warning Systems to Identify Potential High School Dropouts* (Heppen, & Therriault, 2008), is a useful resource and contains instructions on how schools and districts can identify students that are on track to graduate or drop out and provides suggestions for the use of this information. They have developed a Microsoft Excel template for schools to enter information. It can be accessed at http://www.betterhighschools.org. Most or all of these data are usually available and assessable at the school or district site.

Your Turn: Gathering and Analyzing Data and Strategies on Early Warning Indicators

Gather data for K–12 or at the high school level in your district using the information in the text and in Table 3.2. You can begin by only looking at high school data. You can access the Microsoft Excel spreadsheet cited previously. Heppen and Terriault (2008) suggest that three performance indicators should be collected for each student: (1) freshman course failure with an emphasis on core academic courses, (2) freshman grade point averages, and (3) credits earned at the end of each quarter, semester, or trimester. We suggest critical inquiry questions such as: What patterns emerge? What Gaps and gaps are visible at each schooling level? How should these data systematically be reviewed over time? What decisions should be made to modify practices and change the trajectory for students while time still exists? How are elementary and middle schools held accountable for their contributory practices? What can high schools do to articulate with their K–8 partners? What resources need to be redistributed?

Table 3.2   School-Based Indicators That Link to Nongraduation and Dropping Out

Indicators	Citation	Elementary	Middle/ High School
School attendance less than 80% Receiving poor final grade in behavior from their teachers Failing either mathematics or English	Viadero (2006)	X (Grade 6)	
Grouping practices beginning at elementary school	PRINCIPAL's Exchange (2005)	X	
Repeating a grade in elementary or middle school Repeating ninth grade	Viadero (2006); Flores-Gonzalez (2002); Haney et al. (2004); Heppen & Therriault (2008)	X	X
Placement in special education	Holzman (2006); Haney et al. (2004)	X	X
Suspensions or expulsion	Holzman (2006)	X	X

Indicators	Citation	Elementary	Middle/ High School
Lack of qualified teachers	Orfield (2004); Flores-Gonzalez (2002)	X	X
Missing more that 10% of instructional time	Allensworth & Easton (2007)		X
Number of course credits earned course grades and attendance in ninth grade (On-track indicator) Attendance (number of absences during the first 30 days of school during the ninth-grade year; failing ninth grade)	Allensworth & Easton (2005) Neild & Balfanz (2008)		X

GATHERING DATA

Looking at the K–12 patterns of graduating and dropping out underscores the push for longitudinal data systems that would follow students on their journey through school. Jerald (2006) provides information and describes how to develop early warning data systems. Accurate information is needed in order to inform what policies and practices need to be reformed or put into place to improve and measure schools' holding power. Even though it will take time to put systems in place, we urge schools and districts that have the capacity to collect data on K–12 institutional systemic issues that are forecasters for students in danger of not graduating or dropping out. We need to take stock of what we know about high schools and K–8 schooling leading up to high school, what conditions students need to be successful, and what schools should be planning with the end in mind to ensure that all students are successful. Systems must be set up to measure how many students who start high school actually graduate, with an eye toward cumulative K–8 issues.

Systems should be established so the data can be gathered at the institutional, teacher, and student level over time. Inquiries should include the following: What happens to students as they move through the system? Who stays, who leaves, and for

> Systems should be established so the data can be gathered at the institutional, teacher, and student level over time.

what reasons? What does the picture look like in kindergarten and at twelfth-grade graduation for different students? Do students leave the system better off than when they entered? What do we expect our students to be able to do when they leave the system? For example, our expectation is that all students should complete high school and receive the academic preparation to make the choice to enter a baccalaureate degree-granting institution.

We must ask: What is our collective imperative as a community of student advocates? What story does each figure tell about the school? What questions are left unanswered? What information provides the clearest picture of on-the-ground conditions at the school? What picture emerges when the figures are disaggregated by groups?

What are the appropriate responses and successful interventions to keep students on track to graduation and beyond?

COLLEGE READINESS

Students who begin school in kindergarten can one day either officially drop out or simply disappear, or they can graduate from high school. But is graduation enough? The U.S. economy is shifting from low-skilled to higher-skilled jobs that will require greater education. Jobs that previously required only a high school diploma are now requiring that applicants successfully complete courses that were formally considered college preparatory (Gewertz, 2009b). President Obama, in his 2010 State of the Union Address on January 27, reaffirmed his position on the need for all students to pursue their education beyond high school graduation. National policymaking bodies such as the National Governors Association Center for Best Practices, the Council of Chief State School Officers, and others stress the need for students to continue their education beyond high school. This has tremendous implications for high schools. High school graduation is a historical symbol of success in this country, a goal that most school systems are built to promote. As described earlier in this chapter, high school graduates have distinctive life advantages over nongraduates. However, a second stated goal of most school systems is to prepare some students for college. The "some" however, needs to be expanded to greatly increase the representation of African Americans, Latinos, Native Americans, and low-income students.

Olson (2006b) reports that a college graduate will annually earn on the average of $23,441 more than a high school graduate. The difference in annual earnings between a college graduate and a high school dropout is $31,595. According to Swanson (2009), students with a high school diploma, GED, and little preparation after high school can expect to earn $12,638 annually, compared to those with a bachelor's degree who can expect to earn $59,113 annually. Table 3.3 presents statistics on the percentage of total

Table 3.3	Distribution of the Adult Population Educational Attainment Levels and Their Percentage of Total Income	
Level of Education	**Percent of Adult Population**	**Percent* of Total Income**
Less than high school	13%	6%
High school graduate	29%	20%
Some college	29%	26%
Bachelor's degree	19%	27%
Advanced degree	11%	22%

*Rounded to nearest percent

Source: Distribution of the Adult Population Educational Attainment Levels and of Their Percent of Total Income. *Education Week's Diplomas Count 2009.* Reprinted with permission from Editorial Projects in Education.

income for adults based on their educational attainment levels. Clearly, completing postsecondary education is a financial plus. The adults with the advanced degrees are only 11% of the population, but represent 22% of the total income. Earlier information in this chapter described quality-of-life benefits that are beyond the financial advantages, such as the opportunity for more job security (Olson, 2006b).

High school graduation is not a guarantee that a student is prepared for college. Many states currently wrestle with how to define college readiness, and there are those that challenge the notion that we should prepare all students to be college ready. *Diplomas Count* (2009) devoted an entire issue to this topic. We endorse their definition of college readiness:

> [Each] state has formal expectations for what students will need to know and be able to do in order to be admitted to state's two-year and/or four-year institutions and enroll in credit-bearing courses. State approaches to defining college readiness have been classified into the following categories: course, skills, standards, and tests. Some states' definitions may include elements that do not fall into categories established for this analysis. (Editorial Projects in Education, 2009, p. 38)

Districts and states report college-related statistics differently. To be certain, it is challenging to collect accurate information on what path students follow once they graduate from high school. Some states use the number of students who take college-entrance exams (SAT, ACT) as counts of college readiness. Other systems report data from high school self-reported senior surveys about post–high school goals. Another approach is to articulate with higher education institutions and to receive data from them on how many high school graduates from specific high schools enrolled as freshmen. While each of these data sets are relevant, none paint a complete picture of what graduates do with their high school education.

In order to decide what *other data* to collect, schools and districts must reach an agreement on what the goals are for their graduates. While this seems like a simple task, it is not. In fact, beliefs about students and the *inevitability assumption* described in Chapter 2 often make it extremely challenging for educators, parents, and students to reach a consensus on the goals for high school beyond graduation. In our experience, we have witnessed the most creative language exchanges, replete with unvoiced subtext and high emotion, in conversations about what a high school diploma should leverage for students. The following is an excerpt of a transcript of one such conversation at a district graduation task force meeting for a diverse district in a working-class neighborhood. Participants included elementary, middle, and high school teachers and principals, counselors, parents, students, district office administrators, and board members. The task was to decide on official district goals for K–12 schooling in the district.

> In fact, beliefs about students and the inevitability assumption described in Chapter 2 often make it extremely challenging for educators, parents, and students to reach a consensus on the goals for high school beyond graduation.

Facilitator:	Do we agree that the first goal of schooling in our district is that all students will earn a high school diploma in four years?
Task Force:	Yes.
Facilitator:	Is there another goal?
Elementary Parent:	I want my child to be able to go to college after high school.
Facilitator:	Are you suggesting that our graduates should be college ready?
Middle School Parent:	Yes. My son wants to become a teacher.
District Administrator:	Why don't we say that all our graduates will be ready for postsecondary educational options?

Facilitator:	How does that sound to the group?
High School Counselor:	That is good because many of our graduates want to join the military or attend trade schools. Most jobs today require some training after high school, either at the community college, through adult school, or on the job. Some of the trade unions have their own training programs as well.
Facilitator:	Fine. Then, the second goal proposal is that all our graduates will be ready for postsecondary educational options.
Fifth-Grade Student:	May I ask something? Does that mean I can go to college? I want to go to college.
High School Counselor:	Of course, but what do you want to do when you grow up? You know that many jobs do not require traditional university degrees. Also, most students begin at community colleges and then decide whether they want to transfer to universities. There is plenty of time to decide that.
Facilitator:	How would we monitor a goal that all our students graduate ready for postsecondary education? Would we count all students who are in any type of schooling after graduation? I know another district that was able to make impressive gains in this statistic by counseling their students into the community college. In fact, 95% of all their graduates enroll in the local community college now.
High School Parent:	I work for an attorney and my boss has children that go to school in another neighborhood. I asked him about this and he said that at his children's school, parents expect their students to study for professions that require university degrees. The whole school is set up for all students to go on to university, not community college or other training. I asked him about students who want to go to the military or trades. He said that the requirements to get to the university are harder than any other option, so that by preparing all students for university, they are making it so that they have all the choices available to them.

Middle School Teacher: That's an interesting approach. However, I believe that the most responsible approach for us is to agree on a goal that we know is most applicable to our students. There are many, many jobs that earn good salaries that do not require university degrees. Those students who want can take the more advanced courses. But for the general population, I agree that we state our goal using the "postsecondary educational options" language. That gives every student the choice about what they want to work toward.

Elementary Teacher: Hmmm . . . I am concerned. Over the years, most of my students have told me that they want to be teachers, doctors, engineers, etcetera. I am often dismayed when they come back and visit me as they go onto high school. Even as seniors, many of my former students seem lost, not knowing what they will do after high school. Those who tell me they are going to "college" most often name the local community college and do not seem at all clear about college-to-university requirements. One student told me that she was going to the community college to become a lawyer!

Middle School Teacher: I think some students go to community college because it is cheaper than university. However, I think more often they probably did not complete the entire sequence of university prerequisite courses or maybe were not prepared for the entrance exams. That's why they end up at the community college many times. The truth is that most of our students who graduate university prepared can qualify for financial assistance to help them with the costs of a four-year institution.

Board Member: Do we have statistics on how many of our graduates who go to community college actually complete a four-year degree?

District Administrator: We have incomplete data on this, but I think the numbers are not very good.

Board Member: Shouldn't we be clear on this point? When we report the number of graduates who go onto college, do we disaggregate to see how many enrolled in four-year universities versus other types of postsecondary training?

District Administrator: I'm not sure.

High School Principal: Actually, I don't think so. We have articulation agreements with various institutions that send us reports of how many of our graduates enroll in their programs. Our clerks add up the numbers from all the reports and turn in that number in November of each school year.

Board Member: So when we say that 68% of our students go onto college, we really don't know what that specifically means?

Elementary Teacher: Oh boy, I always thought that number meant university graduation with at least a bachelor's degree. During parent conferences I always make it a point to encourage our parents to keep their children in our district, especially the stronger students, because of our college-going rate. I'd better revise what I tell them. I guess I cannot publicize that many of our students go onto the university.

Facilitator: Thank you for all your input. Are we ready to propose a second goal for our students?

Fifth-Grade Student: I am not sure what this is about too much. But I just want to say that I want to go to college to be an engineer. I'm good at math, I love building things, and my teacher said I'd make a good engineer. I want to be the first in my family to be a college graduate. Please let me do that.

High School Student: You can do that the way it works now, but you probably won't. Only certain students get the classes they need for university. I'm not sure how that works . . . I thought I did. I was planning to go to the university, but I just found out that my life science class is not an approved university class. I should have taken biology but it conflicted with choir. I love choir, and the counselor gave me a choice. I think she asked me what I wanted to do after high school. And I think I told her I wanted to go to college. I guess I should have said university. Now I am not sure if I will have enough space in my schedule to finish all my sciences. There are lots of tricks like that at my school.

High School Principal: This student is correct. There are lots of these little options in high school that students may not quite understand. We have options to help students be more successful, but I almost wish we didn't have all of these options. It would make scheduling easier and maybe more students would qualify to get into universities.

High School Parent: It seems like the school where my boss's children go don't have all those choices. I don't even know if they have life science. What is that anyway?

Facilitator: Well, it seems like we are in agreement that we want our graduates to have as many options available to them as possible. While many successful people do not have university degrees, there is no denying that graduating with the university prerequisites opens up the greatest number of post–high school options, from vocational training programs through four-year university admission. Also, we have heard that the lack of a stated goal may result in programming students into lower-level courses. Maybe we are saying that while a high school diploma was the primary goal upon which our entire school system was based, it is time to change.

Board Member: I propose that we agree on the following goals for our students:

High school graduation *and* university preparation. I know that these goals will force us to change many things we do from elementary to high school, but I think it is important to our students' future.

Facilitator: All in favor?

Task Force: Aye.

Fifth-Grade Student: Does that mean I can become an engineer now?

Task Force: Yes!

Fifth-Grade Student:	(Looks over at the high school student for confirmation.)
High School Student:	Yes.
Fifth-Grade Student:	Well all right then!

Source: Based on actual comments recorded by PRINCIPAL'S Exchange.

Your Turn: Finding Out About College Readiness

1. Reread the transcript and jot down comments that in your opinion indicate beliefs and inevitability assumptions about students. What is your personal response to the concluding remarks?

2. Dialogue with other group members about the implications related to those beliefs and assumptions. What are the implications?

3. Have you had a conversation in your district and schools about college readiness? If not, is there a need for a conversation and possibly some actions? Is the transcript conversation reflective of what would happen in your district? What might be some next steps?

Keeping Track of College Readiness

The University of California (UC)/ACCORD (All Campus Consortium On Research for Diversity) has designed a very unique and powerful indicator to monitor a high school's college preparation of ninth through twelfth graders. In order to become college ready students must complete the university-preparation course sequence upon high school graduation. The College Opportunity Ratio (COR) begins with ninth-grade cohorts and traces them through their senior year to see how many complete the university preparation course sequence. In addition, the methodology disaggregates the data for historically underrepresented groups. This is critical information to document in order to address equity issues. Table 3.4 shows an upper-middle class suburban high school's report. Asian students and White students have a graduation rate of 92% and a college readiness rate of 61%. However, the COR in the same district for the historically underrepresented groups of African American, Latino, and Native American students is only 71% for graduation and 29% for college ready. There is a 32% difference in college readiness between the two groups. There is no doubt that this should be treated as a major equity issue. Especially interesting is the fact that the 29% represents mostly upper-middle class students. (Refer to Chapter 1

	Underrepresented (African American, Latino, Native American)				White and Asian American			
Table 3.4 Sample High School College Opportunity Ratio (COR)	Number of Students				Number of Students			
	Ninth Graders	Grads	College Ready	COR	Ninth Graders	Grads	College Ready	COR
High School	91	65	26	100:71:29	254	233	154	100:92:61

Source: http://ucaccord.gseis.ucla.edu/indicators/assembly/maps/ad44.html

for a discussion of the research on how race and ethnicity often override socioeconomics, counter to prevailing wisdom.)

These type of data offer another way to use *other data* to peel off layers of historical educational practices and build the *equity muscle* required to challenge the *inevitability assumption* that some students simply are not meant to reach the same academic levels as others. Districts can calculate the COR for their high schools, disaggregated for racial/ethnic groups, gender, socioeconomic group, or designated program (Special Education, GATE, and so on), to honestly reveal the degree to which schools are either limiting or promoting options for graduates.

Your Turn: Calculating Ratios for Your High School

Find the ratios for your high school. You may want to disaggregate the data in other ways such as by gender, language groups, program groups, and racial and ethnic groups.

	Underrepresented (African American, Latino, Native American)				White and Asian American			
Template 3.2 College Opportunity Ratio by Disaggregated Groups	Number of Students				Number of Students			
	Ninth Graders	Grads	College Ready	COR	Ninth Graders	Grads	College Ready	COR
High School								

Source: http://ucaccord.gseis.ucla.edu/indicators/assembly/maps/ad44.html

COLLEGE ATTENDANCE AND FAMILY INCOME

Even when low-income students are accepted to college or university it may not translate into enrollment in college. Generally, there is an assumption that high college attendance is attributed to high achievement in college preparation in high school. There is also an assumption that low-income students' low college attendance can generally be attributed to lack of preparation. However, preparation may not be the only issue in accessing higher education. There is a disturbing report from Haycock (2006) that shows that high-income students who score at the lowest achievement quartile attend college at virtually the same rate as low-income students who score in the top quartile. Only 36% of low-income students in the lowest quartile attend college. There is a disparity in college attendance and achievement at every income level. For example, at the third quartile, 63% of low-income students attend college, while high-income students have a 90% attendance rate (Haycock, 2006). These data on income and achievement dispel myths about meritocracy. Low-income students are not accessing college opportunities at the same rate as similarly achieving high-income students. The educational journey of many low-income students is being aborted. This can be attributed to finances or other factors, such as being knowledgeable about the institutional culture of higher education and how to negotiate the maze of college enrollment. College campuses may feel like a foreign country. These students often do not possess the social and cultural capital to negotiate these middle-class institutions (Noguera & Wing, 2006). Having the support to negotiate the financial aid requirements, secure housing, complete course enrollments, and succeed in timely payment of fees while also meeting the academic demands may be overwhelming for students who are the first in their family to attend college. These students need advocates and support both early in their schooling careers and beyond the day they receive their diploma. This requires gathering *other data* on those students who may be facing large challenges. High schools and colleges may need to provide safety nets from college acceptance through the first year of college attendance and to establish data systems to monitor leakage of students from the educational-attainment pipeline. Stanton-Salazar (2010) discusses the need for high-status non-kin institutional agents who have high positions in the organization and who are able to provide these students with critical forms of institutional and social support. All of these issues need to be explored and addressed. If finances are the major factor for nonattendance for low-income students, colleges and universities need to examine the distribution of their financial and support resources to low-income students. Many of the answers as to why high-achieving, low-income students are not attending college will probably come from the students themselves and their families.

Student Voices as Other Data

We believe some of the richest, most compelling, and probably some of the most useful data for schools and districts are available at the local level. Students' experiences as they move through the system can point to relevant strategies to stem the leakage in the pipeline. As in the opening scenario with the case of Kyle, as well as the task force transcript, students have a lot to say about their aspirations, why they stay, leave, or return to high school, and what they end up doing after high school. We suggest studying and reviewing resources that help educators elicit the student voice and using them to gather *other data* to change practice. Some suggestions for resources to get started are: Anderson, Herr, and Nihlen, 2007; Flores-Gonzalez, 2002; Johnson, 2002; Ladson-Billings, 1994; Noguera and Wing, 2006.

> Students' experiences as they move through the system can point to relevant strategies to stem the leakage in the pipeline.

Students and educators can have very different perceptions about educational conditions and realities. The voices of students are often left out when we assess school cultures and expectations. This is particularly true in schools where there are large numbers of low-income children. The educators make assumptions about the aspirations of both parents and students based on limited data. Students' opinions are frequently not valued. Because they may not respond in the communication idiom validated by educators, students are presumed to be uninterested or indifferent to their educational experiences. We have found in data that we have collected and analyzed and data from others that this is simply not true. The expectations and aspirations among young people for educational attainment are high (Johnson, 2002). As illustrated so poignantly in the scenario of Kyle, cultural dissonance often exists between the school and the students in the manner in which information, knowledge, and access are transmitted (see Flores-Gonzales, 2002; Irvine, 1990; Shade, Kelly, & Oberg, 2004). It is important to record these missing voices and use these *other data* to help peel off layers of reality in order to help shape effective reform strategies.

When should you elicit student voice? Although all approaches to eliciting student voice are useful, each has distinct drawbacks and benefits. You'll need to think about how to protect students and ensure confidentiality, particularly if they'll be addressing subjects that arouse adults' anxiety or hostility. Table 3.5 may help in selecting the best

Table 3.5 Tools of the Trade: Using Student Voice Strategies	
Student Voice Approach	**Benefits, Drawbacks, Considerations**
Focus groups (to brainstorm issues and get a sense of priorities; to explore a limited number of issues and get greater depth of understanding)	Benefits: Students feed on each other's comments and go into more depth than in written forms of response; responses from many students are obtained in the time it would take to interview just one; students like to talk. Drawbacks: System is time and labor intensive to set up; individual stories and detail are lost; sometimes unusual experiences don't get expressed because of peer pressure to discuss shared concerns. Great way to discover overall themes and patterns, get a sense of priorities, gather reactions to ideas, hear student words.
Surveys and questionnaires	Benefits: System is relatively easy to administer; interview responses are obtained from many more students than through focus groups; anonymous responses can provide more protection for students and sometimes more honest responses. Drawbacks: Any written form of response is harder for students and often yields less depth and "meat" than speaking formats; students often do not take surveys seriously; format restricts responses to forced-choice or relatively simple responses. Good for finding out the extent of a problem and acquiring responses across large numbers of students; can be difficult to design a good questionnaire.
Quick-writes (quickly and informally written response to a given prompt)	Benefits: System is easy to administer; takes little time, and can generate lots of students' responses; it encourages writing; it can be done across multiple classrooms without any particular teacher skill; responses are in students' words (compared to surveys in which they choose prewritten responses). Drawbacks: Sometimes students' writing abilities and comfort levels filter and limit what they say; responses are restricted to a single prompt. Good for eliciting responses to a specific prompt.
Panels	Benefits: Real students talking to real teachers and other educators produces powerful face-to-face contact; format provides some protection for students; responses are in the voices of students. Drawbacks: Students can become shy or intimidated by the face-to-face "in front of the room" format; teachers need to be prepared to listen respectfully.

(Continued)

Table 3.5 (Continued)	
Student Voice Approach	**Benefits, Drawbacks, Considerations**
Shadowing and observing	Benefits: System allows teachers, counselors, and administrators to really see and feel what a student's day and life are like in a school; it offers more holistic information about student experience than a report from students about their experiences. Drawbacks: This is a one-on-one activity and very labor intensive; it is hard for many teachers to participate or for any single teacher to shadow or observe more than a few students.
Fishbowls (a few people have a discussion, often in response to a prompt, while others listen in)	Benefits: System is less structured and less scary than a panel, yet still allows educators to see students and hear them talk; the discussion format allows students to spin off each other and the facilitator to probe for deeper responses; it requires less preparation than a panel. Drawbacks: System allows less depth in individual stories than interviews or panels.
Interviews	Benefits: System is good for gathering individual stories and perspectives in depth, for reconstructing someone's experiences and history, and for eliciting perspectives about an issue, etc.; it can be more comfortable and often powerful for students because they talk to a real person (compared to surveys); it is more revealing than surveys or questionnaires because of depth of responses and opportunities for probes; there is more opportunity for hearing individual voices than in focus groups or panels; powerful teacher–student connection can develop. Drawbacks: System is very labor intensive; interviews take a lot of time to prepare, conduct, and analyze.

Olsen, L. & Jaramillo, A. (1999). *Turning the tides of exclusion: A guide for educators and advocates for immigrant students* (pp. 299–300). Oakland, CA: California Tomorrow.

approach, keeping in mind the students' level of trust, comfort, and adult receptivity. California Tomorrow, a nonprofit organization whose mission promotes opportunity and participation of historically underrepresented students, has developed this useful document that describes some strategies for using student voice as well as the benefits and drawbacks of each strategy. This can serve as a useful tool in designing inquiries that include students.

CONCLUSION

How students experience their schooling journey has a tremendous long-term impact on their lives. Research has identified school, district, and societal indicators that influence students' educational attainment. Great benefits accrue for some students who have access to the best resources the school has to offer. These students do not leak out of the K–12 pipeline and are most likely to enroll in college. On the other hand, there are those like Kyle who are unintentionally silenced and invisible. Kyle was not necessarily causing any problems. Unfortunately, he was placed in a grouping pattern that denied him access to a high-quality education. He became a high school dropout, not graduating and possibly suffering a lifetime of unfavorable financial and social consequences. His dream was deferred. He had aspirations to possibly go to college and become a teacher.

There is a stream of research that consistently stresses the importance of graduating from high school with postsecondary preparation. There are schools that are making progress in this area. It is critical that all groups have equitable access to both academic and cultural knowledge that will enable them to make positive contributions to themselves and the nation. It will be important to raise expectations for all groups and to use *other data* skillfully to describe conditions that affect student success, and to use data to guide policies and practices that view all children regardless of background as potential high achievers. Then we need to diligently monitor progress toward that outcome.

4 Special Education and Gifted and Talented

SCENARIO: PRECIOUS CANTOR

Precious Cantor began experiencing trouble in school in kindergarten. By the second grade, it was clear that Precious was distractible, unfocused, and academically behind her peers. Her second-grade teacher, concerned with her lack of progress, initiated a student study team (SST) meeting of key school staff and Precious's mother. At the SST, Mrs. Cantor shared that Precious's father was in prison and came from a gang-affiliated family. Mrs. Cantor also shared that the family was struggling financially. She was raising Precious and four younger children on her own. The impact of that information on the team was notable, and the team immediately requested a full assessment for Precious. The results determined that Precious had auditory processing problems and qualified for special education services. She was placed in a resource specialist program (RSP) where a special education teacher or aide "pushed-in" to the general education classroom several days a week, for several hours, to help her keep up in class.

Though Precious made some progress, it was slow. Both the general education and special education staff members were frustrated with the rate of progress, but they reminded themselves of her unfortunate family circumstance, and were grateful that she was able to progress at all. Precious participated in this RSP program the entire year, but fell further and further behind.

When Precious began third grade, her little sister, Valerie, started school. Within the first month of school, the staff recognized her as Precious's sister. As her kindergarten teacher heard more and more about Precious and the Cantor family from other staff, she was able to notice subtle potential problems in Valerie's learning profile. Valerie had a short attention span, liked to move around frequently, became tired in the afternoon, and often forgot to return homework. As a result, she requested that Valerie be assessed for possible learning disabilities. The district discouraged special education testing for young students, so instead an SST was held where the discussion centered around reducing the academic expectations for Valerie because of her difficult family situation and her presumed limited abilities. She was given easier class work, and homework was reduced and made optional for her. Also, communication with Mrs. Cantor was kept to a minimum because the staff assumed that this would contribute negatively to her already challenging life. By the end of the following year, Valerie was placed in RSP.

When Precious started fourth grade, a new RSP teacher and a new assistant principal in charge of special education began working at the school. Their arrival heralded a dispositional transformation in the culture of the school and the way in which special education students were valued. At the first IEP (individualized education plan) meeting of the school year, they noted that Precious had met each and every goal set forth in the previous year's IEP, yet her academic performance was extremely low. Upon further examination, they realized that she had met her goals because the goals were written at a first-grade level. They questioned previous teachers about her lack of progress, and were reminded that she was an RSP child and that it was great that she had made some gains.

Uncomfortable with the response, the new RSP teacher spoke to Mrs. Cantor to better understand Precious's academic history. The mother explained her husband's absence from the home and that Precious was the eldest of five children. In the conversation, Mrs. Cantor showed the teacher a letter that her husband had sent her from prison that had amazing artwork bordering it. The teacher admired the artwork and listened to Mrs. Cantor share how Precious received two very positive gifts from her father—an eye for art, and the ability to sing. The next day, the teacher asked Precious to demonstrate some of her talents, and, in fact, discovered that she was a gifted artist and an amazing vocalist. The teacher and assistant principal convened an IEP meeting to purposefully encourage art and singing with Precious to develop her confidence and self-esteem, and also rewrote her academic goals to match grade-level expectations. The overriding question for them was, "What conditions would be necessary for Precious to reach grade level in two years?"

The first issue discussed was whether it was reasonable to expect Precious to ever reach grade-level expectations, as a "special education" student. The teacher *and assistant principal reminded the team that in order to qualify for RSP, Precious was assessed to have average cognitive ability, and they posed the question, "What conditions would be necessary for Precious to reach grade level in two years?" The next issue discussed was the difficulty of the home situation and its likely negative affect on Precious's ability to focus. In response, the teacher and assistant principal shared samples of the incredible, intricate artwork Precious had produced, obviously requiring an immense degree of focus and persistence. They then repeated the question, "What conditions would be necessary . . ." The general education teacher stated that she was not opposed to helping Precious more, but in light of the large class size, felt it impossible to devote the necessary amount of attention to any one child. The assistant principal responded by appreciating the teacher's willingness to be supportive and acknowledged the challenges of meeting the diverse needs of an entire classroom of children. She then restated the question clearly and deliberately, "What conditions would be necessary for Precious to reach grade level in two years?"*

The IEP meeting continued this way for a long time, until the general education teacher finally stopped and said, "You really and truly believe that if we could stop finding reasons why we cannot help her and put our energy into coming up with the right plan, Precious could actually be on grade level before she leaves our school, don't you?" The RSP teacher and assistant principal responded, "Absolutely." After a moment of collective silence, the team took a big breath and set out to design a plan built on the premise that Precious would be on grade level by the end of the fifth grade.

The specific plan and related issues will follow, but the end of this true story (only names have been changed) is that Precious made significant gains during her fourth- and fifth-grade years, actually meeting minimum grade-level expectations in all subjects and meeting the criteria to exit from RSP prior to entering the middle school. Having been given multiple opportunities to develop and share her artistic and vocal abilities, she came to be seen as somewhat of a child prodigy in school and around the community, winning art competitions and regularly performing to amazed audiences. The culmination was that Precious performed an original song at her fifth-grade promotion ceremony, to not a dry eye in the audience, fully confident, and on grade level.

As an aside, Precious's remarkable achievement caused the RSP teacher to reassess her little sister, Valerie. While the current general education teacher continued to feel that Valerie required major program modifications in order to keep up, the school psychologist's assessments determined that Valerie was within normal ranges in all areas. They decided that Valerie would benefit from a new experience, so they changed her class and assigned her to a teacher who had been on the IEP team for Precious. Soon, the new teacher reported that while Valerie did not have the same creative talents as her sister, she was "just as sharp as her sister," and was doing well with the unmodified grade-level curriculum, receiving the same degree of support that many of her other students required. By the end of that school year, Valerie too was exited from RSP.

The footnote to this story is that when Precious was promoted to the middle school, her little brother, Gabriel, started kindergarten. Since the Precious and Valerie stories were well-known sources of school pride by this time, Gabriel's arrival was much anticipated. After a month of school, his teacher described him as energetic, enthusiastic, and excited to learn. A "typical little boy," Gabriel was sometimes scattered and forgetful—just part of his charm—another great Cantor child. No referral was ever made for him.

A true story, as reported by
the assistant principal of a large
urban elementary school in a
Southern California school district

OVERVIEW

In Chapter 3, we discussed the power students' school experiences have on their academic achievement and the K–12 indicators for graduating and dropping out of school. One of the indicators of students who drop out is placement in special education (Haney et al., 2004; Holzman, 2006; Olson, 2004). Our opening scenario about Precious illustrates how the decision-making process in a school impacts the lives and future opportunities of individual children. In this chapter and the next, we discuss three programs found nationally in public schools: (1) special education, (2) gifted and talented, and (3) programs for English learners (EL). Using real-life examples, we highlight the equity issues and the types of indicators that should be diligently and consistently collected, analyzed, and used to monitor the placement patterns and effectiveness of special programs. The dynamics of these labeling and selection processes have enormous implications for equity and are associated with long-term life consequences (Harry & Klinger, 2006; Olson, 2004; Swanson, 2008). In this chapter, we present substantial information on special education and disproportionate mislabeling and placement for certain populations of students, which often results in segregating them from their mainstream peers. We hope that this information will heighten awareness and present a sense of urgency for schools and districts to examine their practices. In a similar vein, we present data on over- and underidentification of certain populations in gifted and talented programs. We consider not only programs with the label of gifted and talented, but courses that are usually considered advanced, such as honors and Advanced Placement. Suggestions for types of indicators to collect and monitor are included.

We embark on this journey fully realizing the political divisiveness that historically characterizes discussions about specially designated populations

> Our intent is to highlight the need to unravel processes and assumptions in some school and district cultures that result in identifying students to receive special program services.

(such as special education, gifted and talented, and English learners). Issues about perceived funding encroachment, entitlement, free and appropriate education, legal compliance, and feasibility are frequent topics of debate. We do not engage in these debates nor do we present a textbook manual on the Individuals with Disabilities Act (IDEA) laws and requirements. Our intent is to highlight the need to unravel processes and assumptions in some school and district cultures that result in identifying students to receive special program services. This information can provide a framework for discourse on current school practices that may contribute to disproportionate identification of some groups of students for special education or other services.

We begin each section by presenting the broad context and an overall quantitative picture of who receives special education and gifted and talented services and some of the implications related to this picture. In the special education section, we examine and analyze the case of Precious and how this case exemplifies windows into belief systems, the predictability of assumptions, and the normalization of failure. We use the true case of Precious to put a human face on the dynamics of how learning opportunities are enhanced or squandered. It is a compelling story about possibilities. Precious and her family are not an isolated case. They typify our experiences in schools and districts and what much of the research tells us about how these scenarios are played out daily in our nation's schools (Artiles, Klinger, & Tate, 2006; Blanchett, 2006; Harry & Klinger, 2006; Olson, 2004).

The typical data sets that describe disproportionate outcomes for students will be presented. Then we will peel off layers of wallpaper to show *other data* that highlight some of the cracks and pitfalls that, in the end, may fail the students they were intended to support. For each area, we will uncover some hidden data sources and present a thoughtful analysis of the underlying issues—deep beneath the layers of educational, cultural, and historical wallpaper—that result in daily decisions made on behalf of children like Precious and her siblings.

STUDENTS RECEIVING SPECIAL EDUCATION SERVICES: THE BROAD CONTEXT

Legislation passed in 1975, the Individuals with Disabilities Act (IDEA), mandates that all public schools provide all eligible children with disabilities a free public education in the least restrictive environment to meet the child's needs (U.S. Department of Education, National Center for Education Statistics, 2007). IDEA was reauthorized in 2004 with some additional policies and procedures. Most notably, a procedure named response to intervention (RTI) provides for alternative strategies for diagnosing learning disabilities. Ostensibly, this procedure holds the promise of reducing the segregation and labeling of students and for the transformation of how instruction is delivered in the general education system. The story of Precious could be considered a prime example of how this should happen. RTI outlines three levels of intervention to diagnose learning problems. These include: (1) regular classroom instruction, (2) intensified small-group instruction, and (3) individual instruction. If a student has not responded to the third level, which is the most intensive, they may be considered for special education (Swanson, 2008).

The intent of special education services is to employ teachers who are specially trained in appropriate instructional techniques that will give students the special learning support they need to be academically successful. IDEA also mandates other supportive services, including extra support from counselors and other professionals. Blanchett (2006) states, "In its original and subsequent conceptualization, special education was not a place but a service delivery structure" (p. 25). In spite of these good intentions, special education has, in all too many instances, become a segregated operating system with its own complex administrative structure and culture.

Until recently, many in general education treated special education as an invisible, unfamiliar system with its own legislation and administrative rules. No Child Left Behind now requires that districts and schools be accountable for the performance of students receiving special education services and at least 95% of them must take state-mandated tests. This has caught the attention of administrators and others in the general education population. Special education systems can no longer function in a parallel manner with minimal intersections with the mainstream (Artiles, Klinger, & Tate, 2006; Blanchett, 2006).

According to Olson (2004), there are nearly six million children between ages 6 and 21 receiving some category of special education services—67% percent of those students have specific learning disabilities such as speech or language impairments and 20% spend most of their school day outside regular classrooms. Fewer than 12% of students are diagnosed with significant cognitive disabilities, such as mental retardation or traumatic brain injury. Most special education students, 88% in fact, are in categories with relatively subjective criteria, such as mild mental retardation, learning disabilities, and

> Eighty percent of the children who are diagnosed with specific learning disabilities have problems with reading.

emotional disturbance. Eighty percent of the children who are diagnosed with specific learning disabilities have problems with reading. This returns us to the scenario of Precious. When she was given the opportunity to learn via appropriate instructional strategies, her academic performance accelerated. The focus was on services and not labels. These data on special education categories have significant implications for the transformation of general education programs (Olson, 2004).

O'Connor and De Luca Fernandez (2006) contend that "disproportionality plagues judgmental but not nonjudgmental categories of special education" (p. 6). Because of the equity implications, we find it necessary to draw attention to the categories that demonstrate the overrepresentation or underrepresentation of different groups. If students in special education overwhelmingly met with academic success, as is the intention, we would all welcome the disproportionate placement patterns. However, the data on achievement of special education students is dismal, particularly for minority and low-income students. These conditions should invoke major equity concerns and actions.

Olson (2004), in a special report on special education in *Education Week's* 2004 issue on special education, reports that students receiving special education perform at levels below students in general education. Both Olson (2004) and Swanson (2008) present data that show the range of academic performance for students receiving special education services. Although some score in the high ranges, most score in the lower ranges. When the data is disaggregated, the higher performers include students with visual or speech disabilities, students who spend more time in general education classes, and those children who have fewer disabilities. However, most special education students' experiences include:

- Lower levels of academic achievement (Olson, 2004; Swanson, 2008).
- Very low graduation rates. For example, in 2001 to 2002, only 32% of special education students received a standard high school diploma (Olson, 2004). Those that do finish are more likely to receive an alternative (e.g., Certificate of Completion) rather than a regular diploma (Swanson 2008).
- A dropout rate about twice the rate of students in general education programs (Olson, 2004).
- Lower performance on state proficiency exams compared with general education peers.
- Higher rates of suspension and expulsion (Swanson, 2008).

Your Turn: Collecting Data on Special Education Students

Collect comparative data on the performance of your special education students in academic achievement, graduation, dropout rates, proficiency tests, suspensions, and expulsions. Disaggregate by ethnicity, gender, income, and special education categories.

Template 4.1 Collecting Data on Special Education Students

Programs and Services (Labels are only samples. Use labels that describe programs and services in your setting.)

Indicator	Specific Learning Disability	Mental Retardation	Emotionally Disturbed	For Students Receiving Special Education Services				
				Male	Female	Low Income	Ethnicity 1	Ethnicity 2
Language Arts Achievement								
Math Achievement								
Graduation Rate								
Dropout Rate								
Suspensions and Expulsion Rate								
(add your own indicators)								

NCLB requires special education students to meet the same standards and take the same tests as general education students, unless it is specifically stated in their individualized education plan (IEP) that they should be exempt. Previously, students receiving special education services may have taken the tests but were excluded from the total school score calculations, or else simply not tested. Because of waivers for these students and pressure on districts to increase high-stakes test scores, many students who may have otherwise remained in the general programs were identified for special education programs. For example, Viadero (2004) reports disturbing trends that occurred in Texas. During the first five years of the state's testing program (1994–1998), the state's special education enrollment doubled. African American and Latino students had the largest growth in special education placements. These types of increases subsided after the districts were required to report achievement results for all students receiving special education services. Now, nationally, 95% of students receiving special education are required to take accountability exams, make annual yearly progress (AYP), and be reported as a group.

Great debate exists regarding the appropriateness of testing all students receiving special education services. Certainly, requiring severely cognitively delayed youngsters to take a grade-level exam is unreasonable. However, as demonstrated with Precious, the majority of students receiving special education services are considered intellectually within "normal" ranges. They are in the program either because of a specific, diagnosed learning challenge, or, more often, because they did not receive effective first teaching and are struggling academically with no specific identifiable cause. Therefore, excluding them from testing implies that they are not expected to meet the same academic expectations as their peers. The special education label sets off assumptions and a chain of events that often limits students' educational opportunities over the course of their academic careers. Harry and Klingner (2006) observe, "The paradox arises when the classification system, instead of serving those in need, does them greater harm" (p. 13).

While the story of the Cantor children is a favorable one, it almost was not, and, all too often, the story is far from happy for too many children. What were the conditions that propelled Precious from severe academic deficiency to grade-level achievement? The success was a result of the leadership of the assistant principal and a team that carefully crafted an inquiry that resulted in a plan that was

built on a set of accurate and specific assumptions,

encapsulated in a clear belief system, and

framed within a context of equity and moral imperative.

In the following sections, we present an analysis of the underlying issues always present when dealing with struggling students but rarely discussed openly. The elements of the Cantor family educational plan will be used as examples embedded in each issue.

WINDOWS INTO BELIEF SYSTEMS: THE INEVITABILITY ASSUMPTION AND THE NORMALIZATION OF FAILURE

The language adults use when discussing students provides insight into their assumptions, beliefs, and expectations about children. Further, when the assumptions, beliefs, and expectations become institutional norms, entire systems begin to accept, mobilize, and operate under the assumptions and beliefs, with expectations connoted by the organizational vernacular. This fact often results in dire consequences for struggling students when the assumptions, beliefs, and expectations are inaccurate. A kind of educational apartheid can evolve in schools whereby students such as Precious get sorted into permanent categories.

. For example, Neal, McCray, Webb-Johnson, and Bridget, as cited in O'Connor and Deluca Fernandez (2006), found that students who moved in styles associated with African America culture such as *strolling* were seen as more aggressive. They argue that being poor in and of itself may not cause students to be academically underdeveloped, what does is "how the culture and the organization of the school situates minority youth as academically and behaviorally deficient and places them at risk for special education placement" (O'Conner & Deluca Fernandez, 2006, p. 6).

Figure 4.1 shows the results of a national survey of teachers by *Education Week*. They found that teachers have different expectations of performance for their general students than those receiving special education services. Even though teachers believe that all of their general education students cannot score proficient on state tests, they had even lower expectations for students receiving special education services. For example, teachers expected that 51% of their general education students could score proficient versus only 15% of their special education students (Olson, 2004).

Figure 4.2 shows that 84% of the teachers surveyed believed that students receiving special education should have alternative standards and should not expect to meet the same set of standards as students in the general population.

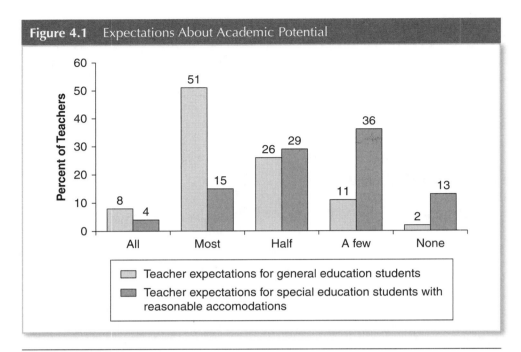

Figure 4.1 Expectations About Academic Potential

Source: How many of your students would be able to score proficient on state tests for students in their age? *Education Week's Quality Counts 2004.* Reprinted with permission from Editorial Projects in Education.

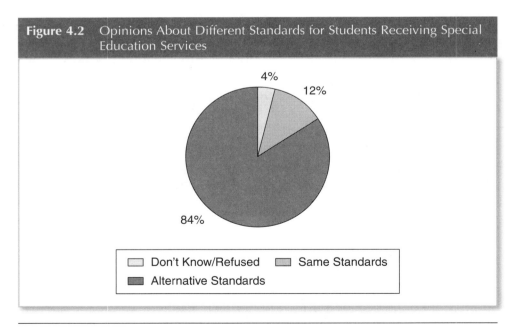

Figure 4.2 Opinions About Different Standards for Students Receiving Special Education Services

Source: What Standards Are Appropriate for Students Receiving Special Education Services. *Education Week's Quality Counts 2004.* Reprinted with permission from Editorial Projects in Education.

Your Turn: Teacher and Administrator Expectations for Students Receiving Special Education Services

Survey teachers and administrators in your setting and tally responses in Template 4.2. What are the teacher and administrator expectations for special education and other students in your school/district? Are they similar to or different from the national sample? Are there any surprises? What might be the implications for your findings? Do other data need to be collected? Are there some necessary actions?

Template 4.2   Expectations

Questions	Teachers	Administrators
How many general education students should be able to score proficient on the state exam?	All Most Half A Few None	All Most Half A Few None
How many students receiving special education services should be able to score proficient on the state exam?	All Most Half A Few None	All Most Half A Few None
Should students receiving special education services be expected to meet the same standards as students in the general population or should they have alternative standards?	Don't know Alternative Same	Don't know Alternative Same
Other questions?		

Table 4.1 Language Samples Collected and Analyzed by the New Assistant Principal

Lower ability.

Working to her *potential.*

Doing the best she can.

Trying to keep up with the *brighter* students.

All we can ask is that she *try her best.*

Let's give her goals that she *can actually meet.*

She's an intervention student.

She is an RSP student.

She is *learning disabled.*

Created by authors based on information from an urban school.

> While this language may seem benign, in the case of Precious, these comments resulted in a shared perception about her that was limiting and inaccurate. We contend that simple comments have the power to evolve into an institutional reality that then becomes the basis for decisions and actions that affect the lives of students in profound ways.

In the case of Precious, for example, belief systems expressed by language played a significant role in her educational plan. On the occasions when her first teacher noticed some learning problems in class, when the first meetings were held, and when her mother was interviewed, the school team used language when describing Precious that was inaccurate and unchallenged until the new RSP teacher and new assistant principal arrived and began to peel off the wallpaper. Table 4.1 highlights qualitative data of some of the language samples collected and analyzed by the new assistant principal. She subsequently used these data to bring to light the underlying, implied, yet operating assumptions about Precious. These assumptions, which later proved to be erroneous, resulted in educational decisions that had clearly impaired her academic progress. Whether individuals intended it or not, the result of this language was the acceptance of a perceived reality about the child's academic capacity that led to institutional acceptance and became the rationale for decisions that actually harmed Precious.

While this language may seem benign, in the case of Precious, these comments resulted in a shared perception about her that was limiting and inaccurate. We contend that simple comments have the power to evolve into an institutional reality that then becomes the basis for decisions and actions that affect the lives of students in profound ways. Table 4.2 lists the previous team's language samples and highlights the possible corresponding interpretations and conclusions about Precious. This issue is not limited to special education but is linked to and reflects the institutional culture of school, and it affects how all students are perceived. The language used can also result in positive outcomes such as those descriptions used for students who are in gifted and talented programs.

Table 4.2	Language Samples and Possible Interpretations
Language	**Possible Underlying Beliefs/Interpretations**
Lower ability. Trying to keep up with the *brighter* students. All we can ask is that she *try her best.*	She was just not born as smart as other students and therefore will never be able to do as well as her classmates. Because of her low-income background she is intellectually underdeveloped.
Doing the best she can. Working to her *potential.*	There is a fixed, predetermined, and inborn limit to every person's intelligence. We, as professionals, are able to determine that point for students. There is no sense trying to insist that Precious perform beyond this point because it is simply not possible.
She's an intervention student. She is an RSP student.	The programs and services Precious receives define her as a student and as a person. She is qualitatively different from other students and just not as good a student.
But she is learning disabled.	She is not able to learn as well as other students. Her academic deficits are inevitable and we are powerless to change that.
Let's give her goals that she *can actually meet.*	She obviously cannot reach high levels of academic achievement and we do not want to be held accountable for her lack of success. Her failure will make the school look bad and make the adults feel terrible. Therefore, let's set lower goals so that we can document that Precious has at least met the legal requirements that she meet individualized education plan (IEP) goals and maybe she and the adults will feel better about themselves.

Created by authors based on information from an urban school.

Your Turn: Identifying Language Patterns Used in Your Setting

Find opportunities to record the language used when describing different groups of students in your school. Identify repetitious language patterns related to students in different programs.

- What are the possible meanings and interpretations associated with these language patterns?
- What assumptions, expectations, and beliefs might be associated with these language patterns?

Template 4.3   Language Samples and Possible Interpretations

Language	Possible Underlying Beliefs/ Interpretations

Limited ideas and dialogue about Precious led to her receiving an ineffective version of a push-in RSP program. In a push-in program, RSP staff (occasionally the teacher but most often the aide) spend time in general education classes three times per week, for one hour each time, hoping to help identified students "keep up." When asked how they were specifically addressing Precious's needs, the general education teacher said she relied on the RSP staff to help Precious when they came into her room. When asked why Precious was receiving special education services, the teacher said that Precious was "RSP." When asked why Precious was RSP, the teacher said that Precious "qualified." When asked how she qualified, the teacher said she had a "learning disability." When asked what the disability was, the teacher became silent. The RSP teacher and aide answered in like fashion, noting that they had not reviewed her IEP for a while, but that Precious had trouble learning. This resulted in an abdication of responsibility for Precious's academic achievement.

For Precious and her siblings, the power of the expectations held for the children was almost the single-most significant variable in their academic trajectory. At first, well-intended adults had sincere compassion for the difficult home situation to which they could hardly relate. Based on their perception of what it must be like to have a father who is incarcerated and also be part of a low-income, single-parent home with five young children, the adults at the school made flawed decisions about how best to help the children, decisions that actually magnified their learning challenges. Precious's IEP goals were written several grade levels below her grade, and any slight improvement was celebrated. For her sister Valerie, the spillover effect resulted in modifications to her program. As a result, her homework demands were reduced, her class work was simplified, expectations for her to develop age-appropriate study skills were eliminated, and a decision was made to avoid communication about her deficits with her mother.

Also, while the district discouraged identifying young children for special education services, the school used "alternate methods," heavily reliant on subjective teacher rating sheets, as a means of identifying Valerie as learning disabled. The prevailing beliefs about Precious and the Cantor family circumstance were so strong that they colored even the assessment process that is perceived to be objective. In fact, belief systems are so strong that even "objective" assessments used for special education identification often contain elements of subjectivity. Even in an assessment context, human judgment and interpretation can lead to very different decisions and outcomes for students. The difficulty is that belief systems and attitudes about individuals and groups are taboo conversational points in most educational arenas. Therefore, decisions based on differential expectations go largely unnoticed and are usually not contested. Recall the decisions made about Valerie. In "anticipation" of her presumed academic struggles, the teacher made some incorrect decisions. Valerie was not expected to do grade-level work, her homework load was reduced, and

> In fact, belief systems are so strong that even "objective" assessments used for special education identification often contain elements of subjectivity.

> While at one level these accommodations seem reasonable, thoughtful introspection leads to the understanding that these decisions express the inevitability assumption and assume that failure is "normal" for some students.

communication with her mother ceased. While at one level these accommodations seem reasonable, thoughtful introspection leads to the understanding that these decisions express the inevitability assumption and assume that failure is "normal" for some students.

CHANGING EXPECTATIONS AND BEHAVIORS, CHANGING OUTCOMES

There were three elements to the revision of Precious's education plan. The first element of the revised educational plan was to gain clarity on what part of her specific learning profile negatively affected her learning and to use accurate language to represent her profile. In fact, the original multidisciplinary assessment determined that Precious had specific auditory processing deficits. This is like dyslexia of the ears. Her hearing is perfect, but her brain jumbles the language she hears, making it difficult for her to fully comprehend language, and especially affecting her literacy development. It also manifests itself in seeming lack of focus or attention, as the strain of trying to understand the massive language input she receives in school become fatiguing. This identification was used to qualify her to participate in RSP, and then was never again highlighted. The generic language of "special education" or "RSP" was the focus until the new RSP teacher arrived. Simply attaching a RSP or special education label to a student is not informative or helpful in developing an acceleration plan. In fact, the labels RSP and special education often mistakenly connote "less intelligent."

> Simply attaching an RSP or special education label to a student is not informative or helpful in developing an acceleration plan. In fact, the labels RSP and special education often mistakenly connote "less intelligent."

It is useful to ask questions like the following:

- How do IEPs align to performance expectations outlined in state and national standards?
- What instructional strategies are used to push students ahead?

The first part of the plan was to ensure that everyone involved with Precious discussed her in light of her "auditory processing deficits," and all subsequent plan components stemmed from that premise. Further, the assistant principal established a norm that the team would make a concerted effort to use language accurately when discussing Precious, and made it the expectation to challenge any language that stated or implied anything that was beyond the determination of the assessment data (such as intelligence, potential, ability, low-income status, and so on). The focus of discussion would be on her present performance levels and ways to get her to grade level, acknowledging her learning profile.

A second element of Precious's plan was to clearly state, verbally and in writing, that the goal was for Precious to reach grade level in two years. Rather than writing oversimplified goals that were within her immediate reach, the school derived quarterly goals by benchmarking backward from fifth-grade standards, assuming accelerated learning would take place beginning in the fourth grade. This acceleration was required for Precious to close the achievement gap between her present level of performance and grade-level achievement by the end of the following school year, and the plan was built so that the necessary conditions would exist for that to occur.

The new RSP teacher and assistant principal were relentless in insisting that the adults supporting Precious accept the premise that she would reach grade-level expectations. In order to achieve this goal they

- explicitly rejected the *inevitability assumption* that certain students are bound to be underperformers, regardless of any educational treatment they receive;
- frequently stated the grade-level goal, wrote it into the IEP, and based all decisions about Precious on that foundation;
- closely monitored the weekly and quarterly achievement data to assess her progress and made recommendations for plan refinements if the pace of acceleration was not acceptable; and
- collected data on the implementation of the plan by visiting the general education classroom and pullout room frequently, observing the teacher collaboration sessions, and shadowing Precious during different points in her school day.

These data were critical in order to monitor that the high expectations set for Precious were being honored in daily practice. These data also helped determine that Valerie's first teacher held beliefs that were helping to perpetuate her learning struggles. Recognizing that changing the teacher's mindset would take longer than Valerie had, a decision was made to move Valerie to another teacher who exhibited very high expectations for every student. This change proved to be pivotal in Valerie's acceleration and ultimate exit from the RSP program.

Important as well are the expectations that parents have for their children and that students have for themselves. While schools cannot control the incoming belief systems of parents and students, experience has taught us that schools can have a powerful influence on them. Schools that develop a culture of high expectations and make decisions based on those beliefs tend to have students who feel more empowered to achieve and parents who expect their children to be academically successful. Conversely, schools filled with excuses for why students are not achieving, that blame children or family circumstances, or ascribe underachievement to cultural, racial, or income variables, tend to have students who accept their academic levels as inevitable and parents who appear complacent about their children's schooling (Harry & Klingner, 2006).

TIME IN GENERAL EDUCATION

History and research teach us that beliefs exist not only for individual students like Precious, but also for different populations of students. Once identified, most minority students are significantly more likely to be removed from the general education program and be educated in a more restrictive environment (Losen & Orfield, 2006) in spite of a drive for students with disabilities to spend 80% of their school time in a general education classroom. The percent of children spending time in general education classrooms is increasing. Between 1995 and 2005, there was an increase from 45% to 52% overall of students receiving special education services spending time in the general population. While that can be good news, there is still cause for concern when the data is disaggregated by race and ethnicity. For example, data from 2004 to 2005 reveal that White students with disabilities spent 57% of the day in general education settings; African American students, 41%; Latino, 48%; Asian/Pacific Islander, 50%; American Indian/Alaska Native, 51%. The range between White and African American students is 16% (U.S. Department of Education, National Center for Education Statistics, 2007). Given that students with special needs benefit most when they are educated in the least restrictive environment to the maximum extent appropriate, these data raise questions about the quality of special education services provided to African American, Latino, and other minority students compared to Whites. This highlights the need for schools and districts to examine the amount of time spent by students receiving special education services in the general population. These data should be disaggregated by race/ethnicity, gender, and income by schools and districts. Compare time in general education to how students are achieving. If inequitable patterns exist, inquiries with meaningful dialogues should occur in order to change these patterns.

Your Turn: Time in General Education for Students With Disabilities

Collect data and complete Template 4.4 to check for the amount of time students with disabilities spend in general education and their achievement levels. Disaggregate by group to look for patterns. What story do the numbers tell? What other questions come to mind? What *other data* would help more completely tell the story?

Template 4.4   Time in General Education and Achievement

Focus Areas	Programs and Services (Labels are only samples. Use labels that describe programs and services in your setting.)							
	Resource Students	Special Day Class	Speech or Hearing	Male	Female	Low SES	Ethnicity 1	Ethnicity 2
Percent of Day in General Education								
Language Arts Achievement								
Math Achievement								

DISPROPORTIONATE REPRESENTATION

The overidentification and participation of some groups in special education is a major equity issue. Disproportionality was identified over thirty years ago in 1968 (Dunn, 1968, as cited in Artiles, Harry, Reschly, & Chinn, 2001). The same groups that are overrepresented in special education are also overrepresented in other areas such as low track placements, dropping out, suspensions, and the juvenile justice system. On the other hand, these same groups are underrepresented in high-status programs such as gifted and talented programs (Losen & Orfield, 2002).

In an effort to shed light on this problem from a social justice perspective, a theme issue journal published by the American Educational Research Association (AERA), *Educational Researcher* (2006), was devoted to the representation of students of color and low-income children in special education. There are several terms that are used such as *misrepresentation, overrepresentation,* and *overidentification* when describing equity concerns. These terms have a similar meaning to disproportionate representation, a term which many researchers use. Artiles and colleagues (2001) define the term *disproportionate representation* as "unequal proportions of culturally diverse students in (special education) programs" (Artiles & Trent, 2000, p. 514). Swanson (2008) explains, "In principle, the idea behind overrepresentation is that a given characteristic or condition appears within a particular group at a rate higher than it 'should,' relative to that group's inherent level of risk for experiencing the condition" (p. 10). Swanson describes three ways to measure representation of groups in programs. Each are valid, however, each statistic answers a different question. Educators should decide what questions are relevant to their context and then determine which calculations would best answer those questions.

Table 4.3 uses a hypothetical student population as a basis to calculate the three measures. This information should not be limited to looking at disproportional representation in special education only, but should be used as a tool in schools and districts to calculate representation of groups in a wide variety of educational settings.

Composition Index—This statistic answers the question, "What percentage of students in a program (such as special education) is comprised of a particular group (racial, ethnic, language proficiency, gender)?

Example: A special education population is composed of fifteen individuals, three of whom are Latino and six of whom are African American. The composition index for Latinos is three out of fifteen, or 20%. Twenty percent of students in special education are Latinos. However, they only

Table 4.3 A Hypothetical Student Population: Numbers of Students in Programs

	Students With Disabilities	General Education Students	Total
African American	6	24	30
Latino	3	7	10
White	6	54	60
Total	15	85	100

Source: A Hypothetical Student Population: Numbers of Students in Programs. *Special education in America: The state of students with disabilities in the nation's high schools.* 2008. Reprinted with permission from Editorial Projects in Education.

comprise 10% of the total population. Forty percent of students with disabilities are comprised of African American students. They are 30% of the total population. White students are 60% of the total population, but only comprise 40% of students identified with disabilities.

Gibb and Skiba (2008) argue that there are some limitations with the Composition Index. For example, the composition index (1) does not yield information for direct comparison across groups, and (2) has less meaning in situations where one group is 90% or more of the population. It is suggested that other measures be used or used in combination with the composition index. These other measures include the risk index and the risk ratio, which are described in the next section. To become more knowledgeable about these calculations, we suggest reading Gibb and Skiba (2008).

Risk Index—This statistic answers the question, "What percentage of a particular group participates in a program?" In other words, how at risk is a group of participating students in a program?

Example: Among a group of ten Latinos, three are identified as students with disabilities. The disability risk index for this hypothetical population as a whole is 15%. The index for Latinos being identified as students with disabilities is 30%.

The risk index can be calculated for any group, including the entire school or district. For example, the average risk of being identified as a student with disabilities for White students is six out of sixty, or 10%. The average risk for African Americans is six out of thirty, or 20%. The average risk of being identified as a student with disabilities for the entire school is fifteen out of one hundred students at the school, or 15%.

Risk Ratio—This statistic answers the question, "How does the risk of being identified for program participation compare from one group to the next?" Is any group more or less apt to be identified?

Example: Imagine that the question is how the risk of being identified for special education services compares for Latino, African American, and White students. The disability risk index value for Latinos is 30%, for African Americans it is 20%, and for White students it is 10%. The risk ratio for Latinos compared to White students is 30:10, or 3, which means that the risk of being identified for special education is three times greater for Latino students than for White students. The risk ratio for African American students is 20:10 or 2 when compared to White students. The chances of the being identified as a student with disabilities is two times greater for African Americans than for White students. Gibb and Skiba (2008) explain that risk ratios over or under 1.0 indicate disproportionate representation of a group. Although there are no national standards regarding disproportionality, Gibb and Skiba indicate that a generally accepted standard for concern is when a risk ratio is above 1.5.

The three aforementioned statistics answer some of the most relevant questions about representation of student groups in particular programs, compared to themselves as a group, compared to the schoolwide population, and compared to each other. Many equity issues can begin to be uncovered by analyzing these data. However, one data point that is missing from this conversation is the one that describes what is reasonable or expected for any group. That is, knowing that 6% of White students are identified as students with disabilities, that Latino students are three times more at risk, and that African Americans are two times more at risk does not answer the question of what level of participation in special education is reasonable or expected for a population. For example, 9% of students nationally are identified as students with disabilities (Swanson, 2008). Is that reasonable or expected for a school/district population?

Figure 4.3 (see page 118) shows a broader view of the disparities in education that reflect the over- and underrepresentation of students according to ethnic groups in categories of suspension, mental retardation, and gifted and talented. The chart shows that African American students are overrepresented in suspensions and being labeled for mental retardation, but underrepresented in gifted and talented. In contrast, White students are overrepresented in gifted and talented and underrepresented in suspension and being labeled mentally retarded. Latino students are not overrepresented, but underrepresented in the areas of mental retardation and gifted and talented. All of these areas involve some subjective judgments (Blanchett, 2006). The patterns in Figure 4.3

Your Turn: Measuring Representation

Gather data on your school or district using Template 4.5 or a template of your own. The template is an example of one you might use to measure the composition index comparing the compositions of groups in the general population and in special education. The table can also show calculations for the risk index and risk ratio for each group or the total population. You might want to disaggregate by special education categories. Measure the representation and disproportions. You may want to use all three measures. What stories do they tell? Which measures are the most useful for your setting? What are your findings? What are the possible implications for further actions? What other inquiries are necessary?

Template 4.5 Measuring Representation for Student Groups

Group	Number of Students With Disabilities	Composition of Students With Disabilities	Number of General Education Students	Composition of Enrollment in General Education	Risk Index	Risk Ratio
African American						
Asian						
Latino						
Native American						
White						
Total						

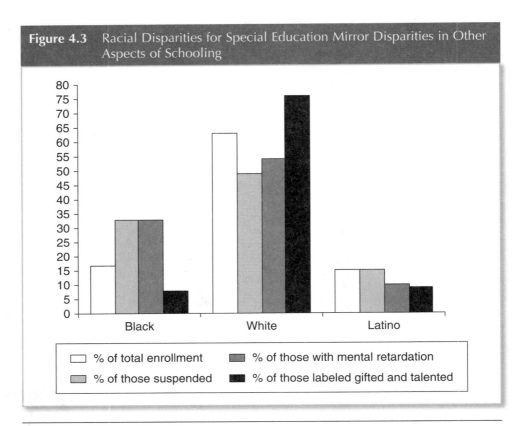

Figure 4.3 Racial Disparities for Special Education Mirror Disparities in Other Aspects of Schooling

Reprinted with permission from *Racial Inequity in Special Education*, edited by Daniel J. Losen and Gary Orfield (Cambridge, MA: Harvard Education Press, 2002), pp. xvii. For more information, please visit www.harvardeducationpress.org or call 1-888-437-1437.

indicate that African American students in particular are judged as less intelligent and behaviorally flawed. Blanchett suggests the need for schools and districts to examine policies and practices related to how schools and districts allocate their resources, whether their curriculum and pedagogy is culturally appropriate, and whether teachers have adequate preparation.

> The categories that are of concern for disproportionate representation are the high-incidence categories that are subjective and designated by school personnel.

The categories that are of concern for disproportionate representation are the high-incidence categories that are subjective and designated by school personnel. These categories include learning disabled (LD), mentally retarded (MR), and emotionally disturbed (ED). African American students have a higher incidence of being identified as mentally retarded and emotionally disturbed (which is

Your Turn: Racial, Ethnic, and Gender Student Enrollment by Special Education Categories

Gather the data for Template 4.6 for your school or district. You may want to expand disaggregation to include children such as those in foster care who are frequently overrepresented in special education (Weinberg, 2007) and other categories relevant to your setting. Complete the table by indicating the percentage enrolled in the school or district and the proportion of each group in a designated program. Again, you might want to expand the calculations to include the risk index and risk ratios. The table will have to be modified or another table may need to be created. Once the data is ready for presentation, meet with the data or leadership teams and discuss questions, such as those that follow, and how the data will be used. This type of information can show the school at a glance that there appears to be some groups that are being over- or underindentified in certain categories.

Template 4.6 Proportion of Students in the Special Education Program by Group

Percent of Group in Program	African American Female	African American Male	Asian Female	Asian Male	Latino Female	Latino Male	Native American Female	Native American Male	White Female	White Male
School/District Enrollment										
Specific Learning Disabilities										
Speech and Language Impairment										
Mental Retardation										
Emotional Disturbance										

connected to disciplinary issues) and are placed in more restrictive environments. According to Swanson (2008), "African American students are identified with disabilities 40 percent more often than the national average and are twice as likely to receive diagnoses for mental retardation and emotional disturbance. Native Americans are also numerically overrepresented in special education, while Asian Americans are underrepresented. White and Latino students are close to the national average" (p. 1). Males are identified at twice the rate of females (Swanson, 2008).

Inquiry Questions

- Does your data mirror Figure 4.3?
- What are the implications from these data?
- What types of actions and other information are required if there are patterns of over- or underrepresentation of groups in these different categories?
- What groups are disproportionately represented? In which programs? Are we satisfied or uncomfortable with the findings? Do we consider these data normal and acceptable?
- Do these data reflect our beliefs and values? If so, in what ways?
- What types of action are required if there are patterns of over- or underrepresentation of groups in these different categories?

PEELING BACK TO EXAMINE OTHER DATA

Research demonstrates how students can perform and achieve differently based on who teaches them. Artiles, Harry, Reschly, and Chinn (2001), in referring to a study by Harry, Klingner, Sturges, and Moore (in press), state that ". . . this research revealed that child study teams seldom take into account information regarding the atmosphere and practices obtained in the classrooms of referring teachers. In the study, several children were referred from classrooms where very poor instruction and classroom management were the norm, making it impossible to know whether the children's difficulties might have been mitigated in more effective classroom environments" (p. 8). We are reminded of Precious's sister Valerie, who had a life-changing experience when the assistant principal realized that she needed another teacher in order to achieve at high levels.

Other data to look at include course placements. Figure 4.4 shows data from an urban high school that is disaggregated by special programs. Special education students and English as a second language (ESL) students had the highest percentage of students enrolled in "below grade level" courses. It would be useful to peel these data back further to look at how different student placements compare. For ESL, it would be useful to look at the levels of ESL, time in program, and course placement. Talented and gifted (TAG) have the opposite profile. An interesting consideration is that not all identified gifted students excel in math, yet they tend to automatically be enrolled in advanced math courses. What math classes do students in special programs take?

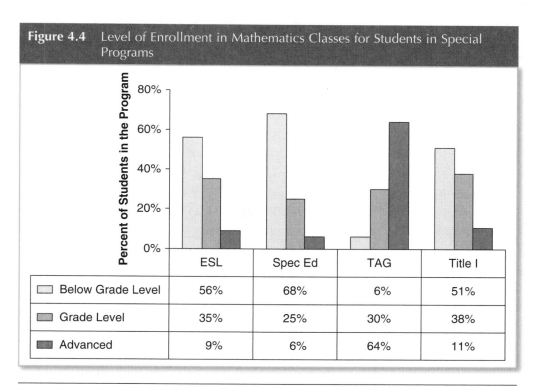

Figure 4.4 Level of Enrollment in Mathematics Classes for Students in Special Programs

	ESL	Spec Ed	TAG	Title I
Below Grade Level	56%	68%	6%	51%
Grade Level	35%	25%	30%	38%
Advanced	9%	6%	64%	11%

Created by authors based on information from an urban school.

Figure 4.5 shows the percentage of students in special categories that are passing mathematics classes with a C or higher. What percentage of students is passing with a C or higher in math classes?

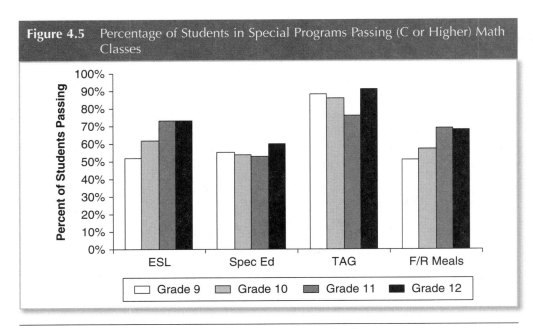

Figure 4.5 Percentage of Students in Special Programs Passing (C or Higher) Math Classes

Created by authors based on information from an urban school.

Although these methods are useful, there are more puzzle pieces that need to be found in order to get a fuller picture. Other ways to peel off the wallpaper and expose other information include: longitudinal and historical information, disability, feeder school, groups within groups, and category (see Johnson, 2002, pp. 44–45). Consistency is important when looking at different groups. Groups are categorized and labeled differently by federal and state governments and researchers. When reporting the data it is useful to have explanatory information about who is included in these groups.

The following section includes examples of the hidden data that should be considered in addition to the required data routinely collected.

Though these data points cannot be collected during a classic psychological or educational assessment, they are the types of *other data* that, when presented to school teams charged with helping struggling students, often inspire people to exercise *equity muscles* that may otherwise remain weak, and advocate the creation or refinement of educational plans that lead to authentic academic gains, such as in the case of Precious and the other Cantor children.

A DISCUSSION ABOUT CULTURE

Circumstances external to school are a part of the total experience a child has and contribute to how the child functions. As we acknowledge this, we

Your Turn: Gathering Information on Instructional Strategies

Consider each data set in Template 4.7 and answer whether or not each is used routinely in your own school or district.

Template 4.7 Examples of Other Data to Collect, Analyze and Monitor Instructional Strategies			
Information	**Yes**	**No**	**Not Sure**
An accurate and present level of student performance compared to grade-level expectations.			
Pacing of acceleration, described in quarterly increments, required for a student to reach grade-level expectations by a fixed target date (for students with disabilities assessed not to have significant cognitive deficits, as in the case of severely mentally retarded, etc.).			
A careful analysis of previously attempted instructional strategies and their effect on student learning.			
Observational profiles of the students' responses to instruction in each of the learning contexts, throughout the day.			
Interview data from each adult working with an identified student to gain insights from each individual's point of view, that may be included in the educational plan.			
Observational data, collected frequently, of instruction in every teaching setting, to check for degree of adherence to the intent of the educational plan.			
Reflection data collected from identified students and parents to assess their perception of the students' learning status, the effectiveness of their educational plan, and their expectations for accelerated learning.			
Collection of informal language samples describing students' progress or learning situations.			

are not of the mind to throw up our hands and say, "What can we do?" Although there is frequently an association of poverty and special education's less desirable classifications and low achievement, we believe that we should be more concerned with our response to the child. According to Artiles and colleagues (2001), there are indicators that have been identified in school and district culture that contribute to disproportionate representation, and they argue as do we that these equity factors need to be addressed. The categories include: (1) structural and institutional factors including funding, resources, and quality of schooling; (2) school size, climate, and achievement; and (3) personnel qualifications, student demographics, and instructional issues.

Other factors that have been identified as contributing to disproportionate representation are high referrals; inaccurate placements and plans; poorly trained, inexperienced teachers and administrators; classroom management problems and inappropriate discipline policies and procedures; perceptions and beliefs related to the students' capacity based on their demographic and income backgrounds; and inappropriate assessments (Artiles et al., 2001; O'Connor & DeLuca Fernandez, 2006).

Similar to the factors in the case of Precious, taking the time to know and understand students is critical to their welfare. O'Connor and DeLuca Fernandez (2006) state that "Without examining 'what' (poor) minority students 'are' we lose sight of how schools systematically marginalize the developmental expressions and competencies of children. Schools thereby fail in practical and pedagogical terms to build on the capacities with which the children enter school" (p. 9). Culture plays a role as well. Viadero (2004) cites a comment from a teacher in Atlanta: "There's almost this push sometimes on the part of some administrators to almost encourage you to fill out the paperwork to get things moving to get kids into special education. It's almost invariably black boys with behavior problems" (p. 25). The data would lead us to believe that African American boys have more mental retardation and emotional disturbance than the rest of the population.

The impact of the child and family culture, as well as the school environment, needs to be taken into account when assessing a child's learning needs. The examination of behavioral issues and how they are responded to is critical, particularly for African American boys. How do these factors influence decisions for placement and the permanency of the placement? These conditions are not inevitable. There are positive systems that can be constructed that include outside-of-the-home associations with supportive adults who are advocates for students as well as effective schools where high levels of education occur (Artiles et al., 2001).

A powerful process in gathering data related to special education involves the general education classes and how teachers handle academic and behavioral problems. Poor academic performance may not be a disability, but rather the result of lack of opportunity to learn, poor teacher qualifications, low-level curriculum, and poor instructional strategies. These indicators were clearly shown in the case of Precious. Prereferral interventions that utilize teacher assistance teams (TAT) show promise. These teams review student files, observe students and teachers in the classroom, and develop strategies for intervention by the teachers. Ortiz (in Artiles et al., 2001) found that, in schools utilizing TATs, referrals to special education were significantly reduced (p. 9).

The National Alliance of Black School Educators (NABSE) collaborated with the Individual with Disabilities Act (IDEA) and the Local Implementation by Local Administrators Project, located at the Council for Exceptional Children, to produce a guide, *Addressing Over-Representation of African American Students in Special Education: The Prereferral Intervention Process* (2002). The guide was developed to assist administrators with strategies to reduce the incidence of referrals of African American students in education. This guide was intended to help develop inquiries that gather data related to organizational policies and practices that contribute to overrepresentation. Although this guide was developed with African American students in mind, it would be useful for any school district to use with any demographic. They provide some inquiry questions that schools should try to answer, including the following:

- Are special education referrals being made for appropriate reasons?
- Is there a noticeable pattern in which teachers refer students regularly?
- Do certain teachers and/or schools have particularly high failure rates?
- Is there a high percentage of students whose families have low socioeconomic status or who are culturally and/or linguistically diverse in special education classes?
- Have other possible sources of the problem been investigated, such as limited instructional materials, a nonwelcoming school climate, language differences, poor instruction, and so on?
- What documented interventions were attempted before the student was evaluated for special education?
- Were the interventions instituted, and modified for enough time before they were abandoned?
- What were the results for each child referred? (p. 8)

These questions should be asked about every referral and the results should be examined for each group to determine differential treatment. Inquiries should also be made for discipline, gifted and talented programs, and advanced courses.

SERVICE NOT LABELS

Selecting a schoolwide approach is popular because it is efficient, easier to plan for, simpler to budget, and generally more straightforward than the alternative. The alternative is to look specifically at each student and design a plan that responds to the identified learning profile and targets accelerated academic achievement. In the case of Precious, the new RSP teacher asked the original IEP team how services were decided for Precious. They responded that it was the schoolwide RSP model. When asked how that model specifically addressed Precious's auditory processing deficits and accelerated progress toward grade-level proficiency, the room went silent.

The third element of Precious's revised educational plan was to build her service model based on her needs. After reviewing her performance and observational data, the team determined that Precious had the best chance of accelerating her academic level if the credentialed RSP teacher collaborated daily with the general education teacher for several purposes, which included the following:

- To anticipate what Precious would be learning the following day so that she could be frontloaded by the RSP teacher the day prior in a pullout classroom using strategies that supported her strengths in visual processing.
- To coplan the lessons that would be delivered by either the general education or RSP teacher in the general education class.
- To use the RSP teacher's expertise to plan lessons for the general education class for the time that the RSP teacher was not present in such a way that Precious's auditory processing challenges would be addressed and her visual processing strengths emphasized.
- To reflect on Precious's progress weekly to determine whether before- or afterschool support was also needed for any subject area, recognizing that students who fall behind cannot always catch up in the typical number of daily instructional minutes.

In sum, the plan for Precious included push-in, pullout, coteaching and extended day, and specific instructional and self-help strategies, rather than one schoolwide model. In fact, even within each of the "models," the details of the plans for each lesson, regardless of the setting, were tailored to her learning profile. She received support through the use of graphic organizers to supplement verbal input, she was taught to create symbols and pictures to help her conceptualize linguistically complex concepts, and she was trained to use an agenda with checklists to help herself keep track of instructions, assignments, and homework. Attention to the detail in her plan resulted in Precious making significant academic gains within two months of implementation of the plan.

This section of the chapter highlighted the necessity to peel off layers of wallpaper related to students with disabilities in order to uncover hidden inequities that have long-term consequences for thousands of students. Through the lens of the on-the-ground example of Precious Cantor, we demonstrated that thoughtful, equity-minded leaders can facilitate an inquiry process that results in tangible action with direct and positive results for student achievement.

STUDENTS RECEIVING GIFTED AND TALENTED EDUCATION (GATE) SERVICES

A principal of Orchard Middle School was concerned with the disproportionate representation of students in her GATE program. Her school was 80% Latino and 20% White. A large percentage of the Latino students were children of farm workers, while the White students were generally children of farm owners. The composition of the GATE program was 95% White students and 5% Latino. The principal calendared a meeting with her superintendent to discuss her concerns. At first, the superintendent questioned her concern, as no one had ever before brought this situation to his attention before.

She checked historical records and found that her school always had that GATE profile, as did the other middle schools in the district. The superintendent called the district GATE director to his office to ask for her insight. She explained that she used to be concerned also, but now understood the situation well, and felt it was appropriate. By the end of a lengthy question and answer session, the superintendent and principal learned the following information:

- The middle school is part of a high school district that encompasses Grades 6–12. There are three feeder elementary schools to this middle school that come from the elementary district. One school is predominantly White and the other two Latino. This ethnic distribution is a function of the location of the schools. The school with mostly White students is in the most expensive part of the city, with multimillion-dollar homes. The other two schools are located in the working-class areas. Since students go to their neighborhood schools, the ethnic profile of the schools is very distinctive.

- The elementary schools identify GATE students using criteria adopted by the elementary district. Using their measures, the predominantly Latino schools identify approximately 9% of their students as GATE. The mostly White school reports about 15% GATE each year. The elementary district criteria for GATE include measures of talent in a variety of areas, including generalized intellectual ability, specific academic subject-matter strength, leadership, creativity, and exceptionality in the arts. Measures include tests of cognitive ability, test scores, grades, teacher recommendation, portfolio and performance presentation, rating sheets, and talent surveys. For English learners, assessments in Spanish are used as well.
- When students from the three feeder schools arrive at the middle school, the high school district gives all previously identified GATE students the high school district's GATE test, as criteria are district dependent. In addition, an annual parent meeting is held to explain the GATE program. Parents are able to request that their students take the GATE exam at that meeting. It is a paper-pencil grammar and writing exam. The rationale for this exam is that the GATE teachers are very demanding and require that students have advanced English skills in order to accept them in their classes. Absent the ability to clearly articulate in English both orally and in writing, students would fail the classes.

The result of this identification process is that many students (mostly Latino) identified as GATE in elementary school are taken off GATE rosters and many other students (mostly White) are added.

The GATE program is very successful, as evidenced by the fact that district GATE students have the highest grade-point average, the highest honors and AP-taking rate, the highest rate of completion of the college prerequisite course sequence, the highest state exam scores, the highest SAT and ACT exam scores, and the greatest four-year university acceptance rate upon high school completion.

Overwhelmed by the information, the superintendent and principal thanked the GATE director and asked her to leave so they could reflect on the information. "I am speechless," said the superintendent. "As am I," replied the principal.

What's Behind the Gifted and Talented Wallpaper?

The story of Orchard Middle School exemplifies many of the inequality implications related to GATE. The first question is: What is gifted and talented? The lay connotation for gifted is "very smart, genius." Cocktail party conversation about "giftedness" would probably include references to Einstein and Dr. Stephan Hawking. Some might think of other types of giftedness, such as child prodigies like Mozart or Stevie Wonder. What do you think gifted and talented means?

An interesting fact is that no official source exists for a consistent definition of what it means to be "gifted." At present, each state, and within that, each district, establishes its own definition of gifted and talented. In the accountability arena, No Child Left Behind legislation defines gifted and talented as, "Students, children, or youth who give evidence of high achievement capability in areas such as intellectual, creative, artistic, or leadership capacity, or in specific academic fields, and who need services and activities not ordinarily provided by the school in order to fully develop those capabilities" (Title IX, Part A, Sec. 9101[22]). Yet, some districts narrowly define gifted and talented as academically high performing, and qualify students using grades and test scores, along with teacher recommendations. This condition has resulted in a long history of disproportional identification for gifted and talented education.

The National Association for Gifted Children estimates that there are approximately three million gifted children in Grades K–12 in the United States—approximately 6% of the student population (National Association for Gifted Children, 2008a). The U.S. Department of Education Office for Civil Rights (OCR), as reported by NAGC, finds that while minorities represent 36% of the U.S. school population, only 19.7% of students in gifted and talented programs are minority. White students, on the other hand, comprise 59% of the student population but represent 72% of gifted and talented students (2002). The Office for Civil Rights reports that 10.5% of school-age children are English learners, but only 1.4% of all English learners are identified gifted and talented. Native Americans are significantly *underrepresented* in programs for the academically gifted and talented. The degree of underrepresentation ranges from 50% to 70% (Committee on Minority Representation in Special Education, 2002; Ford & Grantham, 2003). It is not surprising that Orchard Middle School leaders are confused, since the federal government has wrestled with the disproportionate identification issue in GATE for over thirty years as evidenced by the following chronology:

1971: *Education of the Gifted and Talented: Report to the Congress of the United States by the U.S. Commissioner of Education* (U.S. Department of Health, Education, and Welfare, 1971) noted the underrepresentation of culturally and linguistically diverse and poor students in GATE.

1988: U.S. Congress passed the Jacob K. Javits Gifted and Talented Students Education Act supporting gifted students. The major goal was to address disportionality (The Center for Comprehensive School Reform and Improvement, 2008).

1993: The U.S. Government commissioned *National Excellence: A Case for Developing America's Talent* (Ross, 1993), also focused on remedying disporportionality.

2002: The No Child Left Behind (NCLB) Act was signed. The GATE provisions offered grants to states addressing disproportionality, particularly for the poor, English learners, and students with disabilities, as a way to address the achievement gap. (Center for Comprehensive School Reform and Improvement, 2008).

Cracks Behind the Wallpaper: Equity Issues in GATE

Equity issues surrounding GATE begin at the entry point, that is, the process by which students are identified for GATE. This begins with the operating definition of GATE. The case of Orchard Middle School demonstrates how different operating definitions for GATE result in very different identification practices, which in turn results in huge equity concerns. The elementary district definition matched the concept outlined by NCLB and the National Association for Gifted Children (NAGC). It includes intellectual, academic, leadership, and creative exceptionality. This conception of GATE suggests that GATE students have degree of talent, or a potential for such a talent, in a variety of areas and that such students deserve and require nurturing beyond that which a general education program provides. This view implies that being gifted or talented is a predisposition that some people have that can be developed with proper support. Coming from this perspective, NAGC asks educators to consider the following questions when determining identification practices: What assessments are appropriate for limited-English proficient children? Are the instruments culturally biased? Do we recognize potential in students who arrive at school without the advantages of home computers, libraries, and travel experiences (National Association for Gifted Children, 2008b).

This first perspective seems inclusive to some and, while honorable, too open and subjective to others. Some worry that this second stance implies that all students are gifted and talented or have gifted and talented potential. This mentality would have every student identified as GATE, thereby degrading the exceptionality principal that GATE students are qualitatively different form other students and that identification should objectively decide who has and does not have that exceptionality. We have often heard concerns about the "integrity" of the GATE program. Adhering to the thinking of the second camp, Orchard Middle School operates on the premise that entry into the GATE program relies on a current performance level, specifically in English grammar and writing, as measured by their assessment.

On the surface, this appears to be a basic philosophical disagreement, one of the many areas where reasonable people simply agree to disagree. Viewed from an equity perspective, however, issues surrounding the entry point to GATE are riddled with very practical, on-the-ground equity concerns. As in the case of Precious, belief systems about individual students and groups of students drive every aspect of school systems. (See Chapter 7 for a thorough discussion of the relationship between belief systems and school structures, policies, and practices.) Whether conscious or not to individuals working within school systems, those beliefs result in critical decisions that can either boost or limit educational opportunities for groups of students.

The situation seems straightforward, however, peeling off a few more layers reveals some conditions that raise serious equity concerns. For example, at Orchard Middle School, most Latino students previously identified as GATE were "un-GATED" as they entered the middle school, due to their inability to demonstrate the same level of grammatical and writing ability in English. Many Latino elementary GATE students were English learners at advanced English proficiency and scored proficient on state exams. However, as measured by the grammar and writing test, they had not yet achieved nativelike fluency by the end of fifth grade and so were no longer considered GATE. This was the common understanding about explaining why so few Latino students qualified for GATE.

Why were there so many White GATE students identified? Subsequent peeling of *other data* found that of the elementary-identified White GATE students, only half passed the grammar and writing test. All of the parents of any elementary-identified GATE student who did not pass were invited to a special GATE meeting. Parents received the opportunity to enroll their students in a summer GATE bridge program that, if completed successfully, qualified students for GATE. This program had a very high pass rate. Further, the other annual GATE meeting for parents of students not previously identified provided parents the opportunity to request that their students be tested for GATE and also offered the bridge-program option for those who might not pass.

Attendance rosters and interviews demonstrated that Latino parent attendance at both of these critical parent events was very low. When interviewed, many Latino parents reported not knowing about the meetings or not really understanding their significance. In contrast, parents from the elementary school in the wealthy neighborhood were actively encouraged to attend and request the GATE program by neighbors and other parents whose older children already moved to the middle school. These parents shared that their method of supporting public education and not moving their children to private school was to ensure that their children participated in this specialized program at the public middle school, where their children could learn alongside other advanced students. The combination of all of these factors resulted in highly disproportionate ethnic representation in GATE that had little to do with the exceptionality of certain students over others. Faced with these findings, the superintendent held a study session of the board of education, shared the information, and stated, "Our district is at a crossroads that will define our institutional heart. We must acknowledge the fact that our GATE identification procedures are flawed. Otherwise, we are saying that we accept the notion that one segment of our community is dramatically more exceptional and another is severely less exceptional than any typical population. As the leader of this district, I cannot accept that idea."

Implementation and Participation Practices

Disproportionality in GATE identification can be understood from different perspectives using the composition index, risk index, and risk ratio statistics described earlier in this chapter. In addition, the Orchard Middle School example illuminates several other equity challenges. First, since no federal mandates exist for GATE, every state determines policies governing the program. Within that, each district defines gifted and talented in its own way and determines the scope of services students will receive. In our experience, clearly identifiable GATE programs are more often found in schools or districts where savvy parents or board members demand it. In these systems, GATE includes elements such as a defined time period per day, student grouping for part or all of the school day, enrichment experiences, specially trained teachers, additional instructional materials, and strategic curricular approaches, such as accelerated pace. In the lowest level of implementation, GATE identification results in nominal changes in students' educational experience. Sometimes district plans describe "differentiated instruction" throughout the day, with little more definition, support, or monitoring.

Your Turn: Peeling the GATE Wallpaper

Gather any documents regarding GATE in your system and interview a GATE teacher and administrator to complete Template 4.8.

Template 4.8   Peeling the GATE Wallpaper

Questions	Answers	What Are the Equity Implications?
What is the racial/ethnic and linguistic makeup of your school or district? What is the racial/ethnic and linguistic makeup of your GATE program? Are they proportionate? How far from the 6% estimate of the percentage of gifted and talented students is each group?		
What is the operating definition of GATE in your system?		
How are GATE students identified in your system?		
What other questions come to mind?		

Another equity concern is that not all GATE-identified students receive the same enhanced opportunities. In one example, a district found that while 80% of White and Asian GATE-identified middle and high school students were enrolled in advanced courses, only 30% of Latino and African American GATE students were enrolled in those same courses (PRINCIPAL's Exchange, 2007). In another example, the Committee on Minority Representation in Special Education (CMRSE) reports that although students in middle school gifted and talented programs generally are more often enrolled in algebra than nongifted peers, Latino and African American students enrolled in gifted programs are less likely to be enrolled in accelerated classes. The PRINCIPAL's Exchange example and the case sited by the CMRSE found that the downgrading practice is not a result of test scores or grades. Latino and African American students with the same indicators as White and Asian counterparts were routinely placed in less-rigorous or less-enriched courses (see Johnson, 2002).

No simple response answers the question of why all GATE-identified students may not receive equal services. To be sure, human biases and belief systems on the part of adults in the system may play a part. Also, underinformed or misinformed parents may be part of the picture, by not encouraging their students to participate in a more challenging program. In one district, the GATE program at the elementary level required students to be bussed to a GATE magnet school, away from their home schools. Many minority parents declined the offer to send their students to this award-winning program because they did not want their children so far away, and they did not want to separate siblings. From another perspective, programmatic decisions that are not culturally responsive result in inequitable program participation. In the previous example, when asked, parents who declined the invitation to transport their children to the GATE magnet said that they would agree to their children's participation in the program if it were located at their home school or if their other children could also attend the magnet school.

Finally, students play a role. Particularly if the ethnic distribution in GATE identification exists, then minority students who are represented in small numbers in GATE classes may feel uncomfortable and opt out of the program. In one of many such examples, Katie, a sixth-grade, African American, highly gifted student, went to class tardy every period, so as not to be seen by her peers going to the "smart" classes on the other side of the school, carrying different books. Over time, this brilliant student lost her academic motivation and eventually opted out of the GATE program. Underchallenged in her regular classes, Katie eventually did just enough to graduate from high school. She never pursued higher education. In fact, between 18% and 25% of high school dropouts are identified as gifted (Renzulli & Park, 2000; Russo, Harris, & Ford, 1996). Most are culturally and linguistically diverse or low socioeconomic students (Renzulli & Park, 2000).

> In fact, between 18% and 25% of high school dropouts are identified as gifted (Renzulli & Park, 2000; Russo, Harris, & Ford, 1996). Most are culturally and linguistically diverse or low socioeconomic students (Renzulli & Park, 2000).

Ultimately, we must collectively acknowledge that as humans we all hold beliefs and expectations about people. However, as educators and parents, the decisions we make when we are not fully conscious of those beliefs can result in real educational harm for students that can affect them for the rest of their lives. Unlike special education, which is "data drenched," there are not comparable types of information for gifted and talented programs. There is no national database or federal office that monitors gifted and talented programs. The highest level of monitoring may be at the state level. Most of the data for gifted and talented programs at the elementary level are generated locally. These programs come in a variety of structures, from segregated classes, to afterschool programs, to extra assignments, and pullout programs. However, identification at the elementary level usually initiates a process that sets the stage for students to have premium learning opportunities throughout high school, including honors and Advanced Placement (AP) courses, and international baccalaureate programs.

From an equity perspective, it is urgent that conversations occur related to the underrepresentation of some groups in gifted and talented programs and courses. Moreover, there are many who can benefit from the gifted and talented curriculum regardless of the label. The implications for levels of academic preparation have long-term consequences. Wakelyn (2009) reports that by 2014, two-thirds of jobs will require some college. AP courses give students an opportunity to do college-level work and possibly receive college credit if they receive a score of three or higher on the AP exam. There are also possible economic benefits. Receiving college credit can possibly accelerate college completion. In addition, almost a third of colleges use AP credits as a criterion for scholarship decisions (Wakelyn, 2009).

Your Turn: Reflecting on Your GATE Program

Reflect on the GATE program in your setting and answer the following reflective questions.

Template 4.9 GATE Reflection

Reflective Question	Your Thoughts
Is there disproportionate participation (versus identification) in your GATE program? How do you know? What data would answer this question?	
If disproportionate participation did exist, what contributory factors might exist?	
Taking a parent perspective, are there any disincentives to GATE program participation in your setting?	
Taking a student perspective, are there any disincentives to GATE program participation in your setting?	
What modifications would improve equitable GATE program participation in your setting?	
What are the high school implications and life consequences of GATE participation for qualified students?	
What are the high school implications and life consequences of a lack of GATE participation for qualified students?	

National data are available on AP programs from the College Board. The reports are available online, state by state (see www.collegeboard .com/apreport). They also provide information and data on schools with exemplary programs. Figure 4.6 displays the proportion of ethnic participation in AP testing.

Notice, for example, that about half of all African American students and half of the native populations in the nation took and "passed" AP exams. The gap for Latino students appears much smaller. The College Board's *Sixth Annual AP Report* (2010) cites what they describe as the *equity and excellence gap*. This refers to the condition where "traditionally underserved students comprise a smaller percentage of the successful student group than the percentage these students represent in the graduating class.

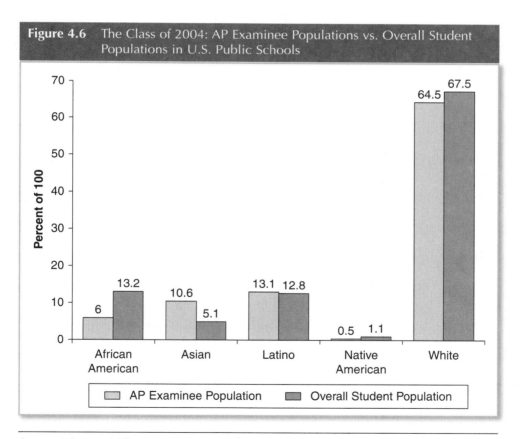

Figure 4.6   The Class of 2004: AP Examinee Populations vs. Overall Student Populations in U.S. Public Schools

Source: Advanced Placement Report to the Nation 2005. Copyright © 2006. The College Board. Reproduced with permission. www.collegeboard.com

Your Turn: Profile of Students in Selected Programs

Complete Template 4.10. What story do the data tell about the three most common programs that cater to gifted and talented students? What additional questions do you have? What *other data* are needed to further your understanding of the complete story? What are the equity implications?

Template 4.10 Profile of Students in Selected Programs

	Percent of Group in Program											
	African American Female	African American Male	Asian Female	Asian Male	Latino Female	Latino Male	Native American Female	Native American Male	White Female	White Male	Free and Reduced Lunch
Gifted and Talented											
Honors											
Advanced Placement											

For example, if 20 percent of students in a state's graduating class are African American, true equity and excellence would not be achieved until 20 percent of the students taking AP Exams and scoring a 3 or higher on them are African American" (College Board, 2010). The recent data show:

- Sixteen states have closed the equity and excellence gap for Latino students.
- Two states have closed the equity and excellence gap for African American students.
- Eighteen states have closed the equity and excellence gap for American Indian or Alaska Native students.

It is very important to disaggregate the results by state, district, and school, in order to peel back the wallpaper enough to reveal potential equity problems. For example, a state-by-state review of the equity and excellence gap data for each racial and ethnic group will reveal different degrees of gaps for each group. While the Latino group appears to have a significantly lower gap as an aggregate group, for instance, individual state gaps for Latino students may reveal very different patterns.

CONCLUSION

How we view a child is critical. Assumptions and decisions about who children are are often linked to long-term beliefs and historical legacies and the use of limited data. Labels are assigned to children that may be inaccurate because we don't have the whole story. The story of Precious highlights that by using *other data*, overidentification in special education can be reduced, and when children are given effective interventions that do not result in labeling, mislabeling, and segregation, they thrive. This gives us hope. We know that inaccurate labels and poor achievement by some groups can be reversed. Orchard Middle School showed how the use of data created opportunities for all groups to participate in rigorous courses. The bottom line is that there are outcomes that schools and districts can influence and change. We highlighted the diligence of dedicated educators who are questioning and probing to explore other possible explanations, resulting in positive outcomes for students.

5 English Learners

In Chapter 4, we presented the story of Precious, a struggling student, as a way to personalize and demystify the complex quagmire of special education. Using one child's experiences through the educational system, we highlight some difficult and hidden issues beneath the surface of special education that impact the lives of millions of students. In this chapter, we focus on another identified group of struggling students, English learners (EL). The label "EL" (also known as ELL, English language learners) encompasses students who are immigrant and U.S. born, beginning through advanced in English proficiency, have been labeled EL from less than one year to up to thirteen years, have studied in their primary language or not, come from formally educated families or not, and are either stable or mobile in a school or district.

Departing from the format of previous chapters, in this chapter we share a case to illustrate how the skillful use of *other data* can help courageous student advocates flex their *equity muscle*, peel off layers of educational confusion, and promote substantive changes that can result in impressive academic achievement gains for all students, including English learners.

OVERVIEW

The achievement of EL students has always been a concern to the educators who serve them. However, the advent of NCLB accountability has significantly increased the sense of urgency around EL achievement. Across the nation, EL students' achievement is significantly behind that of their English proficient counterparts, despite years of state and federal programs and resources aimed at improving EL student success. Over the past thirty years, programmatic options for EL students have included a variety of treatments with labels such as English as a second language (ESL), bilingual, transitional, maintenance, English immersion, dual-immersion, sheltered instruction, and specially designed academic instruction in English (SDAIE). Despite sincere efforts, and some documented successes, English learners as a group are consistently among the lowest-performing groups in the nation on assessments of English language arts and mathematics. For example, according to the 2007 National Assessment of Educational Progress results, only about 30% of EL eighth graders scored at or above the basic achievement level in reading and math in contrast to 75% of their non-EL peers.

Many perceptions exist about the characteristics of English learners in U.S. schools, some accurate and some not. Table 5.1 lists key characteristics of EL students in the United States.

Table 5.1   Key Characteristics of EL Students in the United States

- EL students represent over 5 million students in the United States.
- Almost 80% of English learners are from Spanish-language backgrounds.
- 61% of English learners are primarily concentrated in Arizona, California, Texas, New York, Florida, and Illinois, though EL students reside across the nation.
- Other states have experienced a 300% or higher growth of EL students from 1995–2005 (Alabama, Indiana, Kentucky, Nebraska, North Carolina, South Carolina, and Tennessee).
- One-third of the nation's EL students reside in California (1.6 million students).
- Most EL students in the country are U.S. born.

Source: Payan & Nettles, 2008.

> The sheer numbers of EL students in U.S. schools and their generally poor academic achievement levels make it critical that we address this group of students.

The sheer numbers of EL students in U.S. schools and their generally poor academic achievement levels make it critical that we address this group of students. Several publications exist that treat the issue of EL achievement from various perspectives. Goldenberg and Coleman (2010) recently published a concise summary of major findings from two recent government-funded reviews of research related to EL student achievement. One of the most comprehensive treatments on the subject, this publication demonstrates that much of the existing EL research relates to various specific aspects of literacy development. Research cited in this publication enlightens the educational and political community interested in EL achievement by studying the following types of research questions:

- Does teaching the primary language help or hinder English proficiency?
- What reading methods best help EL students learn to read?
- What are the most effective English language development (ELD) methods?
- How long does it take for an EL student to become English proficient?
- What are the best ways to group EL students?

Readers interested in enhancing their knowledge base in these areas should consult the Goldenberg and Coleman text. Our approach to EL achievement in this chapter takes a different tact, as our goal is different. In this book, we seek to help readers gain the disposition and knowledge on how to use on-the-ground *other data* as an equity tool adaptable to a myriad of educational contexts. Our experiences in addressing EL underachievement with schools and districts across the country compels us to bring to light systemic issues that persistently hinder the ability of educational institutions from effectively addressing key challenges to EL achievement.

CHALLENGING CONVENTIONAL WISDOM ABOUT PROGRAMS FOR EL STUDENTS

Crafting a thorough and meaningful treatment of EL achievement in the context of this book poses several daunting challenges. Most discussions of English learners in the United States are fraught with intense emotion and are entangled with complex adult issues. For example, the politics of economics often cause various factions to compete for slim available resources in schools or districts and in communities. English learner programs and services are often at the center of such arguments. Recently, the national debate about illegal immigration has led to a somewhat pervasive myth that English Learner and "illegal" are synonymous. These types of statements cloud the issues and cause distractions from meaningful conversations about quality education for English learners.

The issues are complex. Decisions about support for English learners in schools can be influenced by lack of information, poor patterns of communication among stakeholders, unclear agendas, and racial and ethnic politics resulting in tension, mistrust, and sometimes dislike among different groups. Historical legacies contribute to an intense effort by some groups to staunchly protect their cultural and linguistic traditions as well as intense countermeasures by other groups to block such efforts. Not uncommonly, the education of English learners becomes a platform for these debates as well, as evidenced by the bilingual education versus English-only decades.

Conducting quality research on EL programs and related systems issues poses some challenging problems due to several fundamental realities, including the following factors:

- **Not all "programs" are the same.** For example, a comparison of different "bilingual" and "mainstream English" programs can be problematic because, in practice, no consistent agreement exists about what constitutes each program. Further, great variability exists even among the different subtypes of programs. That is, two "transitional bilingual programs" may have very different degrees and types of primary language instruction, English language development, or other program characteristics. Such a lack of program clarity makes comparisons of program outcomes highly questionable.   .

- **Not all EL students are the same.** Researchers are challenged when studying EL achievement across contexts because they must be careful to accurately describe and account for the specific characteristics of the EL population they are studying. While most English learners in the United States are American born, their English proficiency spans the entire range, from beginning to advanced. For foreign-born English learners, the number of years in U.S. schools also varies. The educational level of parents of English learners varies as well. EL student proficiency and literacy levels in their primary language are diverse. Therefore, program outcomes must be carefully interpreted in light of the specific students they serve.

- **Not all EL teachers are the same.** Sensitivity about evaluating teaching effectiveness, particularly teachers of EL students, hampers research efforts. While states have different ways to "qualify" teachers to teach EL students, teacher quality and effectiveness vary greatly. For example, teachers who teach in a primary language may range from highly competent to quite limited in the primary language. Also, teachers of EL students may range in their proficiency in formal academic English. Variability in teachers' language proficiency as well as general teaching effectiveness can confound findings of research related to EL students.

- **English learners are part of existing school and district systems.** Programs intended to support target groups of students should never be designed without regard to their effect on students in the rest of the system. As an educational community, we can never accept a program design that sacrifices one group's success for

> As an educational community, we can never accept a program design that sacrifices one group's success for another.

another. Researchers who seek to understand EL achievement must do so in the context of the entire system within which they learn. Failure to attend to the context can lead to incomplete solutions. For example, sometimes EL programs are set up as a "school within a school," or as a separate track from the rest of the school. (Programs for gifted and talented students sometimes operate in this manner as well.) Evaluators may be tempted to study EL achievement of students in the target program. Yet other students, even other EL students to be sure, are enrolled in the school outside of the specific program. Comprehensive studies of EL programs must describe student outcomes within and outside specific programs as well as the effect of the program on the entire system.

A CASE ON TRANSFORMING THE STATUS QUO

Conflicting views surrounding EL education as well as the limitations of current research often result in situations where individuals who want to highlight the need to engage in inquiry about EL achievement must do so knowing that their attempts might cause a negative reaction. For many, it is difficult to pursue this line of inquiry because of the personal and professional risk. For example, one superintendent shared, "I know that our English learners are languishing in our schools . . . just look at the results! But the relationship between the school board, the teachers' union, and that small group of vocal parents makes it too dangerous for me to bring up the need for any changes at this time . . . maybe after the next board election." On another occasion, a new principal shared, "I tried to discuss my EL program with the teachers, just to better understand their direction. Oh boy! The bilingual teachers became very upset that I would question their practice. The nonbilingual teachers openly applauded, even before I finished my question. It felt like a showdown! I quickly realized I was in dangerous territory and backed away from the topic. By the time I made it back to my office, I had a phone message from the county consultant for EL programs wanting to discuss my 'concerns' about the

EL program and 'trusting' that I would continue to support the teachers in the existing program. Yikes!"

Yet, in the midst of these sometimes controversial conditions, some schools and districts have managed to impressively impact EL student achievement, effectively narrowing both the gap between non-EL and EL students at a school or district and the Gap (as described in Chapter 2) between EL students and expected achievement levels for *all* students. How do they do it? Organizations exist where healthy inquiry occurs regarding all student achievement matters, including those related to English learners.

We describe the case of the "Big American Unified School District" (BAUSD), that engaged in a quest to deeply understand the academic profile of their underperforming EL students and their experiences as they attempted to address the thorny issues that arose. This is a composite of actual school district examples that typify common themes related to EL achievement. The purpose of the case presentation is to provide the reader with a window into the process that was used to uncover the most salient issues affecting EL achievement, from the data-gathering stage to the action-planning and implementation phase.

The Context

BAUSD is a large urban school district with 70,000 students and one hundred schools. Almost 30% of the students are English learners. The ethnic makeup of the district is 40% Latino, 35% African American, and 25% White, with 80% of students considered to be of a low socioeconomic background. African American and White communities have resided in the city for generations, while the Latino, community is a combination of American born, second- and third-generation families who have been part of the neighborhoods for some time, and new immigrants. As the economic condition of the city steadily declined over the years, the district struggled to meet the changing needs of the student population and the increasing demands of the various constituencies in the community that sometimes conflict.

Over the past several years, the plight of English learners became a focal point in the district. Spurred by the accountability requirements of No Child Left Behind and the increasing numbers of EL students, EL students became a focus of discussion among factions in the community, at the school-board level, and in the schools. There were heated debates that were at times divisive. Various community sectors were competing for district resources to serve different student populations. There was a general sense that EL students were not as academically successful as other students, but there was a great disagreement as to why (whose fault that was), and how to solve it. The conversations and debates emphasized the types of programs and services EL students should or should not be offered, debating "bilingual" and nonbilingual programs. Advocacy groups representing the various factions became involved in the public debate that extended beyond the district into city and county arenas. The public rhetoric and private conversations were very divisive, with statements from every camp revealing differing belief systems and expectations for groups of students. There was also private talk expressing a legacy of resentment between and among different economically challenged ethnic groups and the middle-class White community.

This strife continued for several years, creating a climate of hostility and negativity, always centered on EL programs, policies, and philosophies. Finally, at great risk to her political standing, one board member came forward to ask whether the district knew specifically how EL students were achieving in the district and in each of the existing programs. She asked for data on each of the bilingual and nonbilingual programs that served EL students in the district. When given snapshot data of the most recent test scores for EL students, she stressed the need to collect longitudinal data. She argued that it takes time to acquire English and any evaluation of EL programs should follow the child's entire trajectory of progress toward desired levels of academic achievement. Further, she asked for a clear description of the characteristics of EL students in the district, including their primary language and how long they had been in the United States or the district. Moreover, she noted that any discussion of proposed solutions to the EL achievement challenge was premature if the district did not fully understand the profile of EL students and their results in existing programs.

Though she was criticized by each of the factions for not automatically supporting their position, the board member asked the superintendent to form a data team to collect the information she requested. The data team was formed and quickly realized that the existing data system in the district could not respond to the types of questions they had. Traditional data sets were available, but data reports using combination statistics or other layered data sets were not readily available and required manual collection. A common challenge is that district data systems often do not store key EL data or have the capability to create combination reports for cohorts of students over many years. The developmental nature of language acquisition requires such capabilities in order to answer substantive EL questions. However, the data team was able to create an EL achievement profile by using a variety of data collection methods.

Their approach was to send one of the members of the data team, armed with the questions generated by the team, to meet with the district director of technology. She explained each of the questions, and together they designed blank tables with row and column headings indicating the data points required to respond to each question. Templates 5.1 and 5.2 were created by the team in response to the inquiry questions.

Once the tables were created, the technology director worked with programmers to create queries of their various databases to retrieve the required data sets to complete the tables. This process was cumbersome, but worked.

A side effect of this process was that the district administration realized they needed to accelerate plans to acquire a fully integrated, longitudinal database system.

Template 5.1   How Long Have EL Students in Each ELD Course been in U.S. Schools?

	1yr	2yr	3yr	4yr	5yr	6yr	7yr	8yr	9yr	10yr	11yr	12yr	13yr
ELD A													
ELD B													
ELD C													
ELD D													

Template 5.2   Analysis of Reclassification Areas of Weakness

What are the areas stopping advanced EL students from meeting reclassification criteria to English fluency? How does the profile compare for the two major EL language groups in the district?

	ELs in country 5 or more years
Total number of students	
Number with total ELD assessment rating of "advanced"	
Number with ELD assessment listening/speaking rating of intermediate or higher	
Number with ELD assessment reading rating of 3 or higher	
Number with ELD assessment writing rating of intermediate or higher	
Number with English language arts state exam score of at least "basic"	
Number with district writing score of at least proficient	

Your Turn: Beginning to Peel Back EL Wallpaper

Using the inquiry questions that follow, collect and analyze information for your school and/or district. Modify the tables and questions as needed. Use Templates 5.1 and 5.2 for data presentations to your team.

- How long have EL students in each ELD course been in U.S. schools?
- What are the areas stopping advanced EL students from meeting reclassification to English fluency criteria? How does the profile compare for the major EL language groups in the district?
- Were there any problems with data availability, location, or collection? If so, what resources are needed?

The following text describes the process that the data team used to compile an actual achievement profile. In order to determine what data to request, the team used a question-and-answer process. The following section illustrates the process of peeling off layers of *other data* in order to accurately portray the status of EL students.

PROFILE OF BAUSD EL STUDENTS

The first challenge for the data team was to reach an agreement on what to measure. The data team represented voices from various perspectives and could not agree on what the goals were for English learners in the district. Recorded from actual meeting notes, the following list outlines some of the questions that were hotly debated as the data team tried to agree on district goals for the education of EL students:

- **Is bilingualism a goal?** Should students be expected to maintain their home language? If so, for how long? If not, then what is the expectation for language development? What is measured?
- **Is biculturalism a goal?** Is it a goal for all EL students or only those in the bilingual programs? Is it a goal for all students in the district? How is that measured?
- **Is academic achievement in English a goal?** Is achievement in English the target, or does that distinction somehow diminish the value of achievement measured in the students' primary language? Is it achievement in the core subjects that is important, regardless of what language is used to measure learning?

- **Is cultural pride and positive self-esteem a goal?** What culture(s) should be promoted and how is self-esteem measured?
- **What about non-EL students?** Should they learn a second language? Is biculturalism a goal for them? In what cultures?
- **Is English language proficiency a goal, as measured by a standardized English language assessment?** Is it the primary goal? It is the only goal? Is it one of several goals?

Conflict surfaced as individual data-team members began to express and push their ideological points of view. Ultimately, with highly skilled facilitation by the team leader and after many discussions, the data team was able to agree on EL program goals and formulated a question that would serve as the first of many layers of inquiry. Table 5.2 displays the overriding question agreed upon by the team and the stated common goals for all programs that serve EL students in the district.

Table 5.2   Initial Inquiry Question and EL Program Goals

Overriding Data Team Question	BAUSD EL Program Goals
How effective are the various district EL programs at promoting and achieving the agreed-upon goals for EL students?	Acquisition of English language proficiency Academic achievement in English language arts and mathematics Bilingualism and biliteracy Biculturalism

Created by authors based on information from an urban school district.

PEELING OFF THE LAYERS

In order to answer the overriding question about effectiveness, the team explored a series of layered questions. In their data-peeling process the team

- asked one question at a time,
- identified relevant data to respond to each question,
- interpreted the data to answer the question, and
- spun off the next logical question to repeat the cycle.

The questions follow as they unfolded over the course of several intense days, accompanied by a narrative of relevant background notes motivating or explaining the rationale for each question.

- **How many EL students are enrolled in the district?** It is important to begin with an accurate baseline count in order to include all students, participating in all programs. BAUSD has 20,000 EL students, which represents 40% of the entire district population. Spanish speakers make up 90% of EL population.
- **How effective is the district at helping EL students become fluent in English?** This question requires peeling back several layers outlined in subsequent text in this section.

Layer 1

How many years have students been EL? EL students are not a monolithic group. An accurate interpretation of EL achievement data requires a complete description of key EL characteristics. For instance, lower academic achievement in English for recent arrivals with limited English proficiency is expected, as it generally takes between four and seven years to acquire formal academic English

> EL students are not a monolithic group.

(Hakuta, Butler, & Witt, 2000). Therefore, achievement results that group recent arrivals with long-term EL students are misleading. A more meaningful approach to determining the effectiveness of EL programs on academic achievement in English is to remove from the data inquiry students who have been labeled EL for less than five years. Using this method, all remaining students in the data set will be long-term EL students who are expected to be academically competitive in English.

Table 5.3 presents data on the number of years current BAUSD students retained the EL label, without reclassifying to fluent English status. Sixty percent of current BAUSD students have been labeled EL for five years or less, and 40% retain the EL label over five years. The immediate concern is for the 40% of students who have been labeled EL for six or more years. These are primarily middle and high school students who began as EL students in the primary grades of elementary school and are still not considered "fluent" in English. Criteria for reclassification to fluent include demonstration of advanced English proficiency as measured by the state ELD assessment, and reasonable academic success as measured by state English and mathematics exams.

Layer 2

How many EL students become English fluent? In addition to current EL counts that show how long students are labeled EL, it is also important to highlight the success stories; that is, how many former EL students successfully met English fluency criteria and are no longer labeled EL?

Table 5.3 Number of Years Current EL Students Retain the EL Label

Number of Years Labeled EL	Number of Students	
<1	2,275	
1	3,300	
2	1,825	13,561 60%
3	3,337	
4	1,900	
5	2,564	
6	2,323	
7	1,299	8,722 40%
8	1,300	
9+	3,800	
Total	**22,283**	

Created by authors based on information from an urban school.

In the BAUSD, 3,700 current students were reclassified to fluent status. This represents about 17% of all EL students. Interpreting this figure from a practical standpoint, however, was tricky for the data team. Is 17% a good number? What does 17% represent? Is there a certain percentage cut point that is the goal? The answer to this question required thoughtful interpretation. The 3,700 students who became fluent will have promising academic futures. However, the academic future for the 8,722 students not fluent after six, seven, eight, nine, or even more years is bleak and may include placement in remedial courses and dropping out. Due to the fact that EL students must demonstrate reasonable academic achievement in English, these "reclassified" students tend to be among the higher-performing students in schools and districts. In fact, several K–12 district evaluation studies conducted by PRINCIPAL's Exchange found that reclassified former EL students in lower socioeconomic schools were among the highest-performing students by high school, surpassing achievement levels of even mainstream English speakers.

Layer 3

What is the gap between the number of reclassified EL students and the desired goal? This answer requires a determination of what is reasonable to expect. Is it reasonable to expect that beginning EL students become fluent in a year or two, or even three? Not generally. Most often, students who come from highly literate backgrounds with years of formal education tend to become fluent in a second language that quickly. Our best understanding of second-language acquisition is that it takes between four and seven years to become fluent in the academic register of English (Hakuta, 2000). While conversational English comes much earlier, English learners generally require more time to gain sufficient mastery in the formalisms of English so that they can apply those skills in rigorous schoolwork. Therefore, one approach is to identify the students who have been EL for over five years, for instance, and set a goal that most of those students should be able to meet English fluency criteria.

> Our best understanding of second-language acquisition is that it takes between four and seven years to become fluent in the academic register of English (Hakuta, 2000).

The data team hoped that any student in the district who had been classified as EL for over five years would be fluent in English, but agreed that at least 75% of the long-term EL students should be able to meet fluency criteria. That would mean that at least 6,541 of the 8,722 long-term EL students should qualify for reclassification. However, they did not meet the criteria. This was a very disappointing finding that a huge number of long-term EL students who should be advanced in English were not.

Layer 4

How do EL students who reclassify to English fluent perform academically? The expectation is that reclassified EL students outperform other EL students. As a district serving primarily low socioeconomic students, it is typical that reclassified EL students outperform even mainstream English speaking students. (Flores, Painter, Zachary, & Pachon, 2009). This, by the way, is a sobering and historically persistent pattern not ameliorated by decades of targeted federal and state monies.

Tables 5.4, 5.5, and 5.6 show that the BAUSD reclassified students consistently outperformed their EL peers who were not reclassified as well as their English-speaking peers. As expected, the majority of reclassified BAUSD students achieved at grade level in English language arts (70%) and math (82%) on annual state exams across the grades and on the high school graduation exam. Tables 5.4, 5.5, and 5.6 present the results of various outcome measures for reclassified EL, EL, and mainstream English speaking students

Table 5.4 Percent of Students Scoring at Grade Level

State Exams Across All Testing Grades (2–11)			
	Reclassified to English Fluent	**EL**	**Mainstream English Speakers**
ELA	70%	22%	29%
Math	82%	25%	34%

Created by authors based on information from an urban school.

Table 5.5 Percent of Secondary Students Taking Accelerated Math Courses (Beginning With Algebra in Middle School) and/or Advanced Placement Courses in High School (Single-Year Snapshot)

Reclassified to English Fluent	**EL**	**Mainstream English Speakers**
80%	5%	24%

Created by authors based on information from an urban school.

Table 5.6 Pass Rate on High School Graduation Exam by Language Proficiency Groups

	Reclassified English Fluent	**EL**	**Mainstream English Speakers**
ELA	89%	31%	37%
Math	86%	34%	35%

Created by authors based on information from an urban school.

in the district. Also, reclassified students participate in advanced courses at a higher rate than other secondary students. The data team lamented that so few students reached that desired level of academic success.

Layer 5

How do EL students perform academically in English the longer they are labeled EL? Sometimes people express the belief that EL students just need more time to develop English proficiency and that this explains their persistently low-achievement profiles in schools and districts. To test this assumption, the team needed to collect on-the-ground data to determine the pattern of academic achievement for EL students as a cohort, over time.

The team started by determining how EL students performed on readily available data, such as test scores in English language arts, the longer they remain labeled EL. They gathered *other data* such as grades, participation in premium programs (gifted and talented, honors, and AP courses), dropout rate, graduation rate, and rate of completion of college-prep courses to more completely answer this question. Many districts, however, do not code or collect many longitudinal data sets, leaving data teams to make reasoned inferences by triangulating whatever data sets are available.

> Many districts, however, do not code or collect many longitudinal data sets, leaving data teams to make reasoned inferences by triangulating whatever data sets are available.

The data team found that BAUSD EL students' achievement did improve up until the fifth year labeled EL, but did not improve the longer

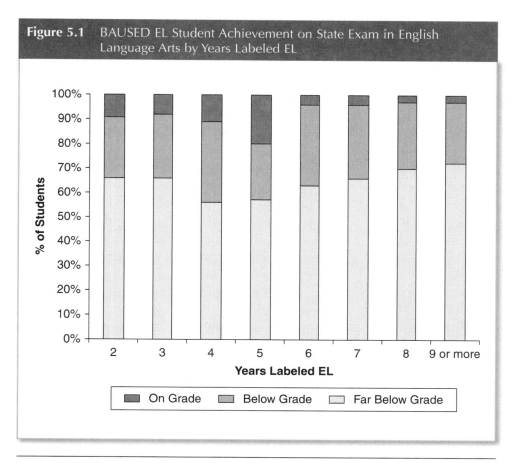

Figure 5.1 BAUSED EL Student Achievement on State Exam in English Language Arts by Years Labeled EL

Created by authors based on information from an urban school.

they were labeled EL after that critical point (see Figure 5.1). There appeared to be no achievement advantage to students remaining in EL programs over long periods of time. Clearly, students who reach sufficiently high English proficiency and academic levels to reclassify to fluent status do much better than long-term EL students. In fact, the achievement gap between groups appears to grow as students journey through school.

Layer 6

How are EL students progressing in ELD? ELD refers to the development of listening, speaking, reading, and writing skills in English as a second language. Research supports the notion that a strong relationship exists between the development of advanced ELD and academic achievement measured in English, across the content areas (Rumberger & Scarcella, 2000; Gersten & Baker, 2000). This is why criteria to reclassify from EL to fluent English status always include demonstration of advanced ELD levels. Obviously, EL students should make annual progress toward becoming English fluent. This is measured differently in every state. However, regardless of the measurement instrument, students should demonstrate measurable growth in English proficiency each year in order to reach English fluency within an average of five years and have the highest likelihood of being among the highest-performing students in the school system. A useful way to conceptualize ELD expectations is to use the term *on track* for EL students making reasonable progress each year and *on watch* for EL students not improving at the anticipated rate. These tags are useful when disaggregating data and determining which students require varying types and degrees of support.

> Research supports the notion that a strong relationship exists between the development of advanced ELD and academic achievement measured in English, across the content areas (Rumberger & Scarcella, 2000; Gersten & Baker, 2000).

> A useful way to conceptualize ELD expectations is to use the term *on track* for EL students making reasonable progress each year and *on watch* for EL students not improving at the anticipated rate.

Overall, EL students in the BAUSD are not making reasonable progress in their acquisition of English fluency. Table 5.7 demonstrates that about 75% of EL students, regardless of program, are on-watch students because they either made no annual ELD level gains or regressed. This was the most surprising and disappointing finding of all for the data team. They realized that the large numbers of on-watch students were among the highest-risk students in the district and that no district program adequately supported them in developing the formal academic English so necessary to overall academic achievement.

Program	Number of Levels Regressed				No Change in ELD Level	Number of Levels Advanced			
	−4	−3	−2	−1	0	+1	+2	+3	+4
Bilingual		<1%	4%	19%	54%	21%	1%		
Two-Way Immersion		<1%	4%	25%	47%	22%	<1%		
English Immersion		<1%	<1%	20%	53%	22%	3%	<1%	
Mainstream English	<1%	<1%	1%	28%	48%	20%	2%	<1%	<1%
Average	<1%	<1%	2%	23%	50%	21%	1%	<1%	<1%

Table 5.7 One-Year Change in ELD Levels for All EL Students in the BAUSD

Source: PRINCIPAL's Exchange.

Layer 7

Which EL program offered in the district is most effective at promoting academic achievement for EL students? This question often raises the greatest degree of emotion, for reasons stated at the onset of this chapter. Advocates of various programs tend to believe very strongly that their favored approach is best in every circumstance. Systematic and thorough data peeling, as well as careful interpretation of those data, is essential if the process is going to result in improved academic gains for students. Recall that the variability in the implementation of programs that share a title, teacher effectiveness, and student characteristics make it extremely challenging to reach conclusive findings about program effectiveness. Various types of outcome data shed light on the question, however, collection of on-site data from interviews and classroom visitations fill out the picture and help educators reach conclusions with greater confidence. In practice, the degree of available resources, including time, money, and people, defines the types and amount of data that can be collected. Data teams must collect whatever is feasible, maintain as much objectivity as possible, and draw the most reasonable conclusions possible based on the available data. Fully answering the program effectiveness question also requires layers of data peeling.

> Advocates of various programs tend to believe very strongly that their favored approach is best in every circumstance.

The following are the programs offered in BAUSD and a general description of each:

Bilingual—EL students are taught using home language while they acquire English. Sometimes the home language is phased out in upper grades, while other times the home language is maintained as part of the program.

Two-Way Immersion—EL and English-only students are in the same class. EL students use bilingual program guidelines while English-only students in the same class are immersed in the second language (such as Spanish) in the lower grades. Ultimately, the program aims to have both groups become bilingual and biliterate.

English Immersion—EL students are taught in English using differentiated methodology to help them acquire English and master content.

Mainstream EL and English-Only—Students are taught in English in the same class.

Available data (displayed in Table 5.8) indicated that none of the EL programs in the district yielded impressive results. There appeared to be no advantage of one program over another. This finding was equally disturbing to everyone on the team, as each member had voiced their hope that their favored program would rise above the rest.

Table 5.8 Percent of Students Achieving at Grade Level on State Exams From Population of Students Labeled EL at Least Six Years *and* Consistently Participating in a Designated Program

Program Type	Mathematics	ELA
Bilingual Program	25%	5%
Two-Way Immersion	13%	5%
English Immersion	30%	10%
Mainstream	20%	15%

Source: PRINCIPAL's Exchange.

Note: These data include former EL students who consistently participated in the programs and met the criteria to be reclassified as fluent in English.

Layer 8

What is the mobility rate of students in each EL program?
Sometimes only in the face of data that challenge individual belief systems does truly open conversation occur. In the
BAUSD example, the absence of compelling
evidence that any one EL program is significantly better than any other created a condition
where members began to ask deeper questions
related to issues of curriculum and other
resources, training, program monitoring,
achievement monitoring, and program leader-
ship. In particular, student mobility is a critical factor because several
EL programs follow a developmental design, with a particular configu-
ration at each grade level, assuming students will move through the
program as a cohort. When this is not the case, class size can fall below
required levels and sometimes other students are placed in these
classes to "backfill" the missing slots. This practice severely compro-
mises the integrity of developmental programs by creating situations
where teachers must modify the intended program design to accommodate the needs of new students.

> Sometimes only in the face of data that challenge individual belief systems does truly open conversation occur.

For example, imagine a second grade bilingual class where a group
of EL students began as kindergarteners where 90% of the school day
was in their home language and 10% was in English. Imagine now
that the program design calls for incremental increases in English
instruction as home-language teaching decreases. By the second grade,
maybe 60% of the school day is taught in the home language and
40% in English. What will a teacher do if student mobility results in
the loss of six cohort students and six non-English speaking new
students are added to the second-grade class roster? In order to accommodate the new students, a teacher will likely modify the ratio of
home language to English instruction, possibly reducing English
teaching to give new students time to catch up. Decisions such as this
fundamentally compromise the integrity of EL programs that are
designed to strategically build from one year to the next. Adaptations
such as these ultimately compromise achievement outcomes for EL
students.

Data indicate that many BAUSD EL students are highly mobile. In
many schools, half of the EL students who begin the school year do not
complete the year at that school. In other schools, mobility is less than 10%
in an average year. These findings led to a serious discussion about

whether developmental programs were equally appropriate in all schools. Peeling off data to look at other conditions in a school or district must be taken into account when deciding what program or service would be most effective for EL students.

Layer 9

How effective are the district EL programs with biliteracy goals at promoting home-language literacy? Some EL program designs have primary language literacy goals for EL students. Most common are some forms of bilingual programs labeled "maintenance bilingual" or "two-way immersion." In the BAUSD, only in the two-way immersion program were students assessed in their primary language. While the data team was pleased with the primary-language results, they took pause at the fact that EL students in the two-way immersion program experienced no advantage in academic achievement measured in English over other program participants. Once again, the data team discussed the variability issues within and across classes with EL program labels. They pondered what *other data* they could collect that would help them more clearly conceptualize factors perpetuating the depressed academic achievement of EL students as a group. Many more layered questions came from this discussion, including why students demonstrating strong primary-language literacy skills did not appear to transfer those skills to English literacy as expected.

The team noted that no readily available data existed to evaluate the goal of biculturalism. They brainstormed *other data* that would respond to this question and made plans to interview and survey students and teachers to evaluate this goal in the future.

DATA AS AN INSTIGATOR OF EQUITY-MINDED ACTION

Ultimately, the time for peeling off the layers of EL issues ended and the data team was ready to move to the next step. They brainstormed as many remaining questions as they could and identified the data sources, including hidden data, necessary to answer those questions. Then they calendared time, over the course of the year, to continue their process.

Your Turn: Remaining Questions

Using the template below, answer the questions below or develop questions for your particular school or district. Create a team that will commit to addressing EL issues and have conversations about the issues and how you should proceed.

Template 5.3 Remaining Questions and Possible Data Sources	
What questions remain unanswered?	**What data sources would respond to each question? (Be sure to include all types of data— traditional and *other data*.)**

Even with the data gathered to that point, the data team felt that their process had clarified a large enough piece of the "story" behind EL underachievement to begin tackling some of the bigger challenges. After a board presentation of their findings, and with the encouragement of the key board member and the superintendent, the data team transformed into a "leadership team." They analyzed each of their major findings, brainstormed possible responses, and then crafted an action plan.

Your Turn: EL Inquiry

After analyzing EL data, brainstorm major findings with your team and develop some possible responses. It would be useful for the team to review some of the recent research on English learners cited in this chapter.

Template 5.4 Major EL Inquiry Findings and Possible Responses

Major Findings	Possible Responses

A key aspect of the team's action plan was the monitoring and evaluation components. (See Johnson, 2002 for more information on using data for monitoring progress.) For monitoring, the team devised a multi-pronged approach to ensuring that plans were thoughtfully and consistently implemented. This approach outlined the responsibility of various individuals across the system to perform monitoring duties designed to support plan implementation.

Your Turn: Monitoring Plan

Decide what needs to be monitored, responsibilities, and possible dates. Discuss the implications on how to plan for, organize, and accomplish monitoring responsibilities.

Template 5.5 Monitoring Points and Responsibilities

Monitoring Activity	Monitors	Monitoring Responsibilities	Dates for Data Collection
	Schoolsite principals		
	Teacher leaders and coaches		
	Parent leaders		
	District office		
	Superintendent		
	Board of education		
	Students		

For the evaluation step, the team delineated what the expected outcomes were for each plan component, what measures they would use to determine the degree of goal attainment, and a timetable of frequent status checks.

Your Turn: Analyzing Evaluation Elements

Complete Template 5.6 with your team. What are the implications for your site?

Template 5.6 Evaluation Elements

Expected Outcomes	Measurement Tools/Methods	Status Check Timeline

CONCLUSION

The purpose of this chapter is to illustrate the process of peeling off layers of *other data* in order to bring to light issues that directly affect student achievement, even in the most complex situations. Highlighting English learners is important not only because of the growing numbers, but also because of the persistent underachievement pattern for large numbers of students. This chapter does not promote any philosophical or political position regarding English learners. Rather, we charge readers to commit to moving beyond debates about program models and approaches, and use the data-peeling process to carefully trace the journey through school experienced by thousands of English learners in every state. We illustrated some of the complexities that exist when trying to objectively evaluate EL outcomes:

- No generalized agreement exists on characteristics of programs carrying the same label.
- EL student characteristics range tremendously, calling into question any reporting of EL achievement as an aggregate group without any disaggregating for variables such as time in the United States, time in program, or primary language level.
- Teachers of EL students, within program labels, display a wide range of qualifications, experience, language proficiency, and overall effectiveness.
- Adult sensitivities create obstacles to open and honest dialogue and data transparency.

These challenges are not unique to the education of English learners. We use this topic as another example, among the many addressed throughout this book, of how to mobilize resources to untangle very intricate webs of data and reveal real outcomes for students. Profound challenges to educational equity result when we spend maximum resources deciding on programs and services without attending to the outcomes in each context. We need to have the courage to ask the outcome questions, collect relevant *other data* layer by layer, openly engage in collaborative discourse to tell the true, on-the-ground story, and then take necessary action to improve educational opportunity for students.

6 Nonacademic Indicators Associated With Achievement Outcomes

SCENARIO: TITAN MIDDLE SCHOOL

Titan Middle School is a midsized school located in a working-class suburban area. The student body is mostly African American, Latino, and White, though a growing number of students are identifying themselves as "mixed-race." After many years of low achievement, the district assigned a new administrative team, charged with improving academic performance. The young, energetic principal and assistant principal vowed to do everything in their power to provide rich educational opportunities to their students.

They learned that the previous administration spent most of its time "putting out fires." Emergencies with facilities, teacher concerns, parent issues, and student discipline consumed their days. Teachers reported that their classrooms had not been visited for years. After much deliberation, the new Titan administrative team decided on what they believed would be a winning strategy. They would focus all of their attention on the quality of instruction that occurred in each classroom. In the spirit of true "instructional leadership," they would be in classrooms daily, would discuss lesson plans with teachers, and would even provide demonstration lessons for struggling teachers if need be. Nothing would deter them from their focus on the classroom.

The team was diligent and unyielding as they spent most of their time each day in and out of classrooms. When the school year ended, they anticipated great increases in test scores and grades. However, when all data were calculated, achievement results improved only slightly, and were certainly not commensurate with the degree of energy the team had expended on classroom practice. Dejected and deflated, the principal asked a retired principal friend to spend time with him to try to understand what happened. After a few probing questions, the friend said, "Oh, you made a classic mistake. Your attention to instruction was admirable, but teaching and learning occur in context, not in isolation. There are systemic issues that affect the academic culture and learning at a school."

The principal thought and thought and then asked, "What systemic issues?" The friend responded, "Finding out the answer to that question should have taken up part of your time last year. Your focus on instruction should have taken up the other part. There are always issues at school, not obviously academic in nature, that are the stage and set upon which the act of teaching and learning take place. You must concern yourself with the backdrop as much as the acting to have a successful production.

With the help of the critical friend, the principal and assistant principal revised their improvement strategy for the second year, continuing the support of effective teaching, but also working to understand the less obvious variables related to achievement that existed at Titan Middle School so that they could begin making changes. They uncovered a host of nonacademic conditions that explained the disappointing first-year results. Little by little, they made necessary changes and were ecstatic when the second-year results indicated significant gains in achievement across the school.

OVERVIEW

In this chapter, we explore some of the less-than-obvious factors that portray themselves as nonacademic variables. These variables influence student achievement in profound ways. The story of Titan Middle School is a composite of dozens of schools that we have supported over the years. Over this past decade, and with the onset of the national school accountability movement, attention has been focused on the elements that are related to teaching and learning. Examples include but are not limited to: acquiring sufficient and up-to-date textbooks, teacher recruitment, credentials and professional development, leadership development, interventions, and assessment. Discussions pertaining to nonacademic issues are rarely heard and are generally not given much attention. There is little thoughtful analysis of how these nonacademic issues may relate to academic achievement outcomes. While previous chapters focused on the multiple methods to address academic achievement, this chapter provides a framework for understanding system issues that have been identified as constraints to achievement. We describe a set of contextual realities, which is shared by many schools. These data need to be disaggregated and combined with achievement measures by student demographic group, teacher, course, and program. Most or all of these data required to look at these issues are at the school site, but they are rarely used, analyzed, or connected to school improvement in meaningful ways.

This chapter presents five major areas that need attention from the perspective of equity and overall improvement of school culture. The areas are time, discipline, attendance, extracurricular participation, and facilities and program quality. There are other areas that schools and districts should identify and conduct inquiries on, such as truancy. In our discussion of these nonacademic issues we provide on-the-ground examples as well as supportive information from the research literature. Titan Middle School's winning strategy was dependent upon the identification of specific systems and elements of school culture that inhibited achievement. This along with a focus on instruction and addressing significant nonacademic issues resulted in impressive academic gains.

RETHINKING TIME

Time is a precious educational resource. Nationally, many schools and districts are calling for extended school days and school years. Often, educators complain that their students never have enough time to learn and teachers do not have enough time to cover what they should. There is the notion that more minutes will equal higher levels of academic achievement. The research suggests that merely increasing the quantity of time without increasing the quality of what happens during that time will not yield higher academic achievement. More of the poor practices do not usually produce results. Silva (2007) stresses that ". . . any extended time proposals must focus on expanding the right kind of time—time when students are engaged in

> The research suggests that merely increasing the quantity of time without increasing the quality of what happens during that time will not yield higher academic achievement.

productive learning" (p. 4). Several factors including allotted time, class time, instructional time, and engaged time must be addressed. There exists evidence to support that increasing instructional and engaged time pays off with achievement gain. Certain students, particularly low-income students, lose learning time over the summer when their middle-class peers have access to enrichment learning opportunities. This puts low-income students on an unlevel playing field. More quality learning time would surely be beneficial for these students (Silva, 2007).

This next section describes several nonacademic conditions occurring in schools that reduce time for learning. Ironically, most of these conditions are mandated with the best intentions by schools and districts. Yet, the unintended consequences can be devastating to student achievement. We examine the mandated 180-day school calendar, teacher-allotted instructional time, and student time.

Calendar Analysis

It is possible to increase instructional time *without* adding one more minute of allotted time. Every school year has a certain number of days, and each day has a legal minimum of instructional minutes. How those days and minutes are utilized varies school by school. We have found that in many schools, particu-

> It is possible increase instructional time *without* adding one more minute of allotted time.

larly low-achieving, low-income schools, that existing time is misspent. Many in the public assume that the 180-day school calendar is devoted to instruction. However, that may be an erroneous assumption when we examine the real world of schools and see that many other activities take precedence over instruction. These decisions are made by design. In many schools where there is an absence of *academic press,* an inordinate amount of teaching and learning time is taken up with assemblies, celebrations, contests, special events, over-testing, regrouping students, and the like. It is not uncommon to find that students must hand in their books two to three weeks before the end of school, leaving students and teachers with the feeling that school is officially over. Table 6.1 shows how allocated time and actual time for instruction differed in Titan Middle School. However, the story told by this table is only the tip of the iceberg. Clearly, much more intensive analysis at the classroom and student level should occur in this particular example. Additionally, a deeper analysis is needed to see how days and minutes may be lost by design.

Table 6.1	Titan Middle School Use of 180-Day Calendar		
Allotted 180-Day School Year Time Schedule	**How Time Is Spent**	**Holidays**	**Total Days Prescribed Instruction**
September 6–October 3 20 days	• Review of last year's work: 15 days (mostly due to lack of finalized class schedules)		5 out of 15 allotted
October 4–October 31 20 days	• Prescribed instruction: 20 days • Unit testing: 2 days	4 holidays	18 out of 20 allotted
November 1–November 30 20 days	• Prescribed instruction: 16 days • Assemblies, holiday parties: 4 days	2 holidays	16 out of 20 allotted
Nov 30–January 31 39 days	• Prescribed instruction: 36 days • End-of-semester testing: 3 days	10 holidays	36 out of 39 allotted
February–March 31 43 days	• Prescribed instruction: 37 days • Presidents' assembly: 1 day • Review and end-of-unit testing: 3 days	5 holidays	37 out of 43 allotted
April 1–May 31 27 days	• Prescribed instruction: 12 days • Test preparation: 10 days • State testing: 5 days	7 holidays	12 out of 37 allotted
May 3–End of school 11 days	• Prescribed instruction: 5 days • Testing, handing in books, trips, other end-of-year activities: 6 days		5 out of 11 allotted
Total 180 days			Total: 129 out of 180 allotted days spent on prescribed curriculum

Created by authors based on information from a suburban school.

Designated Instructional Time

Attention to and critical monitoring of instructional minutes during the day are critical to determine if the structure for time is supporting the school's focus on academic achievement. For example, the Titan Middle School schedule included sixteen minutes of homeroom per day. The homeroom program, once highly structured, had evolved into a more flexible concept. The most recent intent was for sustained silent reading (SSR) to occur at least three days a week, leaving the other two days for teacher-determined activities. With the help of the principal's critical friend, the principal identified homeroom as one nonacademic condition at the school and decided to study its effect on academic achievement. Teacher and student interviews and classroom observations revealed that the homeroom plan was being inconsistently implemented and was not systematically serving the purpose of advancing the school's student achievement goals. On SSR days, no more than 50% of the students in any class were observed engaged in reading. On teacher-determined days, 80% of the classes observed were not engaged in any teacher-directed activity. Over the course of a school year, homeroom represented approximately two weeks of instructional time. As a result of this finding, the leadership team decided to restructure the daily schedule and add the homeroom minutes into the regular teaching periods to provide teachers and students more time to target the specific instructional objectives outlined in the common units recently developed by teachers.

Looking inside the classroom reveals what percentage of the allotted time is spent on instruction or nonacademic tasks, such as classroom management, handing out assignments, and students starting homework during class time. Teachers' plan books used in combination with other data collection can be rich sources of information. Do plans adequately reflect what is actually done in the classroom? Observation logs can be used to assess what and how instruction is occurring. Another type of log should observe how much students are engaged in instructional activities. Shadowing students at different achievement levels can be very revealing. These types of data will provide a treasure chest of information way beyond any type of test score analyses. It is well worth the time to gather these data. They are useful and extremely valuable for analyzing instructional time and assisting teachers with their use of time when it is deemed necessary.

Student Time: Office Aide and Other "Classes"

How many times have you called a school and heard the greeting, "Student speaking"? "Classes" such as Office Aide or Teacher's

How many times have you called a school and heard the greeting, "Student speaking"? "Classes" such as Office Aide or Teacher's Assistant have unfortunately become part of a school culture that epitomizes a lack of "academic press."

Assistant have unfortunately become part of a school culture that epitomizes a lack of "academic press." At Titan Middle School, 175 students received credit for Office Aide, Teacher's Assistant, or Service. Evidence from observations and interviews clearly indicated that credit for these experiences most often required little to no learning. Incredibly, the most common grade for students taking those courses is an A (with an average GPA of 3.95 among the 175 students for these nonacademic assignments). Further, transcript analyses for those students pointed to the fact that 65% of those 175 students were struggling in their core subject areas. Therefore, students could have benefitted and had more opportunities for academic growth from a different use of that time.

We believe that students should be actively discouraged from taking the minimum requirements or from finding alternative ways to satisfy requirements. For example, it is common in high schools that some students are enrolled for less than a full six-period day. (Some schools have as many as eight periods.) At one such high school, counselors reported that 40% of students did not receive a six-period day and that twelfth graders were regularly assigned only five periods. One school year, 285 EL students (14% of student body, 27% of all EL students) did not take six periods (150 students in Grades 9–11, and 135 seniors). Yet, EL students were among the lowest-performing students at the school. It is clear to see how some of these issues can be remedied by looking at these on-the-ground available data.

It is essential to further analyze data on students taking high-credit/low-learning "classes" and data on students not taking a full day's course work. The data should be disaggregated by race, ethnicity, gender, socioeconomic status, program groups, and GPA. All students, regardless of their background, should be programmed into meaningful courses that will prepare them for the postsecondary and workforce requirements of the twenty-first century.

Even when all things appear to be in place, there are students that need more time than others to achieve at proficient levels. Often, difficult choices need to be made in order to give a student more time to catch up in a particular course. For example, a student with a particular subject-area need who qualifies for a scheduled intervention class may also want to take an elective, like band. Solving this conflict involves some creativity and willingness on the part of the school to do everything possible not to make extra academic support feel like punishment to students. Is there a way to help students who need more time achieve standards and have some choices on what courses they take? Keeping track of these students and solving these issues are important at the individual student level as they may affect students' relationship with the schooling process and their long-term outcomes for graduation and beyond. Suggestions have been made that go beyond the school to involve community programs and others to expand learning time. In recognition that it takes some students longer to get through high school, NCLB has modified the high school graduation regulation to give selected English learners and students with disabilities up to five years to complete high school requirements and still be considered on-time graduates (Gewertz, 2009a).

Your Turn: Studying Use of Time

Have your data team gather data about time at your school. Divide up the work by areas you want to look at and are most concerned about. Analyze factors related to time at school, classroom, and student levels. Discuss the implications and design action plans to recover lost time in the existing schedule. Monitor achievement outcomes.

Template 6.1	Findings from Our Time Inquiries	
Area	**Findings**	**Action Plans (Must be related to findings)**
School level		
Classroom		
Student		

DISCIPLINE: EXCLUSION
AND LOSS OF LEARNING TIME

We treat discipline as a nonacademic issue affecting achievement. However, there is a need to discuss the context in which discipline practices are occurring in our schools. Therefore, we will discuss a major policy related to discipline in this chapter rather than in Chapter 7, which is the chapter that focuses on school policies and practices.

Because of perceived and real fear of violence in our nation's schools, we see an escalation in the use of a disciplinary practice stemming from a zero-tolerance stance. This policy had its beginnings in the 1980s with federal drug policies. According to Skiba (2000), "Zero tolerance has been intended primarily as a method of sending a message that certain behaviors will not be tolerated, by punishing all offenses severely no matter how minor" (p. 2). We urge that anyone who is interested in reading more about its inception and the role of zero tolerance in school discipline read Skiba's policy report cited here and in the reference section of this book.

> Because of perceived and real fear of violence in our nation's schools, we see an escalation in the use of a disciplinary practice stemming from a zero-tolerance stance.

In addition, the Civil Rights Project and the Advancement Project (2000) published a brief that summarizes the issues related to discipline and zero tolerance. They contend that under zero tolerance, the punishments may not fit the offense and students are expelled or suspended for reasons that are not related to safety. When school officials use the most severe punishment, it is considered zero tolerance. Nationally, most of the students who are suspended under the zero-tolerance policy have not done anything related to safety. Zero tolerance is popular in many urban districts and is touted as nondiscriminatory, however, disciplinary polices have two categories, mandatory and discretionary. In practice, how the rules get interpreted is subject to human decisions and bias. In this chapter we focus on looking at the data for students and groups and the types of patterns that emerge related to overrepresentation of some groups.

A 2009 report by the American Civil Liberties Unions details the outcomes and implications of zero-tolerance laws on expulsion in Michigan. They outline a school-to-prison pipeline connection (also described by Children's Defense Fund, 2007; Texas Appleseed, 2007; Reyes, 2006) and the lost opportunities for students. They also contend that school offenses are now being criminalized, and students are losing educational opportunities for behaviors that previously would have been handled by schools. One of the major criticisms of zero tolerance is the lack of discretion and consideration of the circumstances by school administrators, the absence of safeguards against cultural misunderstandings, and how behaviors are interpreted. This has become a major equity issue.

It would be impossible in this text to fully cover the research and all the manifestations of policies and programs related to discipline in schools and districts. Needless to say, there are huge costs that are diverted from other programs. What we hope to do is raise some issues for schools and districts to consider based on some common national patterns and to examine local data in light of the facts about gross inequities and overrepresentation of some groups in the discipline pipeline. Sometimes, there is a normalization of negative perceptions that accepts which students or groups misbehave, are disrespectful, or are "disruptive." So when these groups are targeted for punishment, there is little concern or question. We should be asking why this is considered normal and why we accept this condition. Later in the text, we describe how Titan handled their disciplinary issue relative to inequitable practices.

The Civil Rights Project (2010) provides an enlightening summary of the data:

- African American children only represent 17% of public school enrollment, but 33% of out-of-school suspensions. White students, 63% of public school enrollment, represent only 50% of suspensions.
- In Minnesota, for example, 25% of African American students were suspended.
- Latino students are also singled out for discipline; in Tennessee, more than 38% of Latino students have been suspended.
- Research shows that these disparities are not due to poverty or inherently bad behavior. Students of color are more likely to be suspended for nonviolent, minor misconduct such as disobedience, disruption, and disrespect of authority. (p. 2)

A common assumption is that children's academic and behavioral problems are related to family income level. This seems to target all racial and ethnic groups, so it appears to be bias free. However, the argument doesn't hold up when the data are examined. First, it is generally found that males are referred more often and receive more disciplinary penalties than females, and African American males are disproportionate to their percentage in the population suspended and expelled (Holzman, 2006; Skiba, Michael, Nardo, & Peterson, 2002). Collier (2007) found that for the same offense, African American males received harsher consequences than did other students. We pose rhetorical questions that may reveal stereotypes that affect groups (groups mentioned previously) that are typically marginalized in this society: Why is there disproportionality for some groups? Is it cultural? Is it related to school's practices? The data show connections with discipline and low grades. Are some groups less capable intellectually? Are they less moral? Is instruction appropriate? Each of us should take time to ponder our personal beliefs and our institutional practices as they relate to the answers to these questions because our belief systems influence our responses to different populations of students.

When the data are further revealed and the layers peeled off, questions such as this surface: Are we less competent in how we educate and interact with certain students? Skiba, Michael, Nardo, and Peterson (2002) were interested in finding out more about the reasons for the disparities along gender and racial lines. They conducted a study in a middle school that had a disproportionate number of disciplinary actions for African American students. What they found when they unpeeled the wallpaper was evidence of differential treatment at the classroom level. Students were referred more in subjective areas of discipline, such as being disrespectful, rather than mandatory violations, such as carrying a weapon or possessing drugs. It is critical for schools and districts to be skeptical and never accept disproportionality as a normal state of affairs. Once the information about unfair practices for certain groups of students is revealed, educators must change course so that all students have the opportunity to succeed. To address the urgency of this issue it is crucial for schools to examine and respond to these data. Not to do so implicates educators in the false belief that some groups are naturally unruly or even violent. Again, we emphasize that it is vital for disciplinary data to be disaggregated and combined with achievement measures by student groups, by teacher, and at the student level in order to appropriately examine the full impact.

> It is critical for schools and districts to be skeptical and never accept disproportionality as a normal state of affairs.

The joint report by the Civil Rights Project and the Advancement Project (2000) on discipline recommends that schools monitor disciplinary referrals for overuse by teachers in order to find out about problems related to classroom management, discriminatory treatment, or students being singled out. Addressing issues of culture and how they are responded to is paramount. Although the data picture on discipline in our schools is troubling, these data are usually limited to review by deans, counselors, local and district administrators, and, in more serious cases, boards of education. The professionals who are most hands on—teachers—are rarely involved in looking at these data and patterns of discipline in a systematic way. There is seldom a discussion about the connection of the removal of students from class, lost time and academics, and classroom and school climate related to measureable academic achievement. The topic is usually addressed when someone has a concern about disruptive classroom behaviors and/or the perceived need to remove a student with the rationale such as "so other students can learn." Most of the findings show that much of the focus is on how the student behaves, rather than looking at the school conditions and the cultures in which students find themselves (ACLU, 2009; Bay Area School Reform Collaborative, 2001; Reyes, 2006).

We describe discipline at Titan Middle School as an on-the-ground example of how disciplinary practices played out at a school. The school did not have a stated zero-tolerance policy, but students experienced the unintended consequences of this type of policy, such as the differential treatment of certain groups in disciplinary actions. At Titan Middle School, maintaining positive, contained behavior as defined by the faculty and staff was the number one priority. During their first year, the new administrative team began to question some of the school procedures for dealing with discipline but was quickly discouraged from doing so by the staff. Apparently, the previous administration preferred that teachers handle their own disciplinary issues and not send students to the office. In response, the teachers created a detention room where they could send students throughout the day if they wanted to remove them from class. In order to staff the room, each teacher agreed to take five additional students each period in order to release a full-time teacher to manage the detention room.

Discouraged by the staff to meddle with the system, the newly assigned administrators left the detention room alone for that first year. Instead, they spent time in classrooms, observing. The administrators noticed that students were occasionally sent out of classrooms for various reasons, from answering the teachers in ways they deemed inappropriate to forgetting homework or not having a pencil.

During the second year, the principal was encouraged by his critical friend to collect some data and try to assess what the impact was of the detention-room system, a seeming nonacademic variable. Observations clearly indicated that students were regularly sent to the room without any textbooks or assignments and that they spent most of their time there engaged in little or no academic pursuit. Further, the only observable interaction between the teacher and the students was disciplinary in nature. The detention room enjoyed the support of 100% of the teachers, who insisted that they could not allow one unruly student to disrupt the instruction for the rest of the class. Several teachers said they did not use the room often and did not suspect that most teachers did, but that it was necessary for the rare occasions when a student was unmanageable. Table 6.2 indicates how many teachers actually made referrals and how many students they sent to the detention room.

Records indicated that the detention housed between zero and five students on average, in a given day, not all the same period. Further analyses revealed that about one third of all school referrals were from physical education, where adult supervision in the locker room was lacking. Also, teachers with the highest detention-room referral rates generally referred a small number of students multiple times, rather than many students one time each. A few of those students were referred by several teachers, but

Table 6.2 Teacher Referrals to Detention Room	
How many teachers. . .	**. . . made how many detention room referrals?**
10	0
1	1
1	4
2	5
2	6
2	7
1	10
1	12
1	20
1	25
1	30
1	36
All substitutes combined	102
1	156

Created by authors based on information from an urban school.

Your Turn: Detention Room Referrals

Collect your data and discuss the implications on lost instructional time and opportunity to learn.

Template 6.2 Teacher Referrals to Detention Room	
How many teachers. . .	**. . . made how many detention room referrals?**
All substitutes combined	

most by only one, suggesting a possible personality conflict. Finally, in addition to one single teacher who referred students almost every day, substitute teachers referred students most often.

Additional inquiry found that punishments escalated for some students. When students misbehaved in the detention room for their assigned period, they were told to stay after school as punishment. If they did not come after school, they were given in-house suspension to be served the following day outside of their classrooms, to contemplate their misbehavior. If they did not come to school the next day, they were suspended from school for three days.

After the principal presented the data to the staff, the teachers agreed that referral data needed to be disaggregated by grade level, ethnicity, gender, program, and individual students to check for patterns. In fact, clear patterns surfaced that reflect national data:

- Boys were referred more than girls.
- African American boys were proportionally overrepresented and Asian and White students were proportionally underrepresented.
- Mainstreamed students with disabilities were also referred with regularity.

After reviewing the data, the Titan staff decided that they could no longer continue with the practice and opted for professional development and coaching on behavior management, cultural responsiveness, and differentiation for special populations in order to handle the majority of student issues. Administration agreed to take responsibility for the most egregious offenses as outlined by the new school discipline plan that focused on keeping students in the classroom, except for the most extreme cases. The physical education department received additional supervision staff and revamped procedures in the locker rooms. The administration and staff made improved teacher attendance a priority to reduce the need for substitute teachers. They had baseline data and they developed a monitoring plan to track progress.

ATTENDANCE

Other major areas where students lose time are school and class-level absences. Most of the publicly reported data is about average daily attendance (ADA), which includes excused absences and is linked to funding. Our concern is actual time that students are not in class. In-class seat attendance for elementary school, period-by-period attendance at the secondary level, and class tardies can give a more accurate picture of lost time. At the secondary level, there are even more ways that students lose time and fall through the cracks. These other time indicators include school-sanctioned absences such as those that allow for athletes to participate in home and away games. What classes are they missing and how many? What are their grades in those classes they are missing? What accommodations are made for them to make up class time?

We heard the story of a ninth-grade athlete, Glenn, who had his algebra class during the last period of the day. Neither the coach nor his counselor red flagged this issue so his algebra class time could be rescheduled. When basketball season began, he had to miss algebra when there were away games. He missed many periods and was not concerned about the missed classes since the school sanctioned these absences. There was no way for him to receive the instruction he missed in this important college preparatory class. He received a C– in algebra that year and struggled with math all through high school. In the end, he did not have the college preparatory math courses for four-year college enrollment.

Major blocks of time are lost in many low-performing schools via class changes, mobility issues, and master schedules that are sometimes not finalized for months. Moreover, there is a musical-chair effect where the students and teachers are moved in and out of classes for weeks after the first day of school, so teachers do not want to present new material until their class enrollments are finalized. As a result, teachers resort to constantly giving review lessons because the classes are not settled. The students and teachers understand this game of musical chairs, and continue to move along with such practices. These practices waste precious time and deprive students of learning key academic concepts, yet, these issues are rarely taken into account as part of understanding low achievement.

While regular school attendance does not guarantee academic success, not attending school generally guarantees failure. Therefore, accurately checking student attendance is an important exercise and should continue. Typical reports of attendance data, however, are not usually helpful in determining whether student attendance patterns may be affecting student achievement. In this next example, *other data* includes typical attendance data reconfigured to answer some very practical questions.

> While regular school attendance does not guarantee academic success, not attending school generally guarantees failure.

The Titan Middle School staff complained that students were habitually absent, resulting in a high failure rate. A standard attendance report indicated that student attendance was at 95%, higher than the district average of 89% and higher than the country average of 92%. These figures were surprising to staff members who insisted that student absences were a chronic problem. This topic was a priority at several staff meetings, where the discussion continued to center on the belief that student attendance was an issue.

After much discussion, the staff and administration realized that the data reporting a 95% positive attendance rate did not answer their fundamental question: How many days of class were students missing? They grappled with how to request the data, realizing the format of the data report could either help or hamper their quest. They reached consensus that five days of absence in a yearlong course was not likely to prove fatal. However, more than a week's worth of absences could severely hamper a student's ability to master essential course standards. Recall the information presented in Chapter 3 that identifies excessive absences as one redflag indicator that students may not graduate from high school or may drop out. Table 6.3 displays the results.

Table 6.3 Number of Days of Student Absence From School	
Days Absent in One School Year	**All Students (1,448 students)**
0–5	485 (33%)
6–10	332 (23%)
11–15	165 (11%)
16–20	66 (5%)
21–25	22 (2%)
25+	32 (2%)

Created by authors based on information from a suburban school.

Notice that 43% of the student body was absent for more than a week of school and 20% of students were absent for more than two weeks of school. In fact, attendance was a problem for hundreds of students, and the 95% positive attendance figure did not tell the important part of the story. Continued discussion led to concern over the individual students comprising the various absence increments. Who were those thirty-two students missing over a month of instruction? What was causing their excessive absences? What resources could the school direct toward these young people?

Further conversation centered on subgroups of students. Was the absence profile the same for all racial, ethnic, socioeconomic, linguistic, and gender groups? Was the pattern the same for all grade levels and special program participants? The staff ultimately asked questions about whether students were missing entire days, or just certain classes. They requested *other data* that answered whether patterns existed in student absences in certain courses, subjects, particular teachers' classes, or classes offered in different parts of campus (such as bungalows versus main buildings). Figure 6.1 presents the pattern of absences by period. Data indicated that first and sixth period had high absences that were never calculated in the daily attendance counts. The teachers' concerns about student absences were founded on period absences, not daily attendance counts.

Analyzing typical data configured in new ways helped the staff move from an abstract discussion of school attendance rates to an extremely

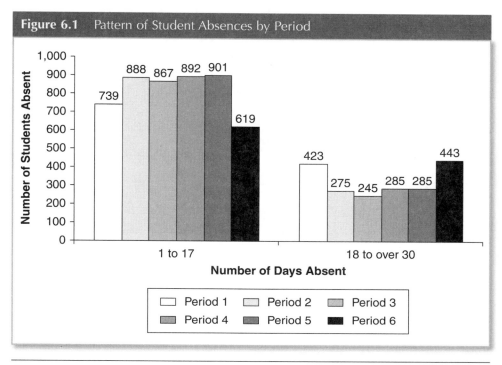

Figure 6.1 Pattern of Student Absences by Period

Created by authors based on information from a suburban school.

practical conversation about concrete strategies for helping individuals as well as specific groups of students.

Other combinations of data can tell more parts of the story. Another common assumption is that students who don't attend school are the nonachievers. However, this assumption, like most, needs to be tested. At Titan Middle School, the majority of students who earned D or F grades in math had 80% or better average school-year attendance. Two students had perfect attendance. Therefore, mere attendance does not guarantee academic achievement. We need to look at what was happening to the students by class, period, course, teacher, disciplinary profile, and so on, to understand why some students who apparently come to school regularly still fail. Could this inquiry be examined further to find out about GPAs and attendance? How much does being in class count? These are very important questions to ask when working to develop a culture of inquiry at a school or district in order to find some key indicators that could direct future decisions on effective use of the school day.

The student attendance discussion and the exaggerated disciplinary referrals by substitute teachers led to the topic of staff attendance. While appreciative of adult sensitivities, the principal collected the teacher absence data and presented it to the leadership team. Table 6.4 presents the results.

Table 6.4 Teacher Absence Report				
Teacher Name (deleted)	**Illness**	**School Business**	**Personal Necessity/Other**	**Total**
A	165	2	18	185
B	150	0	2	152
C	29	19	1	49
D	17	27	4	48
E	22	9	15	46
F	4	25	11	40
G	7	26	5	38
H	12	17	8	37
I	20	10	1	31
J	19	2	8	29
K	18	5	5	28
L	11	11	5	27
M	9	14	3	26
N	1	16	8	25
O	2	13	7	22
P	17	5	0	22
Q	15	0	3	18
R	3	0	12	15
S	13	0	1	14
T	6	2	4	12
U	3	2	7	12
V	6	5	0	11
W	6	4	0	10
X	0	8	1	9
Y	4	4	1	9
Total	559	226	130	915

Created by authors based on information from a suburban school.

Overall, the pattern of teacher absences suggested that continuity of instruction was negatively affected by the inconsistency in teachers' attendance. Some teachers were pulled out the equivalent of a month for school business, including professional development, conferences, and union business. Going back a few years, some teachers maximized their illness days every single year. For a combination of reasons, students had substitute teachers for over 900 classes in one year.

This report led to questions that required peeling more layers, such as:

- Why are some teachers involved in so many days of school business, but others not?
- What can be done to provide instructional continuity in the rooms where teachers are absent with reported illness most of the school year?
- What has been done to ensure that personal necessity absences adhere to contractual agreements?

The principal used the result of this discussion of teacher attendance and collaborated with the district office to establish an attendance incentive program whereby teachers were rewarded for improved attendance. Also, the district established a policy of discouraging professional development during the school day, opting for afterschool or weekend training instead. Finally, individual teachers with a history of poor attendance were counseled and placed on improvement plans to increase their attendance. These measures instituted during the second year of the new administration led to significant increases in teacher attendance and an overall improved sense of staff cohesiveness.

Your Turn: Attendance Analysis

Collect and analyze data on student and teacher attendance using Titan's inquiry as a guide. Are there any surprises? Discuss findings and develop an action plan.

EXTRACURRICULAR PARTICIPATION

Extracurricular activities are most often discussed in isolation of school courses and academics except for eligibility. Interscholastic sports and participation in other activities are increasingly requiring minimum GPAs. There are arguments made that these extracurricular activities may be the magnet to keep disengaged students in school and that academic qualifying criteria are misguided.

On the other hand, some argue that not having academic requirements does students a disservice and lowers expectations. Moreover, in our experiences, we have heard about athletes who have been advised to take easier courses to maintain a GPA. As a result, when these students get to college, many cannot handle the rigorous courses required to complete their degrees. Additionally, teachers and professors have had pressure to change an athlete's grade, particularly if the athlete is a team starter. Some schools may find their data on athletes and course taking very interesting. Key questions should be posed, such as: What are the course-taking patterns of athletes? Are they in honors and advanced courses? If the number is low, why?

The movie *Coach Carter* (2005) deals with this issue of academics, expectations, peers, family and community, and interscholastic athletics. The story is based on the life of a basketball coach, his team, and a community. In this true story, the coach challenged a system where athletes were able to receive poor grades and continue to play. In spite of resistance from the students, school administration, parents, and the community, Coach Carter instituted a strict academic regimen with his players. The students on the basketball team were underperforming in academics, but excelling at basketball. Coach Carter locked the gym and canceled games until their academics improved. In the end, the students responded to the higher academic expectations, and many of the players enrolled in college. This coach is an example of how a significant adult can influence the outcomes for young people, even when the strategies may be unpopular.

Although much of the attention is focused on athletics, there are a myriad of extracurricular activities in schools. A plethora of research exists related to these nonacademic and voluntary activities that are so much a part of many students' school experiences. There are strands of research related to academic connections, affiliation, students' well-being, and the connection between race, ethnicity, and selection of activities (Feldman & Matjasko, 2005). However, the research focuses mostly on athletics. More attention is needed on other extracurricular activities and their affect on students' achievement.

Our interests in this area relate to issues of equity and what types of data schools and districts might collect that could be useful in looking at equity issues with extracurricular activities. The research informs us that there are patterns of students in clubs, athletics, and other activities that are distributed along gender and equity characteristics. Feldman and Matjasko (2005) conducted extensive research on of the key characteristics of this distribution and the influence of these activities on students. We have referenced the work for those who want a deeper knowledge base on the patterns associated with equity. Schools willing to dig deeper into these issues may find that equity issues exist, which can lead to deeper questions such as: Is there an association with student participation in activities and attendance, grades, and so on? Are clubs and activities segregated along racial or gender lines and if so, what are the positive or negative implications? How do advisors work with these groups?

Much of the current research reviewed by Feldman and Matjasko (2005) supports the notion that there is a positive relationship with participation in structured (supervised by adults) and organized extracurricular activities and academic achievement. The literature also supports that sports for both genders is associated with academic achievement, and football and basketball are related to aspirations for higher education. How these aspirations get realized is not discussed. Some argue that the aspirations were preconditions to engaging in the activity. Schools need to look at their particular settings and study these relationships and how they manifest themselves on the ground. Eccles and Barber (1999) found that the peer group is a mediating influence between the activity and participation. A very powerful line of inquiry is the association of peer groups as a mediating factor for enhancing a student's school-staying power (Feldman & Matjasko, 2005) and influencing academic achievement. We recommend the examination of several combinations of information:

- Longitudinal databases.
- Number, types (structured or unstructured), characteristics of activities and membership by grade, race, ethnicity, language groups, and gender.
- Level of student participation in activities.
- Alternative schools and special education student participation.
- Academic achievement of students in various activities.
- Distribution of resources to different activities.
- Student perceptions of activities: Is there a feeling of openness to join different activities, or are there unwritten codes about who should participate in different activities?
- What role do adults play in steering or discouraging participation in high-profile activities such as student council, yearbook, sports, or cheerleading?

Template 6.3 represents data that might be collected on student affiliations for your school or district. Are all students participating equally in all activities? Are all activities equal in terms of providing positive social networking support for future academic pursuits? Why do some groups gravitate toward specific activities and away from others? How else should these data be disaggregated to provide a more complete picture? What other questions should be asked?

Your Turn: Data on Student Affiliations With School Activities/Clubs

Gather data for your school and answer the inquiry questions provided.

Template 6.3	Percent of Students Affiliated With Major School Activities/Clubs			
	Percent Latino	**Percent African American**	**Percent Asian**	**Percent White**
Student Government				
Cheerleading				
Band				
Orchestra				
Choir				
Soccer				
Tennis				
Volleyball				
Football				
Service Club				

Data on extracurricular participation should be integrated into discussions about school climate, student welfare, and its role in holding power and academic achievement for students in school. This is an overlooked area that may hold clues to helping students experience more productive school careers.

FACILITIES AND PROGRAM QUALITY

A strong perception existed at Titan Middle School that limitations with facilities negatively impacted the instructional program. As a result of space shortages, a number of teachers did not have a regularly assigned class-room. In fact, fifteen teachers in the core academic areas moved to at least two different classrooms during the teaching day. Table 6.5 displays the pattern of movement.

Table 6.5 Numbers of Traveling Teachers in Core Academic Areas		
Department	Number of Teachers who Travel per Department	Number of Classrooms Teachers Travel to in a Day
ELD	3 out of 3 teachers	1 teacher moves 1 time 1 teacher moves 2 times 1 teacher moves 4 times
English	2 out of 5 teachers	1 teacher moves 3 times 1 teacher moves 4 times
Mathematics	5 out of 5 teachers	2 teachers move 2 times 3 teachers move 3 times
History/Social Science	1 out of 5 teachers	1 teacher moves 4 times
Science	4 out of 5 teachers	3 move 2 times 1 moves 4 times

Created by authors based on information from a suburban school.

A thorough review of the movement patterns indicated that the "roving" situation impacted the program in several ways:

- Instructional time was impacted for roving teachers due to time used to pack materials and change classrooms.
- Subject areas that should provide students with lab or experiential learning activities were not implementing the programs as designed, in part due to barriers related to setting up lessons while changing classrooms.
- Instructional lesson planning was impacted by the practical need to find a location conducive to supporting careful instructional preparation. The need for storage and filing space challenged teachers to remain organized.
- Roving and nonroving teachers had less ownership of their classroom environment because of the movement and space sharing. Evidence manifested itself in the absence of posted student work or in traditional furniture arrangement that limits student interaction.

- The practice of assigning newer teachers to roving situations created conditions where new teachers expended energy on issues other than perfecting their teaching craft. As a result, they developed perceptions and beliefs about the teaching profession that did not support the school's long-term instructional goals to significantly improve the instructional program for all students.

As a result of this analysis, portable classrooms were moved to the campus to enable every teacher to be assigned their own classroom. This change had an immediate impact on the quality of instruction, as noted by administrative walk-throughs and benchmark test results.

STUDENT VOICE AND SOCIAL NETWORKS

> Often, clues to nonacademic variables that negatively affect achievement can be mined from the impressions students have of their experiences at a school.

Often, clues to nonacademic variables that negatively affect achievement can be mined from the impressions students have of their experiences at a school (see Chapter 3). The new principal of Titan wondered about this, so he set out to systematically interview a representative sampling of students. That is, he and his critical friend identified the various subgroups that comprised the student body, and then randomly selected a group of students from each subgroup. He asked them some probing questions and then some open-ended questions. The following list represents the findings from four of the subgroups, as an example of the type of *other data* that were collected from them.

Findings for Latino and African American students included the following:

- Their parents wanted them to attend "college."
- Low-performing students had very little to no information about college requirements.
- Low-performing students relied on friends to advise their academic decisions.
- Low-performing students were not confident in their abilities. These students felt they could not compete and reported giving up easily when school became challenging.
- Low-performing students and their parents were not knowledgeable about college requirements and did not actively participate in requesting specific course assignments.

- These students were almost entirely dependent on school personnel to determine their schedule and to advise them on decisions regarding academic and career matters.
- As a group, they were not persistent and insistent on specific program schedules, trusting instead that schools had their best interest in mind.
- AVID (Advancement Via Individual Determination, a national college preparatory program) students were the stark exception, exhibiting much more knowledgeable, proactive influence over their academic direction and program.

Findings for White students included the following:

- They actively participated in the development of their own schedule.
- Their parents expected them to attend a four-year university.
- Their parents "pushed" them to seek changes in their programs when they had problems, even when students did not feel comfortable doing so.
- They and their parents were knowledgeable about college requirements. Much of that information came from community and peer resources, in addition to school information.

These impressions, as communicated by students, provided the administration with a first step in peeling off the layers of more nonacademic variables that influence achievement so profoundly. Educators widely accept the notion that academic achievement is highly related to students' sense of academic direction and control or influence over their academic success. In that regard, Latino and African American students at Titan were at a distinct disadvantage. A critical sixth-grade math placement decision, whether to go into general math or honors math, was highly related to the quality of students' entire program for the duration of their time at Titan. Students who were assigned to honors math in sixth grade were placed with the more dynamic teacher "teams," offering them richer science, English, and history courses as well. Most of their school day was with the same group of students, anchored by that one math course.

More than the accelerated academic benefit, that group of students developed a social network that provided them key information focused on finding ways to navigate the educational system to their benefit. Those students counseled one another to actively influence their class schedules by making multiple contacts with their counselors. Counselors tended to visit those classrooms with greater frequency to provide them with pertinent information related to their academic success. Those classes developed a culture of excellence not pervasive in the lower-level classes, though classes were not labeled differently on the master schedule. Students were keenly aware of what level they were in.

Overwhelmingly, White students were included in those advanced courses, and Latino and African American students were not. Even Latino and African American students with the highest achievement scores were not regularly included in those higher classes. As a result of these placement practices, the majority of Latino and African American students experienced their entire middle school career in the least powerful learning environments with the least motivated, least successful students. This pattern served only to perpetuate the historical underperformance of Latino and African American students in the school.

In stark contrast were the Latino and African American AVID students, those participating in a college-prep elective program designed for middle-performing students whose parents are not college graduates. AVID students, by virtue of their program participation, are part of a powerful information network that proactively and aggressively provides students critical information about college requirements, necessary study skills and habits, and a mindset that convinces students that they are able and deserving of the highest-quality education offered in their school. Latino and African American AVID students performed equal to their White peers on state exams and district benchmark assessments and had similar grades. Students reported that, in addition to the academic supports, the most valuable part of AVID was the information they received about ways to make the school work for them and their academic future. They received more individual teacher time, more counselor contacts, and exposure to information that only students in the higher-level classes typically received. They also gained self-advocacy and effective communication skills so they could better help themselves along the way.

By actively listening to student voices, the school was able to uncover the power of social networks to either promote or limit academic achievement. Making a concerted effort to change that informal information network had a significant impact on the achievement of historically underperforming student groups at Titan, and the impact was felt more strongly each subsequent year that the plan was in place.

CONCLUSION

Nonacademic indicators should be at the forefront of data collection and analyzed in combination with academic indicators. These indicators are linked to academic outcomes. There are major equity issues that must be considered especially in the area of discipline. These data are mostly available at the school level and should be accessible, but it will take time for teams to collect, summarize, and analyze the data. However, it is worth the work, as was evidenced at Titan Middle School. As has been demonstrated throughout this book, leadership plays a pivotal role in supporting teams through the data-peeling process promoting educational equity.

Again, we emphasize the importance of disaggregating the data. As the stark realities about the disproportionality of certain groups being suspended, expelled, or not receiving opportunities to learn surfaces, the issues must be red flagged and addressed. A culture of inquiry should be nurtured until it becomes a part of the legacy and mission of the school or district. All members of educational institutions must give themselves permission at every level to take the time to step back, reflect, and address these nonacademic issues that may uncover inequities that affect student achievement.

> A culture of inquiry should be nurtured until it becomes a part of the legacy and mission of the school or district.

7 Systemic Inequities

Structures, Policies, and Practices

SCENARIO: AWARD-WINNING SCHOOL DISTRICT

A superintendent of an award-winning school district was not satisfied. She was concerned that even though her district's overall achievement was strong, Latino, African American, and Native American students (historically underperforming) performed significantly lower than their Asian and White counterparts. She was particularly concerned with the low numbers of historically underperforming high school students who went on to four-year universities. While she accepted that many of their families faced economic, social, and linguistic challenges, she noted that the Asian community in her district faced similar conditions, as many were English learners and struggled socioeconomically as well. She refused to accept the prevailing belief among staff that some groups of students and parents simply did not value education. She asked a critical friend to engage in a study to help her better understand the issues. It was important for her to know if there were any variables that the district could directly influence, recognizing that family and community issues were beyond her direct sphere of influence.

A critical friend led a study team through an inquiry that included interviews of students in each demographic group; students completing their university prerequisite sequence and those on the lower academic track; teachers of advanced, regular, and remedial courses; and counselors. The team asked a series of questions that led to other questions and were fascinated as they peeled off the layers of the district's past and present practices and uncovered the roots of the achievement gaps in their district. The summary and main points gathered through interviews can be found in Appendix C.

The interviews caused the study team members to have more questions and gather other data *including:*

- *counselor-student contact rosters,*
- *written placement criteria compared to student transcripts,*
- *schedules of counselor visits by class,*
- *ethnic distribution of classes by level, and*
- *facilities maps locating advanced and other classes in relation to information bulletins and counseling activities.*

The process of triangulating the data resulted in the following findings related to the university-readiness gaps between Latino, African American, Native American, and Asian and White students:

- *Advanced classes are 85% Asian and White, and lower level classes are primarily Latino, African American, and Native American. The student population of the district is actually 45% Latino, 20% African American, 5% Native American, 20% Asian, and 10% White.*
- *Asian and White students meeting placement criteria for advanced classes were regularly assigned those classes. Asian and White students not meeting the placement criteria were regularly assigned the advanced classes by parent, student, or teacher request.*
- *The historically underrepresented students meeting placement criteria were offered advanced classes 50% of the time. Qualified students were not assigned to advanced classes if teachers did not recommend them or if students opted out. This was a common occurrence. The only African American, Latino, and Native American students not meeting placement criteria who were assigned to advanced classes were AVID (Advancement Via Individual Determination) students.*
- *Counselors' perceptions were that they gave college information frequently to all English classes because they and their colleagues were out of their offices and in classrooms very often. In fact, only advanced classes received university-preparation information and only those got visited frequently. Lower-level English class students were visited, on average, once each year, and the content was about graduation.*
- *Adult perception was that placing college information on the public bulletin board provided equal access to all students. However, the location of lower-level classes made it highly unlikely that those students would ever be in the vicinity of the board. Because they lacked information about university requirements, they would not likely see relevance in the information even*

if they did walk by the board. In contrast, the board located outside the Advanced Placement (AP) classroom, near the honors classes, provided an excellent information source for advanced students.

The result of peeling off layers of other data helped the superintendent answer her questions: Why was there a gap between the Latino, African American, Native American and Asian and White university preparation rates? Is there anything within the control of the schools and districts that can be done to improve the situation? The answer was clear, that while economic and social conditions related to the gap, they did not entirely explain it. The inquiry conducted by the district revealed systemic inequities that perpetuated the gap and in fact exacerbated it.

As a first step, the superintendent committed to making sure that all students who met the criteria were assigned to advanced courses. Teacher recommendation and student acceptance were no longer heavily weighted for students who met the objective criteria. In addition, students who did not meet the criteria could petition to be in these classes. These changes in practice immediately increased the number of historically underperforming students in advanced classes. The fact that the classes were more diverse made them more welcoming to other Latino, African American, and Native American students as they enrolled. Counselors studied the data and acknowledged that their perceptions of how they spent their time were not accurate. They then modified their visitation schedules and agendas to ensure that all students received important college information. They also redesigned their freshman orientation event, ensuring that the presentation did not communicate subtle messages that university was for some students and graduation/community college for others. This event included parents as well as students.

Initially, some teachers began to come to terms with their flaws in their perceptions about groups of students. Other teachers took a bit longer. If Latino, African American, and Native American students were not academically oriented or not interested in challenging themselves, then why were their AVID peers so successful in advanced courses? They acknowledged that AVID provided students a social and academic support system that enabled them to compete equally in the most rigorous courses. This awareness helped many teachers consider modifying their teaching methods as more Latino, African American, and Native American students enrolled, and over time, many more of these students found success in challenging classes.

As counselors began to visit regular-track classes with university-preparation material, teachers realized the need to upgrade the level of their courses to match their title "college-prep." As those courses improved, students from the "college-prep" course track, not the advanced track, also began applying and getting accepted to universities.

Each year, the superintendent and the study team reconvened to review data to determine the effect of the structural changes. On every indicator, the gaps between Latino, African American, Native American and Asian and

White student university-preparation rates were reduced. More historically underperforming students than ever in the history of the district were completing the university-prerequisite course sequence. Of course, conditions were not perfect. Some students resisted taking harder classes, some teachers fought to keep some students out, and other teachers fought to keep students in who were not succeeding. Stereotypes about students persisted. As the team discussed these daunting challenges, the superintendent concluded by saying, "We began our quest by focusing on the systems over which we had immediate control. Our students benefited from those changes right away. However, we will work to change belief systems also; they just won't change as quickly. We now have more students achieving at higher levels who defy former expectations . . . Over time, that will change beliefs about students. Until then, we will continue to create a college-going culture in our school system that behaves as if everyone believed that all students should graduate college and be university ready."

OVERVIEW

Schools and districts are part of systems with interacting components working in tandem to provide schooling for students. Solutions from a narrow perspective may create problems in other areas. In other words, neglecting systems thinking when approaching educational challenges can bring about unintended consequences. This chapter is about uncovering systemic inequities that influence differential achievement levels. We provide readers with a framework to examine systems that bury some students and catapult others.

> Neglecting systems thinking when approaching educational challenges can bring about unintended consequences.

Structural features, processes, and practices are components of systems that affect students' well-being and academic outcomes, but little time is spent in systematically looking at the everyday workings of the institution. There are over thirty years of research (Cicourel & Kitsuse, 1963; Delpit, 1988, 1995; Edmonds, 1979; Flores-Gonzalez, 2002; Ladson-Billings, 1994, 2001; Lezotte, 2010; Losen & Orfield, 2002; Noguera & Wing, 2006; Oakes, 1985) that give clues as to effective and ineffective institutional practices. There also is an abundance of literature on how institutional practices affect equity. Collecting, analyzing, and using broad-ranging quantitative and qualitative information about school and district policies and processes can help to crystallize the real need for appropriate reforms that have the potential for positive long-term effects on students. This deeper level of reflection must continue as schools and districts establish visions, set goals, and implement strategies.

COMMON ROOTS OF SYSTEMIC CHALLENGES TO EQUITY AND ACHIEVEMENT

Our collective sixty years of work in schools and districts afforded us ample opportunity to observe systemic successes that positively affected achievement, as well as failures that limited educational opportunity. While the specific system characteristics are fascinating, even more interesting is that most often, systemic flaws are not idiosyncratic. Systemic impediments to educational equity are most often attributable to a set of prevailing suppositions. The following section outlines our analysis of seven suppositions regarding systemic challenges to equity and achievement, including descriptions of on-the-ground examples and supporting evidence from the literature. These suppositions are:

> Systemic impediments to educational equity are most often attributable to a set of prevailing suppositions.

Supposition One: More is better.

Supposition Two: Conventional wisdom is always wise.

Supposition Three: Low achievement is inevitable for some (the inevitability assumption).

Supposition Four: Implementation is the goal.

Supposition Five: School systems are fair.

Supposition Six: Everyday inequities are normal and natural.

Supposition Seven: Adult interests should take priority.

Supposition One: More Is Better

In Chapter 6 we addressed the issues related to more time. Here, we discuss the common practice of adding more programs and initiatives to existing school days. A report from the Steering Committee Consortium on Chicago School Research (Bryk, Easton, Kerbow, Rollow, & Sebring, 1993) described the add-on program mentality as "unfocused academic initiatives." Two of the categories they describe, "peripheral academic changes" and "Christmas-tree schools," paint a vivid picture of fragmentation and add-on efforts:

1. "Peripheral Academic Changes"

- Add-on programs with little innovation
- Limited focus on improving core teaching

- Absence of coherent planning
- Little active resource seeking (Byrk et al., p. 15)

For example, "Struggling Elementary School" illustrates the supposition that more is better. It is located in an impoverished urban area, and has been persistently low performing for at least ten years. In 2006, only 12% of their students were on grade level in any subject. Fed up, the new board of education demanded reform, and, in lieu of closing the school, they gave school teams or other community entities an opportunity to submit school transformation proposals. The team submitting a plan with the greatest chance of turning the school around would gain control of the school. One community team proposed changing the school calendar from year-round to traditional. Another team wanted to impose school uniforms. A school proposal asked for parent literacy classes. A final submission on behalf of the teacher's association was to change the composition and meeting schedules of the "professional learning communities" (collaborative teacher teams) on campus.

After considerable debate about which proposal had the best chance for success, the board president observed that while each proposal had merit, none dealt directly with issues central to teaching and learning. All of the suggested "reforms" were positive, but none was focused and targeted on drastically improving the poor instructional conditions at the school, a situation that resulted from years of weak leadership. As a result, no proposal was accepted, and the board reconsidered its intervention plan. This "tinkering around the edges" approach stems from a lack of solid understanding of fundamental equity issues that can be uncovered through a systematic process of peeling off layers of data.

2. "Christmas-Tree Schools"

- Showcase schools with many new programs
- Multiple "add-ons" with little coordination
- Little attention to strengthening organizational core
- Entrepreneurial principals actively seeking resources (Byrk et al., p. 15)

Often, educators become program shoppers, looking for the silver bullet that will create the needed change. A high school principal complained that after years of such "shopping," there were so many programs in her school that she could not keep up with them. The principal was constantly calling substitutes to stand in for teachers going through new training programs. Although all of the programs had the greatest of intentions, she was not sure specifically what each was supposed to achieve, how, and for which students. There seemed to be overlap in many of the goals and activities, but the teachers involved in the different initiatives rarely communicated, much less collaborated.

Frankly, the principal felt that many of the programs had been forced on her by central administration. She wished the school could focus more in depth on improvement efforts already begun before adding new programs. A colleague asked her, "Why don't you just say that you don't want any more programs?" Her reply was, "Oh, I can't do that. I am fearful that people would think that I don't want to improve my school!" Still, the principal wondered whether there was any way to determine which programs were best for her school and which were not particularly effective.

Subsequently, the principal and some staff members attended an institute where they were challenged to analyze the disparate programs at their school. The principal realized it was the first time in a while that she had been encouraged to think solely in terms of what was best for her students. The principal, with the assistance of the data team, began analyzing program impact at the school, getting familiar with all of the efforts, collecting data, and finding out how others evaluated the programs—including students and parents. They presented this research in a coherent way to support whether particular improvement efforts should be kept, modified, or eliminated.

Some of the findings from the team included the following:

- **ISD Class.** The in-school detention class kept students who were tardy out of class for a whole period. During that time, no academic work was given or expected to be completed. No provisions were made for missed academic work.
- **Academic Study Hall.** This class was a consequence for students who did not turn in homework. This was a mandatory elective to help students complete homework and to receive academic assistance with concepts and test preparation. There was no guidance for the teacher, little collaboration with the students' teachers, and no evidence as to whether this class was working to raise student achievement.
- **Double Periods.** This structure was designed to give students extra math periods. Because it cut across the lunch period, many students cut class and went unnoticed as they blended into the lunch area. There was no mechanism for monitoring attendance or effectiveness.

- **College Preparatory Programs.** Many programs labeled "college prep" had a remedial label until the district eliminated remedial courses. However, the course content in the formerly remedial classes did not change. Expectations for achievement and behavior varied from teacher to teacher.
- **English Learner Programs.** Separate classes were offered for EL students. Classes included new arrivals and long-term EL students. The curriculum was below grade level but not aligned to the English proficiency levels of students. These students received core class credit for these courses.

Many more programs or initiatives were also identified. With the participation of the leadership team, the data team, and the school community, this evaluation had a major impact on how the school progressed. The epiphany was that the school simply did not have the capacity to implement, with technical soundness, all of the specialized programs they offered. While their intent to serve students was commendable, the sheer number of efforts was impossible to manage and monitor in order to ensure quality. They realized that human and fiscal resources are finite, and that adding more elements to the school without attending to systems considerations was part of the reason the school was declining. Over time, the school reformed the content and the way the programs were implemented in order to devote concentrated energy on the efforts that showed the best promise of raising achievement for all students. Data were always used to defend decisions. The central administration did not entirely change its views, but the principal's immediate supervisor supported the new direction of the school.

Supposition Two: Conventional Wisdom Is Always Wise

Countless systemic failures stem from the mistaken assumption of what "everybody knows." These assumptions seep into the system and are accepted as truths and not challenged. The "everybody knows" phenomenon occurs when decisions are made without adequately studying issues, peeling data, applying an equity lens, and deeply understanding conditions.

> The "everybody knows" phenomenon occurs when decisions are made without adequately studying issues, peeling data, applying an equity lens, and deeply understanding conditions.

Your Turn: Examining Current Programs and Initiatives at Your Site

Collaborate with a study team to complete Template 7.1 to identify the programs and initiatives currently in place in your setting and to begin the evaluation of those efforts. Are your efforts "peripheral" or focused on achievement? Do you suffer from the Christmas-tree syndrome? What is the effect of the efforts on student achievement? How do you know?

Template 7.1: Examining Programs

Programs/ Initiatives	Who's Involved?	Initiated by Whom?	Impact on Student Achievement			Documentation (Multiple Indicators)
			High	Medium	Low	

From Johnson, R. S. (2002). *Using data to close the achievement gap: How to measure equity In our schools.*

For example, "everybody knows" the following:

- struggling students should be retained to help give them more time to catch up,
- grades are the best, most objective criteria for program placement,
- struggling students should be offered simpler classes so that they can be more academically successful, and
- students with disabilities need to be taught basic skills rather than core grade-level curriculum.

In fact, each of these "everybody knows" statements is counter to much of the evidence and systems based on these beliefs serve to exacerbate existing inequities.

- **Struggling students should be retained to help give them more time to catch up:** Giving students another year of the same has not proven effective. Retained students are among the largest group of dropouts (Viadero, 2006; Flores-Gonzalez 2002; Haney et al., 2004; National Association of School Psychologists, 2003).
- **Grades are the best, most objective criteria for program placement**: Grades are extremely subjective in most cases, not usually calibrated from teacher to teacher, even if they teach the same subject and grade. Abt Associates (cited in Johnson, 2002; U.S. Department of Education, 1994) found that when test scores are compared to grades that students receive, an A in a low-income school would be a C in a high-income school. Therefore, attaching high stakes to grades, such as placement in premium or lesser pathways is highly objectionable and unreliable.
- **Struggling students should be offered simpler classes so that they can be more academically successful**: Offering simpler classes for struggling students rarely accelerates growth. Our extensive experience in schools indicates that students in homogeneous lower-level classes experience the greatest degree of failure by almost every measure, including grades and test scores. Further, years in this lower track put students further and further behind. On a related point, schools need to assess whether low-level content is masquerading as being on grade level or college preparatory when it is in fact below grade level. When this happens, we are setting students up for academic ridicule by making them less academically competitive (Adelman, 1999; Mathews, 1988; Barton & Coley, 2009; College Board's National Task Force on Minority Achievement, 1999; College Board, 2010; Johnson, 2002; Oakes, 1985).

- **Students with disabilities need to be taught basic skills rather than core grade-level curriculum:** Students with disabilities include a huge range of cognitive and academic levels, most of whom could receive educational benefit from core curriculum if presented with appropriate differentiated strategies (Harry & Klinger, 2006; Reid & Knight, 2006).

> Vigilant equity stewards ensure that such assumptions are challenged and tested using *other data,* such as combination indicators, and making sure to delve into the research prior to agreeing on solutions.

The point is that sometimes what "everybody knows" is simply not accurate. "It's not what you know that hurts you. . .it's what you know that isn't so" (Coker, 2009). Instituting a formal or informal policy based on faulty assumptions creates systems that result in very different outcomes for students. Vigilant equity stewards ensure that such assumptions are challenged and tested using *other data,* such as combination indicators, and making sure to delve into the research prior to agreeing on solutions.

Supposition Three: The Inevitability Assumption

The story of Precious in Chapter 4 exemplifies the harm that comes from assuming that low achievement is inevitable for some students. It also demonstrates the benefit that comes from challenging that belief. The now famous story of Jaime Escalante, the math teacher at Garfield High School, made famous in the movie *Stand and Deliver* (1988), is a classic example of a system built upon the *inevitability assumption.* Prior to his arrival, the common mindset was that advanced mathematics was not appropriate for large numbers of students from East Los Angeles. The prevailing belief was that poor Latino students from the barrio could not succeed at the level of advanced algebra and calculus. Escalante challenged that assumption and, from 1979 to 1991, grew the number of students taking AP exams from 2 to 570, with an unbelievably high pass rate.

These two examples demonstrate the power of challenging the inevitability of failure or mediocrity for some students. In the absence of such a challenge, many harmful systems are built and perpetuated. For example, if the belief is that some parent groups do not value education because they do not attend evening or school-day functions, then important parent outreach and education initiatives are discontinued. When that assumption is challenged, schools or districts seek to understand why parents do not attend during those hours and find other ways of communicating with them. Working parents cannot always afford to miss work. Sometimes cultural or neighborhood norms do not support being away from home in the evening hours. However, some schools and districts have experienced great success accessing parents through weekend events during the day, home visits, or coffee klatches in familiar community venues.

This book is filled with suggestions about how *other data* can be gathered. Much of this information provides red-flag areas that warrant deeper probing to uncover inequitable practices. The more difficult systems to uncover are the hidden norms and unwritten policies that get played out in the interactions between and among the humans in the school environment. Observations in natural settings between students and teachers; teachers and parents; students, parents, and counselors; students, parents, and deans; and administrators or child study teams are not always available to document. However, those who are diligent and skillful can access other information to see what inevitability assumptions may underlie behaviors and decisions.

What other questions come to mind from this analysis? What *other data* can be gathered to test decisions based on these assumptions? How can the effect on students' achievement be determined for various subgroups?

Supposition Four: Implementation Is the Goal

Outcomes are the goal. Implementation is the means to an end. Frequently, a rush to address a challenge results in haphazard or short-changed planning and premature implementation of new systems. Undoubtedly, this rushed process leads to unintended consequences with great equity implications. This is where, by design, the best intentions can lead to negative outcomes or no support for some students— not intentionally, but as an unintended side effect of a solution not thoroughly studied.

For example, we asked an administrator to observe the new tutoring program recently instituted at his high school. Quarterly progress reports indicated that many students were not meeting expectations, so he and a team of teachers designed an afterschool intervention. He admitted that since the program began, he had no idea what happened during tutoring sessions. He found out that the sessions were poorly

Your Turn: Identifying the *Inevitability Assumption* in Action

Spend a defined time period (a meeting, a day, a week) observing and listening as your school or district operates as usual. Make a journal entry on Template 7.2 each time you suspect that the *inevitability assumption* is operational. If you have the opportunity to question policies or practices, ask the following question: Why is it this way? Listen for clues in language such as: "That's just how it is." "We do our best, considering . . ." "Those are the rules." "That will never change." "What more can we expect."

Template 7.2 Language and the Inevitability Assumption

What language, event, or observation captured your attention?	What *inevitability assumption* do you suspect is at play? (teachers don't care, parents don't care . . . students can't learn X because Y so . . .)	What is the potential harm to student achievement if this assumption is at play?

attended and the students receiving tutoring were not getting low and failing grades. They were C or above students. The students and the teachers had a created a climate that was informal and socially friendly. There is nothing inherently wrong with having spaces like this in schools for students, but the targeted group was not receiving the services.

When the vice principal dug deeper to find out where the students were that needed the academic support, he found that some could not attend the afterschool intervention. They had jobs, some did not feel it would help them, and others just forgot and no one was pushing them to go. Of those who did attend tutoring, there was no communication with the classroom teachers to find out if the tutoring was effective. The vice principal began to give more attention to tutoring and other support programs. In collaboration with the teachers and counselors, he developed a set of monitoring documents and worked with students to develop strategies to get them to consistently attend. This attention and focus by leadership made a difference and also let the staff and students know that this program could work and be effective. He also changed personnel. He wanted to staff the program with people inclined to promote opportunities for struggling students.

Table 7.1 (see page 208) demonstrates how popular ideas, even those with solid research backing, can have negative consequences for students if the implementation is not well planned or monitored. Do any of these initiatives exist in your setting? How do you know that the efforts are yielding intended results? What other initiatives exist in your school or district that should be studied for potential unintended consequences? What interventions are necessary to get the reform back on track?

Supposition Five: School Systems Are Objective and Fair

Often, systemic barriers to equity stem from the erroneous belief about objectivity. That is, systems are constructed on the premise that schools operate objectively, without human bias. In truth, without safeguards in the system, human beliefs about different people and students creep into daily school life and ultimately affect student achievement.

In this true story, James, an African American student, and Jim, a White student, are best friends and attend the same public high school. They are

(text continues on page 211)

Table 7.1	Potential Unintended Consequences of Reforms and Initiatives	
Examples of Reform Initiatives and Policies	**Intended Outcome**	**Potential Unintended Consequence (exacerbated in low-SES schools) and Points for Monitoring**
Class-Size Reduction	To lower the student-teacher ratio and increase student achievement.	In order to fill the staffing demands, more classrooms may be staffed with unqualified teachers. Also, the need for additional facilities may result in classes being taught in less-than-ideal spaces (cafeterias, shared classes, even hallways).
Block Scheduling	To provide secondary students with additional time to participate in each learning period.	Teachers who are not skilled at teaching "bell-to-bell" in a traditional 50-minute period are even less successful at effectively executing lessons for longer time periods (as much as an hour longer). Given the fact that remedial and lower-level classes are often assigned to less experienced teachers, struggling students in blocked periods can experience most of an entire day in settings where, for long periods of time, little productive learning occurs.
Eliminating Low-Level Classes	To align instruction to rigorous academic content and performance standards and increase expectations for student achievement levels.	Students can continue to fail under such a system if the necessary interventions (such as teacher training to address differentiated instruction or providing extra instructional time) are not in place to provide struggling students with needed scaffolding and support in order for them to achieve. Course rigor may get compromised and watered down.
Frequent Formative Assessments Administered to Students	To provide teachers and administrators with incremental feedback on the effectiveness of the instructional program for individual students so that tailored modifications can be designed based on those data.	Assessments can become so time consuming that teachers sacrifice a significant amount of potential teaching time in order to complete assessments. This problem is exacerbated if assessments are administered in a one-on-one student to teacher setting, resulting in the majority of the class doing busywork for extended periods of time while individual assessments take place. The problem is worse when teachers focus on the administration of the assessments and not the meaning behind the data that results from the assessments.

Examples of Reform Initiatives and Policies	Intended Outcome	Potential Unintended Consequence (exacerbated in low-SES schools) and Points for Monitoring
Sustained Silent Reading (SSR)	To promote the love of reading and improve reading proficiency by providing students extended, uninterrupted opportunities to engage in independent reading.	If not properly implemented, students can have extended periods of wasted time (often between 15 minutes to almost an hour, depending on the grade). Struggling students, especially, can become disengaged during SSR, filling the time with a host of unproductive activities. This may reduce the amount of available time for powerful instruction and can promote a climate of laxness and low expectations.
Homeroom/ Study Hall	To provide students with time, during the day, to do homework, read, organize their materials, or orient themselves as students.	If not properly implemented, students can have extended periods of wasted time (often between 15 minutes to over an hour, depending on the school). Struggling students, especially, can become disengaged, filling the time with a host of unproductive activities. Often, these minutes are defined as "noninstructional" by contractual agreement with teachers' associations, severely limiting the types of experiences for students. That time is often limited to activities that do not require teachers to have to plan. This reduces the amount of available time for powerful instruction and promotes a climate of laxness and low expectations.
Professional Learning Communities (PLCs)	To provide educators with a process of engaging in collaborative inquiry and professional growth with the ultimate aim of improving educational opportunity for students.	The intent of the professional learning community can be lost to the rules and structures surrounding it and can result in no tangible benefit to students. PLCs can deteriorate and simply become another "meeting," as in the phrase, "We PLC every Tuesday." Sometimes, it can connote meetings with specific rules, such as: (1) administrators may not direct the agendas, only team members may attend, (2) meetings must occur during the contract day, (3) only two PLCs can be held a month, and so on. Absent clear school- or districtwide academic targets or strong leadership, "PLC time" can translate into systemic nonproductive time.

Your Turn: Reflecting on Systems

When addressing equity and achievement, policies, structures, and practices, a school or district should be scrutinized for potential winners and losers. Template 7.3 is an example of a table that can serve to display these data and be used as a basis for dialogue. Set aside time to examine some policies and practices in your school/district. Discuss the implications for different groups of students. What are the implications?

Template 7.3 Policies				
Policy	**What Is the Intended Outcome?**	**What May Be the Unintended Consequence?**	**Who Benefits?**	**Who Loses?**
Academic Grouping				
Instructional Supervision Process				
Promotion				
Support Programs				
Special Education				
Discipline Policies				
Teacher Assignments				
Student Assignments				
Principal Assignments				
Student Transfers				
Attendance Monitoring				

in the same activities and classes at school. Both are sophomores planning to attend college. In the fall of their sophomore year, both were experiencing problems in chemistry. They usually studied together, but in this situation they could not help each other. They both had the same counselor, but had individual appointments to discuss the problems they were having in their chemistry class. After meeting with the counselor, they met and shared their experiences.

Jim told James that the counselor gave him information about a support program at a local college and other resources that were available that could help him. James's experience was different. The counselor told him that the chemistry was probably too hard for him and that he should drop it. There was no attempt to suggest support strategies or share information about the possible consequences for dropping chemistry.

This was not the only incident concerning differential access to information. Jim consistently shared with James tips he received from his meetings with the counselor. James was not receiving the same valuable information. James ended up taking chemistry in summer school in an attempt to catch up, and meanwhile fell off of the track for advanced chemistry. Currently, as a senior, he is an International Baccalaureate (IB) English, history and math—so clearly he could have stayed on track. Jim is currently in IB chemistry and on track for a full IB diploma, which is no longer possible for James. This story mirrors the differential treatment that certain groups were experiencing in the scenario.

> The point is, however, having no controls to check for potential bias assumes that humans always behave objectively.

We have no way of knowing why the counselor provided different information and guidance to both students. More probing is required to completely understand whether this is a unique case or whether other students are receiving differential guidance by this counselor or other staff. The point is, however, having no controls to check for potential bias assumes that humans always behave objectively.

Was there agreement on all topics? If not, what themes emerged from the debriefing discussion? What systems are in place that assume an objective base, but may actually include subjectivity? What are the equity implications? What are the implications for student achievement? Can you identify any fertile areas to exercise *equity muscle*?

Your Turn: Objective or Subjective?

Organize in groups of three. Two team members stand back-to-back, each holding one sheet of paper with black and white halves and another paper all shaded gray. One at a time, the third member reads aloud each topic in Template 7.4. The back-to-back pair listen to each topic, and after a three-second pause, holds over their heads one of the two papers: If the topic is objective, they hold up the black and white page; if the topic is subjective, they hold up the gray sheet. They cannot see what the other holds up, but the third team member records their responses on Template 7.4. After all topics have been read and "rated," share the results and discuss the implications. Blank cells are left for leaders to add topics relevant to your sites.

Template 7.4   Objective or Subjective?

Put a tally mark in either cell as the back-to-back members hold up the pages.

Topic	Objective? (Black and white sheet)	Subjective? (Gray sheet)
Grades		
Grades if policies standardize weights (such as: homework is 30%, tests 30%, class work 30%, participation 10%)		
Placement procedures for special education		
Placement procedures for GATE		
Placement procedures for advanced classes/groups		
Teacher evaluations		
Common assessment results		
Scoring of student writing		
Evaluation of English learner programs		
Disciplinary practices		

Supposition Six: Everyday Inequities Are Normal and Natural

Noguera and Wing (2006) describe in great depth everyday inequalities that are practiced at Berkeley High School in northern California. The high school is in a city with a progressive history. In spite of this context, vast inequities exist related to White and African American students. Regarding discipline, the researchers portray a process of mostly subjective judgments, which results in punishments, such as transfers to an alternative school, for a disproportionate number of African American students. While this pattern is disturbing, more alarming is the finding that neither the school nor the community made any attempt to address the inequities after the data were examined and clearly presented. One would expect that the data alone would cause a sense of urgency, and some kind of outrage in the community. How is this passivity explained? Noguera and Wing state, "The only explanation we could come up with was that the figures we shared reflected what the faculty and community had come to consider as normal and natural. Whether we were talking about the achievement gap or the discipline gap, the disparities among groups have become so commonplace that they are taken for granted" (p. 142). Nationwide, in study after study, the research about discipline and race produces findings that merely "'prove the obvious: African American and Latino students are more likely to get into trouble" (p. 142).

> "Whether we were talking about the achievement gap or the discipline gap, the disparities among groups have become so commonplace that they are taken for granted" (Noguera & Wing, 2006, p. 142).

Most often, when schools with large populations of poor students and students of color are required to implement programs where all students must take algebra in eighth or ninth grade, it seems *not* normal. What seems appropriate is to have lower-level classes that are disproportionately filled with low-income students and students of color. Leaders must challenge the normalization of failure. These leaders include the superintendent in the previous scenario, teachers such as Jaime Escalante and Dr. Shabazz, whose teaching practices defied the expectations and accelerated Latino and African American students to high levels of achievement in mathematics (Mathews, 1988; Hilliard, 1991), and mentors such as Coach Carter. It is important to compare what schools and districts espouse as shared norms and values (for example, all students will learn) with institutional action (such as offering only some students premium educational opportunities). There is a need to create new a "normal" and to deem inequitable outcomes as not normal or acceptable.

A structural feature in schools that seems normal and natural, and takes place every day in schools, is student scheduling. Every school has some kind of schedule. These can be rich sources of information about equity issues. For example, the high school master schedule can be used as a constraint and can impact certain students' opportunity to learn. We constantly hear, "We can't change this or that because it will cause havoc with the master schedule." These appear to be normal and natural everyday occurrences. Usually, a few people in the school influence the design of the schedule. The final high school master schedule might be determined by a few people or even just one person, such as the head counselor, department chair, or an administrator, with some input from others. Many times, the master schedule is the engine that drives the school, but it is not always user friendly for students or teachers. Because of the rigidity of the schedule, students are tracked with the same groups throughout the school day. Therefore, if a student qualifies for honors math, but not honors English, they may not be able to access that class.

Schools with small learning communities (academies, houses, "small schools") need careful analysis related to issues of access and equity (Conchas & Rodriquez, 2008). This structure can lead to tracking and segregation of student groups. A typical scenario results in student electives (such as band, athletics, spirit groups) determining house placement rather than other educational criteria. This has serious implications for student placement. For example, generally, athletes and spirit groups take their electives at the end of the day so that their practices can extend beyond the school day. Students cannot participate in extracurricular programs unless they meet satisfactory academic achievement criteria. Therefore, placing those students in the same house results in one grouping of students that are the most involved, successful students. Other houses may, for the same reason, contain all the honors or AP students. Therefore, by default, at least one house will generally contain more of the students who are not "connected" to school and who are not as academically successful. As one student interview revealed, "Some houses are the 'in-houses' and that one is the 'out-house!'"

Table 7.2 exemplifies an everyday, on-the-ground example of how schedules that promote inequities are considered normal and natural. This table shows a high school math department teacher schedule and how teacher talent was distributed based on teaching credentials. Overall, the department lacked experienced credential teachers. However, the hardest workload fell on the most inexperienced teachers. These teachers taught the students with the greatest academic needs. For example, Teacher 3, a long-term substitute, had four different preparations and five classes of students who were repeating the first or second half of a two-year algebra

Table 7.2 Mathematics Courses by Teacher

Teacher	Status	Period 1	Period 2	Period 3	Period 4	Period 5	Period 6	Preps
1. Illness Leave	Long-Term Sub 5 Months	ALGC/D 9	ALG/D 9	ALG A/B 10–12	ALG C/D 9	ALGC/D 9		2
2. Regular Credential	21st Year/Retiring	ALGA/B 9		ALGA/B 9	ALG1 9	ALGC/D 10–12	ALG1 9	3
3. Long-Term Sub	Long-Term Sub—1st Year	ALGC/D Repeat	ALGC/D	ALGA/B Repeat		ALG2 Repeat	ALGC/D Repeat	4 and 4 repeat classes
4. Non-Credential EL Teacher	2nd Year		ALG EL	ALGA/B EL	ALG C/D EL	ALG1B	GEO EL	5
5. Non-Credential Teacher	2nd Year—Does not have clear teaching credential. Is on an emergency permit to teach.		ALGC/D	GEO	GEO	ALG A/B 10	GEO	4
6. Intern/Department Chair	4th Year—In teaching intern program working to complete credential requirements		ALG 7/8C114	MATH 7/8 C152	ALG ABC 111			3 and traveling and Dept. Chair

(Continued)

Table 7.2 (Continued)

Teacher	Status	Period 1	Period 2	Period 3	Period 4	Period 5	Period 6	Preps
7. Intern	2nd Year Teaching—Intern	ALG C/D T&T	MATH 7/8	ALG1	ALG1 9		ALG A/B9	5
8. Credentialed Teacher	23rd Year—Retiring	ALG2	COMP APPL		ALG2	ALG2	7TECH	4
9. Credentialed Teacher	Fully Credentialled—4th Year	GE09	GEO	APCALC	ALG A/B 9		GEO	4
10. Substitute	Experience in another state—Having transcript evaluated	GEO	CAHSEE MATH	ALGA/B		CAHSEE MATH	GEO Repeat	4-1 Repeat and 2 CAHSEE
11. Credentialed Teacher	Fully Credentialed	Physics		Advanced Math	Geometry	Advanced Math	Physical Science A	4—2 Science

Created by authors based on information from an urban school.

program. Teacher 4, who did not have a credential to teach English learners (ELs), was only in his second year of teaching and had five preparations. Teacher 6, the department chair, was an intern teacher of four years who traveled from classroom to classroom. Data are missing on the number of students enrolled in each class, but often reveal further inequities. What are the policies that fuel these teacher assignments? These practices had been occurring for years and seemed normal and natural to the staff. There were no loud protests about injustices against inexperienced teachers or students. In fact, the teacher contract that favored senior teachers over student need exacerbated the conditions. The principal at the school had never analyzed teacher assignments, background, experience, and talent. The counselors and teachers did the assignments. The information, at the very least, points to a school that needs clear guidance and support. The schedule of classes indicated that many students were failing or repeating classes, and there were few higher-level math classes, among many other concerns.

Supposition Seven: Adult Interests Should Take Priority

This is another area where public rhetoric and private talk differ greatly. Rarely do members of the education community, including teachers, administrators, parents, students, or community members, openly admit that some systems are designed to satisfy adult interests at the expense of student achievement. For some, the mere mention that this could occur is highly objectionable. Maybe some have never thought about the notion that adult interests can trump student needs. We suspect, however, that many readers will relate to some of the following examples from our on-the-ground work in schools and districts that make it difficult to claim that students always come first.

> Maybe some have never thought about the notion that adult interests can trump student needs.

One low-performing middle school decided to become a math and science magnet school for the district. Teachers, administrators, parents, and students wanted to increase the rigor and reputation of their school and orient their students toward careers of the future, many of which involve math and science. The master schedule was developed, replete with challenging math, science, history, and English classes. Electives included either preview-review classes to accompany core classes for struggling students, or math and science application classes, such as rocketry or pre-engineering. Student welfare was at the core of program development except in one situation.

While most teachers either held multiple subjects or subject-specific credentials in core areas, one teacher on staff held a rare vocational credential, hired when school needs were different. For the past eighteen years, the master schedule was developed to include five sections of shop class to fill his assignment. The design team was perplexed about how to plan his assignment with the change in emphasis for the school. Additional troubling data included the counts of students who needed preview-review companion classes of core classes in order to be able to compete in rigorous courses. The school needed teachers to teach sections of the preview-review course. Only the vocational education teacher was left unassigned by credentialing restrictions, and could not teach anything but his subject.

The design team was clear that they needed multiple-subjects teachers or subject specialists to teach the support classes in order to offer the struggling students help for advanced courses. The entire premise of the magnet was that with high expectations and if given proper supports, all students could access the highest levels of curriculum. The design team was clear on the student need, but the principal explained that he needed to discuss certain issues with the district.

After several days, the principal reported that the district could not add a teacher to the staffing ratio, so the team was directed to create assignments for all existing teachers. Though the teachers' contract allowed for teacher transfers based on program need, it had never been done before and the district did not feel comfortable pursuing that path. Many difficult discussions later, the design team assigned five sections of students to the vocational class, thereby reducing core support class opportunities for students.

Educators are all too accustomed to experiencing situations such as this where adult interests override student need, though few will speak of it publicly. Of course, we are not naïve to the complexity of how system components interact and the dynamic of the human business in which we are engaged. However, are these practices equally applied in all neighborhoods, equally affecting all students? Are they ever acceptable? What role should adult interests have in school and district decisions that affect students? How should a school system appropriately handle adult interests such as the one in the scenario?

At what point do we draw a collective line in the sand and admit that all systems, even failing ones, are perfectly built to get the results they are getting? Rather than blaming students, parents, or society for poor academic achievement for some students, let us take a critical look

> At what point do we draw a collective line in the sand and admit that all systems, even failing ones, are perfectly built to get the results they are getting?

at decisions we make about structures, policies and practices, and the underlying belief systems to determine if anything within our sphere of influence might be a help or hindrance to equity and academic achievement for all students.

Your Turn: Introspection

We ask that readers initiate the conversation of adult interests in educational systems with only themselves. That is, take some quiet time to privately reflect on one day in your life in the educational arena. Ask yourself if you interacted with any decisions, policies, or practices that benefit adults but not students? Make a list. Are any of those decisions or systems harmful to student achievement? Are all students equally affected or are some students impacted differently from others? What needs to be done to change this picture?

We recommend that readers repeat this activity several different days to see if patterns emerge.

CONCLUSION

This chapter highlighted structures and policies that affect equitable outcomes for students. Mounds and mounds of quantitative data can only act as signals to begin the probe. Most of the time those structures, practices, and policies are designed and instituted with good intentions. But when they are implemented, sometimes they may have unintended consequences that do more harm than good. School systems are complex and built on layers and layers of beliefs and assumptions that are deeply rooted in historical legacies and perceptions about diverse groups of people. Therefore, it is important to examine existing and proposed systems to assess how they play out on the ground in schools and classrooms. There should be rigorous monitoring, especially in the implementation of new initiatives. The questions that we must constantly ask about systems are: Who benefits? Are there any students who don't benefit? What needs to change and how? In order for all of our children to thrive we need to create new legacies that are embedded in everyday equitable structures, policies, and practices.

Part III

Changing Our Current Normal

8 Increasing Equity Muscle

OVERVIEW

The dilemma in writing this chapter is what can we say that is new? Much of the discourse about differences in achievement among racial, ethnic, language, and income groups has been rehashed over many decades. Many in the education profession are already familiar with the streams of research since the 1970s and prior that have informed us about inequities and the conditions in schools, districts, and society that inhibit or enhance learning for children. In spite of this information, many schools and districts continue to underachieve. There are differing views about the reasons for the inequities. This chapter does not focus on those debates. Rather, we emphasize the imperative to respond and to develop strategies to strengthen individual and collective *equity muscle*.

In this chapter, we will set the context for the need to uncover and use *other data* as a lever to focus on school factors that influence students' school and life careers. We provide a historical perspective of the challenges in creating schools where all children are seen as capable learners. Examples of how to use *other data* combined with effective actions, similar to what have been described in previous chapters, are provided. The chapter is designed to draw attention to topics that are not often highlighted and that are uncomfortable to talk about. We discuss the need to transform our perceptions of what we recognize and believe is "normal," and the need for conversations to take place in schools and districts to challenge inequitable norms. We offer some suggestions on ways to approach these issues. It is our stance that the current inequitable levels of achievement described throughout this book are unacceptable, but not unchangeable, and that positive steps can be taken in places where there are genuinely effective advocates for young people. These advocates must have the will, passion, knowledge, and skills to *do the right thing.* Next, we provide some suggestions on how to organize, collect, analyze, and use the *other data.* Then, we discuss the need for culturally relevant practices in order to interpret the on-the-ground data and the issues that should be addressed in seeking authentic improvement. We emphasize the interplay that should happen between research and school inquiry. Because leadership is a key factor in creating and supporting equitable school reform, we discuss and describe key leadership behaviors. The chapter concludes with a call for a specific brand of student advocacy that results in schools and districts actively surfacing their hidden inequities and tackling them.

THE CONTEXT: THE NEED TO INCREASE EQUITY MUSCLE

The national picture continues to show large Gaps of African Americans, Latinos, Native Americans, English learners, and students receiving special education services from desired goals on state exams, NAEP scores, advanced courses, college readiness, and enrollment in college, and gaps between them and their White and Asian peers.

In 1966 a report by Coleman funded by the U.S. Department of Education concluded that background factors such as income and parents' education were responsible for low-income children not learning, and schools could not make a difference no matter how the children were taught. In response to these conclusions, Ronald Edmonds, who at the time was the Director of Urban Studies at Harvard University, countered with a different viewpoint. He knew there were schools where students from low-income backgrounds were achieving and set out to identify them and the school factors that contributed to their success. Other scholars, such as Larry Lezotte and Wilbur Brookover, joined him in the quest to find and describe those schools. They identified achieving schools with populations of low-income students and students of color where adults mitigated

> Their view argues that schools can influence academic achievement for populations who have had historically low patterns of academic achievement.

perceived achievement barriers in schools. These schools defied expectations. Out of these efforts, the effective schools movement began. Their view argues that schools can influence academic achievement for populations who have had historically low patterns of academic achievement (Lezotte, 2010). Edmonds (1979) observed that "(a) We can, whenever and wherever we choose, successfully teach all children whose schooling is of interest to us, (b) We already know more than we need to do that, (c) Whether or not we do it must finally depend on how we feel about the fact that we haven't so far" (p. 23).

Other more recent pioneers who have created equitable places for students include individual teachers, administrators, schools, and community leaders whose students have excelled despite their poverty profile. Many have been cited in this text. There are some promising charters such as the Capital Preparatory Magnet School in Hartford, Connecticut, and the Knowledge Is Power Program (KIPP), located in several cities nationally. Two teachers initiated this program. There are initiatives that work directly with students, such as Village Nation in Los Angeles. They have seen phenomenal improvement in the performance of African American students. This initiative was started by three high school teachers who saw a need to change outcomes for these students. The Chicano Youth Leadership Conference, also in Los Angeles and in operation for over forty years, has demonstrated dramatic effects on Mexican-origin and other Latino students in four-year college completion rates. These and other efforts demonstrate astronomical growth and dispel myths. They can provide inspiration for others who would like to make a difference.

Another initiative that has received a lot of attention is a comprehensive baby-to-college pipeline community-based project in Harlem, New York. The Harlem Children's Zone (HCZ) spans ninety-seven blocks in central Harlem. This model concentrates on ways to connect parents and communities to schools. These are just a few examples. Information on these and other resources can be found in the References and Resources sections of this book. We provide contact and web information to find out more about these beacons of hope.

There are other educators in more traditional settings who are creating schools that make a difference in the lives of children by developing conditions that increase students' academic standing. Several groups document these schools, but their efforts are not coordinated, which makes the hunt for successful schools a challenge. Educational Results Partnership (www.edresults.org), for example, identifies Star Schools, high-poverty, and achievement-gap closing schools, in California. They also provide the list of top ten comparable schools for every school in the state. That is, we are able to input the name of any school, and the website provides achievement data for ten schools with similar demographics, that represent the highest-scoring schools in the comparable group. EdSource published two reports, "Similar Schools, Different Results" and "Similar English Learner Students, Different Results: Why Do Some Schools Do Better" (Williams, Hakuta, Haertel et al., 2005; Williams, Perry, Oregon et al., 2007). National sources for information about high-achieving schools include Education Trust, The NCLB Blue Ribbon Program, state websites, professional publications such as *Education Week,* and many of the organizations in the Resources section of this book. The Center for Rural School Resources has issued a publication on differences between low- and high-achieving rural high schools.

These sources help school and district teams challenge the inevitability assumption about students just like their own. However, we do issue a cautionary note. The primary indicators of achievement still rely on state test or other test scores because they are the most consistently available indicators to compare schools within a state or nationally because all of the students are tested on the same test. However, some use multiple measures such as the 90/90/90 schools (90% of students were eligible for free lunch, 90% were members of ethnic minority groups, and 90% or more met district or state standards in reading or another subject (Reeves, 2003). They used state, district, and school-based measures to identify high-performing 90/90/90 schools. Throughout this book, we have examined data that goes beyond test scores. Therefore, it will be important to search for and find out about other related indicators to find out if the schools are consistently high performing in critical areas such as course rigor. Ask to examine the high school master schedule, looking at sorting patterns and other equity identifiers. Many of these schools will probably be showing gains on a broad set of indicators, so the test scores may serve only as a place to begin the search for authentic achievement.

REFRAMING AND CHALLENGING WHAT APPEARS "NORMAL" AND NATURAL

We repeat: There are places that are defying conventional wisdom about the achievement of historically underachieving groups. Unfortunately, high-achieving schools are akin to lighthouses isolated on islands that are surrounded by waters of struggling schools and districts. There are still far too many schools that need to drastically improve. These schools share commonalities with lighthouse schools in that they have human resources, similar groups of children, teachers, principals, and other staff in ancillary positions. Then what is different? Achieving schools believe, as Ron Edmonds and others believe, that low-achievement patterns can be reversed. They are visionaries with a mission to succeed in spite of the odds, and they have strong beliefs that they can make a difference. They have high expectations for themselves and their students. They have high instructional standards. They rigorously monitor progress. They have effective strategies to reach out to parents. They have effective teachers and leaders. They don't give up on their vision when they are confronted with challenges.

Our position is that struggling schools do not need to implement more programs, initiatives, or resources until they delve deep into their educational psyche about what is taken for granted as acceptable, "normal," and natural achievement patterns in their institutions. They must embark on a journey to become institutions that value and fight for equitable outcomes for students. If this does not take place, the exposure and use of *other data* likely will have shallow interpretation and action solutions will be mere window dressing. It is unlikely that there will be a challenge to the status quo. If these "normal" and natural patterns are not challenged, there will continue to be achievement gaps that exist even when it appears that achievement might be improving. In previous chapters, we discussed how data on gross inequities are often perceived as "normal" because of the child's background or educational classification.

We fully realize that schools are socializing agencies for both educators and students, and both the content and context of that socialization are very powerful. As a result of a series of educational practices, educational outcomes are affected. When practices are manifested in low expectations, low-level curricula, and essentially low-level instructional strategies for low-income children, low achievement is the outcome. These can become accepted, institutionalized practices, to which administrators, teachers, parents, and students all live out roles that perpetuate these bad practices. Thus, the practices go unquestioned and are systematically perpetuated (Haberman, 1991).

Historically, patterns of gaps, over- or underrepresentation, and educational attainment of groups are seen so often that they are perceived by many as "normal." This is because explanations are constructed in ways that decisions about where children land on the educational ladder are proclaimed as fair. However, these decisions, actions, and behaviors are filtered through lenses that can result in inequitable treatment. Inequities are justified through the use of demographics, community factors, and setting up structures that appear as if they are helping kids (such as remedial groupings). The helping mechanism usually sorts, labels, and segregates students under the guise of helping the student to reach some unknown potential. That underscores the need to expose *other data* that show that the opposite may be occurring. This allows these conditions to be confronted.

Responses and actions that the data generate can give clues about equity dispositions. On one hand, there is a helplessness that translates into "we can't do anything because of the child's *background*." This relegates the use of data to a *prediction* paradigm. These students will continue to achieve in the same manner throughout their school careers. This plays out a scenario of inaction, or the design of pseudo support structures that coexist or exist outside of the mainstream school and district organization, thus not influencing the bureaucratic structures (Winfield, Johnson, & Manning, 1996). These behaviors are evident in how schools and districts structure courses, curriculum, principal and teacher placements, repeat courses, grades, suspensions, expulsions, discharges, placement in special education, redesignation rates of English language learners, and placements in high-end gifted and talented programs and courses.

On the other hand, if we are genuinely committed to eliminate inequities, we must acknowledge that the following outcomes are not "normal" or natural:

- Low graduation rates, low college readiness, low college admission and enrollment, and high dropout rates for low-income, African American, Latino, Native American students and English learners.
- Overrepresentation of certain groups in special education.
- Overrepresentation of certain groups in disciplinary referrals.
- Overrepresentation of retention for certain groups.
- Underrepresentation of certain groups in gifted and talented programs, advanced courses, and college enrollment.
- Highest-need students being taught by long-terms substitutes and the least-prepared instructors, while others experience exciting and engaging learning with instructors who have high expectations for their learning exacerbates inequities.

Next, we should reflect on the following questions and points:

- How do we feel and usually respond to inequities affecting "other people's children?"
- Would we feel about or respond to the inequities differently if they happened to children in our own families?

To change unacceptable "normal," adults are needed who are willing to stand up for students who are experiencing inequities, and codes of silence need to be broken about practices that destroy young people's futures.

Those who want to challenge the current "normal" and natural, but lack the courage and/or skills to take the risks and confront those who appear more powerful, should find others with similar views, become educated on the issues by searching for successful schools, and use the data to challenge inaccurate perceptions. This is often a difficult task for people who pursued a career in education to teach, not to confront a status quo, but it must be done.

We acknowledge that changing the current "normal" will take time and will include more than simply reframing the visions of what schools should look like. It will take major shifts in (1) beliefs, values, and assumptions (dispositions); (2) knowledge (studying and understanding the literature); and (3) skills (how to facilitate and implement what is good for students). It will require developing efficacious adults who believe that they have the genius to create these schools (Hilliard, 1991). Nobody can bring about schoolwide reform alone. Experience suggests that it will take a lot of hard work from a very committed core of individuals. Collaborating in teams creates a shared vision and shared responsibility. Thus, there is more potential to penetrate organizational cultures that negatively affect student opportunities (Anderson, Herr, & Sigrid Nihlen, 2007; Johnson, 2002). Some suggested strategies to consider include the following:

> We acknowledge that changing the current "normal" will take time and will include more than simply reframing the visions of what schools should look like.

1. Establish the need for change: In schools where the culture is resistant to challenge the status quo, and where staff are more likely to blame parents and students than to accept their share of responsibility, it may be necessary to establish an informal leadership team to work to build consensus about the need for changing practices and to push the movement forward. We have found that even in the lowest-performing schools there is usually a group of people that are dissatisfied. In our work in schools and districts, we meet people who are willing to go to bat and take the risks to become advocates for underserved young people. Leaders need to identify that group of like-minded staff, parents, and community members to strategize.

2. Ask questions like the following: What will it take to convince at least a significant number of our colleagues and fellow community members that our school can do better? What data can we present to make our case? Are there lighthouse schools with students like ours? Should we visit more successful schools that have similar students? Do we need pressure from outside—from parents and the community? What research or other information is necessary?

3. Establish study teams wherein the entire team, including office, custodial, and paraprofessional personnel as well as teachers and parents, reads literature and possibly watches videos that can open up knowledge bases and expose participants to information they lack.

Those who are serious about moving forward and contesting what has been the status quo can find information that is hopeful about possibilities for themselves and their students. At one meeting, after a group had read an article on retention, the teachers commented that they had no idea that research has found that retention had long-term negative consequences for students. This type of response can then open up opportunities to look at retention, at who gets retained, alternatives to retention, and the use of longitudinal data systems.

4. Visit places with similar populations, but that have dissimilar results. This can be a very effective, eye-opening, inspiring, and energizing strategy. It can be very convincing for teachers to see their peers accomplishing things they thought were impossible, and how people's hard work pays off. Meet with colleagues before the visit and prepare questions and identify who you might want to meet with. These places can provide valuable resources. Ask for templates, surveys, or other data that they use. Query about technology use and how they get the work done. How do they monitor progress?

5. Bring in people who have done the on–the–ground work. Talk teacher to teacher, principal to principal, and parent group to parent group.

6. In some cases, the group may have to create the moment themselves by challenging the stand taken by their more resistant colleagues. The goal of the team is to be prepared to seize a moment to start a schoolwide discussion about improving teaching and learning. Meanwhile, the process is not at a standstill, because the leadership group is getting ready.

7. However, in the end, the team needs the tools to take risks, challenge their colleagues, and garner energy and will to do the work. They will also need to stay positive against negative forces. Adults need positive peer groups in order to unlock their genius.

8. Team leaders will need to acquire skills to facilitate difficult and uncomfortable conversations that deal with race and ethnicity. In the next section, we discuss the need for dialogue in accomplishing the equity agenda.

THE NEED FOR DIALOGUE

Inclusive dialogue can help to increase *equity muscle*. When people see the data that exposes inequities, especially those involving race and ethnicity, they often become uncomfortable and defensive (Singleton & Linton, 2006).

Educators typically have not examined and discussed race in their schools because they have feared not knowing how to go about this process correctly. Some justify inaction on racial achievement disparities by suggesting that no one knows how to impact them. Saying 'we don't know how' allows educators to claim that they have done all they can do. Such suggestions do not produce improved results.

We suggest that the problem of educators not knowing what to do about racial achievement gaps or how to talk about race is not as devastating as the problem of educators failing to seek solutions to the gaps. (Singleton & Linton, 2006, p. 21).

Eliminating inequities requires conversations about race, ethnicity, language, and income (see Johnson, 2002, Chapter 5). This text cannot cover the topic in depth. We suggest reading Singleton and Linton's text, *Courageous Conversations about Race: A Field Guide for Achieving Equity in Schools* (2006) and the companion facilitator's guide (2007). The book and guide are rich sources for guiding educators on how to conduct and engage the school community in these dialogues. Useful literature sources are included.

> Eliminating inequities requires conversations about race, ethnicity, language, and income.

Becoming skilled in dialogue and using guiding questions such as those throughout this book bring meaningful problem solving and solutions. Saavedra (1996) has successfully used teacher study groups to affect the professional culture of teaching and to create changes in beliefs and practices. She points out that teacher transformation means that teachers study in a context in which they can confront their own cultural, social, and political identities, and the situations that have shaped and continually shape the expression of those identities. "In other words," she says, "through understanding their world and themselves within their world, teachers engage in the process of creating and shifting knowledge, meanings, ideologies, and practices, and thus transform themselves and conditions of their lives" (p. 272). The context for the dialogues is study groups that meet on a regular basis to reflect, analyze, and critique their practices in relationship to how students benefit. By participating in study groups, teachers were able to transform their practices and beliefs about diverse groups of students and their parents. They understood that their practices needed reform.

As schools and districts engage in this journey, usually it is useful to have skilled facilitators from within or outside of the school or district. Professional development is critical so these conversations build rather than destroy. When these dialogues are skillfully conducted over time (this is not an event or activity), schools will become better advocates for all students and move away from comments such as "I see kids, not color," and "disaggregating data is racist." Instead, there will be inquiries about practices and the differential impact they may have on groups of students. Evaluation should take place at the child level. Does it make a positive difference for students? Using *other data* and facilitated conversation, the following are some suggested topics for dialogue:

1. Dialogue needs to occur about remedies for system inequities. When the wallpaper is peeled off and exposes hidden data, it underscores the need for board, district, school, and community leaders to examine system policies, such as leader and teacher placements, contracts, and practices that continue to perpetuate conditions of underachievement. Digging even deeper is required to look at, for example, whether race is more of a factor than income or parents' education (Barton & Coley, 2009; Singleton & Linton, 2006).

2. Dialogue needs to occur about what content is taught to different groups of students. The evidence continues to build around the necessity for all students to engage and become proficient in rigorous curriculum content and problem-solving skills. There are vast inequities in what gets taught to whom, and while many students and their parents are thinking that students are receiving an education that will qualify them for college admission or a "good-paying professional job," in reality their education may be relegating them to low-paying service positions.

3. Dialogue needs to occur about the disproportionality of groups in high- and low-status programs, such as special education and gifted and talented.

4. Dialogue needs to occur about nonacademic issues. There should be an urgency about looking at and analyzing the overlooked nonacademic data to deal with the discomforts on inequitable practices and differential treatments. The area of discipline related to differential treatment and lost instructional time should receive immediate attention. Zero-tolerance policies and the data related to policy implementation should be analyzed. There are cultural aspects that must be examined related to how one responds to behaviors of different groups and how misreading cultural behaviors is resulting in devastating losses for groups of students, such as African American males.

Ultimately, schools and districts must identify their other on-the-ground issues that need to be addressed. Establishing, recognizing, and devoting time to ongoing conversations is what is critical. The content and discussions in faculty, grade-level, and department meetings and workshops should be transformed. The content of the conversations should be substantive. The conversations need to become honest, trusting, reflective,

> Everyone must situate themselves inside the problem and identify their personal role in creating a transformation.

and hopefully ones that result in actions that make a difference for children. Leadership should play a major role in creating climates where these types of conversations can flourish. We state "need to become" because we recognize that this is a process. Everyone must situate themselves inside the problem and identify their personal role in creating a transformation. Parents and students should be part of the dialogue and should also situate themselves inside the problem. Which of their behaviors need to change?

ORGANIZING TO USE THE OTHER DATA

Using whole-school inquiry is a paradigm shift in the current practices of most schools. The on-the-ground data can define a culture that is able to define indicators of progress including the distribution of learning opportunities and test assumptions about students and their experiences. It can also encourage more provocative inquiry about institutional practices that contribute to performance, and constant internal monitoring of progress toward goals. The data generated from school inquiry can not only act as a lever to describe student outcomes, it can also facilitate students' access to meaningful content and effective teaching. Rich dialogue can provide early opportunities to assess and understand the belief and values that drive norms of behavior in the school culture.

If significant inquiry is to take place in the organization, there need to be dispositions, implementation, data skills, and rich knowledge bases. Organizational structures must allow for continuous quality time to engage in meaningful dialogue around the information gathered. The composition of the data team should be representative of the organization and team members who need to understand their roles in the process. Some schools use data coaches. Love, Stiles, Mundry, and Diranna (2008) provide a rich resource for professionally developing data coaches.

We propose that schools and districts build cultures of inquiry with an equity lens. These are organizational cultures that require multiple layers of reflection and investigation by the school community in order to measure the responsiveness of the school to all students and their learning needs. It requires collecting and analyzing quantitative as well as qualitative data of the type that is presented in this book. Schools and districts can then have ways to provide multiple indicators on how the school is performing with different groups of students. Data inquiries

> We propose that schools and districts build cultures of inquiry with an equity lens.

should focus on major issues and measures that will make a difference for students. Once there are multiple indicators and patterns of inequities are apparent, the data and implications should be presented, and discussions should take place on how the inequities will be addressed.

Where and how does the *other-data* journey in a school or district begin? Throughout this book we have demonstrated how *other data* have been used at the district, school, and department level to create change. Superintendent, school administrators, and teachers who were dissatisfied with certain outcomes and felt compelled to change the status quo led these efforts. It might begin with a dissatisfied community or one administrator or board member. Those who want to lead the effort need to discuss the best way to enter or how to build on current processes that hold promise. Know the culture of the desired setting for the change. What are the positive and negative forces? What barriers might need to be dismantled? Reflect on what has been presented in each chapter of this book and discuss the implications for your setting. This book could be used in a study group to prepare teams to increase their own *equity muscle* prior to launching a change initiative. The website that accompanies this book offers an opportunity to access electronic files that support follow-up inquiry and discussion.

Accountability must extend beyond the usual. What do we need to measure beyond test scores? For instance, we have information about how the K–12 school journey takes students on different paths. We know that some conditions for future success or failure in school are set in motion as early as elementary school. Some students experience roads with smooth six-lane highways, others experience two-lane highways where they move slower, and then there are those who are on roads with lots of detours and potholes. They do not reach their destination. Having high schools solely responsible for graduation rates ignores the journey. The research informs us that there are indicators along the journey that are connected to the final destinations. They include: retention in elementary school, placement in special education, being taught low-level curriculum that results in low test scores, course enrollment, attendance, disciplinary infractions, and other indicators. We should be accountable for monitoring those indicators. The organization Jobs for the Future suggests that there be accountability for higher graduation rates and high academic standards (Almeida, Johnson, & Steinberg, 2006). NCLB now requires that high schools track and report Grade 9 or Grade 10 cohort information (whichever is the entry grade for a particular high school) to calculate graduation rates. These longitudinal systems need not only be used for accountability, but as sources

> Some students experience roads with smooth six-lane highways, others experience two-lane highways where they move slower, and then there are those who are on roads with lots of detours and potholes.

of information for prevention and intervention. These are much better strategies then solely using snapshot data. These strategies can focus on where students are lost, particularly at the ninth-grade level, and there are proposals to start at eighth grade. A school that looks like it is improving by retaining, discharging, or sending students to continuation schools can be monitored more closely. Schools that are making authentic progress can be identified so their practice might inform others.

The Data Quality Campaign (DQC) (2009) issued a report on the progress of state data systems. Even though the focus of this report is on state longitudinal accountability systems, it is informative for schools and districts as well. Many districts are considering instituting their own longitudinal systems and DQC's website can be a valuable resource. We view these indicators as useful for high schools and districts. The design focuses on obtaining information on the following points:

- Which schools produce the strongest academic growth for their students?
- Which achievement levels in middle school indicate that a student is on track to succeed in rigorous courses in high school?
- What high school performance indicators (such as enrollment in rigorous courses or performance on state tests) are the best predictors of students' success in college or the workplace?
- What percentage of high school graduates who go on to college take remedial courses? (DQC, 2006, p. 2)

Districts and schools should also set up systems so the data can be gathered at the institutional, teacher, and student level over time. Additional inquiries should include the following:

- What happens to students as they move through the system? Who stays, who leaves, and for what reasons?
- What does the picture look like in kindergarten and at twelfth-grade graduation for different groups of students? What do we expect our students to be able to do when they leave the system? For example, our expectation is that all students should be prepared to complete high school and to enter a baccalaureate degree-granting institution.

Most schools have these data. They should be systematically collected and used while larger database systems are being designed. Yet, a cautionary note is in order. Longitudinal data can be used for description or prediction. The purpose and goal for having and using longitudinal data should be for effective prevention and interventions, monitoring progress, and informing practice. Creating another more sophisticated sorting mechanism is not the goal. The data systems should look at the system indicators as well as student level indicators.

Data must be checked for accuracy. In a climate of accountability, sanctions, and rewards, it is important that achievement gains are authentic. It is important that scores are not looked at apart from other data such as retention, special education placements, or other sorting and isolating mechanisms. Authentic progress needs to be celebrated and rewarded. Year-to-year data should be collected at the same time each year. Data collectors and sources should be identified. Over and over we hear the questions about site-collected data: Where did these data come from and who collected it?

> Data must be checked for accuracy. In a climate of accountability, sanctions, and rewards, it is important that achievement gains are authentic.

We have demonstrated throughout this book that both quantitative and qualitative measures can be used to yield information about students, staff, and the school and district culture. In the education community, there appears to be more trust in quantitative than qualitative data. Quantitative data appears to be more definitive and easier to cite, and most of the readily available data is quantitative, so qualitative data needs to be created and collected in addition. These data provide rich information, but practitioners need to be skilled in using this approach and be informed about the legal rules their state and district have regarding student and interviewee confidentiality rights. Those who would like more information about practitioner qualitative approaches should read Anderson, Herr, and Sigrid Nihlen (*Studying Your Own School: An Educator's Guide to Qualitative Practitioner Research, 2006*) and review some the approaches set forth in this book.

It is critical to have a serious dialogue concerning whose knowledge counts. Whose voices are listened to and which research and what type of research are read? What literature is valued? Who does professional development and what is their orientation? What information gets dispersed and how is it filtered?

Teachers, students, and parents are rich sources and whose voices should be heard. For example, student work is a valuable resource for teachers to analyze, yet this is discussed less than test scores. The information from the student work, however, can give teachers and school leaders different information about their instructional practices and how students are learning. If instruction improves to include rigorous content using engaging strategies based on frequent assessment, learning outcomes will improve, however they are measured.

Critical to this discussion is the issue of who defines the inquires and whose voices count (Smith, 2004). Because of cultural issues involved with the inequities that we see in schools, it is essential that the voices of those from whom data are being collected have valid representation in how research and school-based inquiries are conducted. Although Smith (2004) directs her comments to researchers, we view her recommendations as relevant to anyone who is conducting inquires for data use. She states:

> When studying how to go about doing research, it is very easy to overlook the realm of common sense, the basic beliefs that not only help people identify research problems that are relevant and worthy, but also accompany them throughout the research process. Researchers must go further than simply recognizing personal beliefs and assumptions and the effect they have when interacting with people. In a cross-cultural context, the questions that need to be asked are ones such as:
>
> - Who defined the research problem?
> - For whom is this study worthy and relevant? Who says so?
> - What knowledge will the community gain from this study?
> - What knowledge will the researcher gain from the study?
> - What are some likely positive outcomes from this study?
> - What are some possible negative outcomes?
> - How can the negative outcomes be eliminated?
> - To whom is the researcher accountable?
> - What processes are in place to support the research, the researched and the researcher? (p. 173)

If there is not an understanding of the cultural aspects in using data, points are missed and wrong conclusions are drawn, such as seeing inequities in the data as "normal" and natural. Utilize the voices of students and parents—we have found that they can provide educators with very different points of view about why things are the way they are. There is often a cultural dissonance between the school, the parents, and the students in the manner that information, knowledge, and access get communicated. Assumptions that teachers, counselors, and administrators hold about parents and students from diverse backgrounds need to be tested for accuracy. It is important to get the student and parent voices on record and to use the data in shaping reform strategies. The following real-life scenario describes these misperceptions. There are teacher, student, and parent voices on the topic of homework and other matters.

At a staff meeting where teachers, counselors, and administrators were deliberating on the low achievement of students in their school, the subject of parent involvement surfaced. There were comments such as, "If the parents showed more interest and came to school more often the kids would do better," "They don't care about their child's academic achievement," "The students have no ambition," "They don't want to do the work," and "They don't turn in the homework, so why bother to assign it?"

At a meeting with parents, the following comments were heard: "The homework is never checked by teachers," "We don't understand homework directions," "Kids should have homework every night," "Teachers need to explain homework," "Our children need more homework—twenty to thirty minutes for K–2 and one hour for Grades 3–5," "My child has too many substitutes, and they don't follow the plans the teachers leave," "My child enjoys reading," "We want evening classes for parents," "The school needs to jump-start the program and be consistent from teacher to teacher," "Tutoring needs to be done by a qualified person with a focus on the area for remediation—not old homework," "Videos should not be shown during the week," "How much time goes to special events and draws away from regular instruction?," "There are inconsistent standards at a grade level—and inconsistent expectations for students," "Office personnel need to be more approachable," "The perfect attendance breakfast was great!" "I want my child to go to college—will he be prepared?"

In a meeting with students, the following comments were heard: "We don't do homework because no one checks it," "I don't understand the homework," "I do my homework in class," "I want harder work," "I ask for help, but the teacher has no time to help me," "She leaves right after school," "We can't bring our books home because we have to share them with another class," "The work is too easy," "I'm bored of watching videos all day long," "We always do projects in a group, and I am tired of that."

The team will need to analyze these points of view, address the implications, and take appropriate actions.

THE NEED FOR CULTURALLY RESPONSIVE SYSTEMS

We place emphasis on the need for schools whose populations of students are low-income, African American, Latino, Native American, Asian, and English learners to have the best culturally responsive leaders and teachers. Schools play a significant role in developing the academic muscle of children whose parents cannot afford to have private tutors and college counselors for their children. The children who have the least social and cultural capital to negotiate schools need the most and the best in order to move ahead.

> The children who have the least social and cultural capital to negotiate schools need the most and the best in order to move ahead.

There are complex issues that schools must comprehend and surmount to authentically raise achievement levels for all students. To address these challenges, strategies should be situated within the current discourse on culturally responsive and appropriate pedagogy. A large amount of background literature is currently available from respected scholars (see Delpit, 1995; Hale, 2001; Irvine, 1990; Ladson-Billings, 1994,

2001; Lee, 2006; Nieto, 2000; Shade, Kelly, & Oberg, 2004). Comprehensive inquires that involve seeking and analyzing *other data* have the potential to demonstrate the need for culturally responsive pedagogy. Inquiries, such as those throughout this text, need to be coupled with culturally responsive actions. These create the guidelines for planning and focusing leadership, curriculum, and school practices. Inquiry strategies provide a useful and necessary way to measure the ongoing effectiveness of the institutional culture and its outcomes (Johnson, 2002; Johnson & Bush, 2006). Approaches are needed that build on, rather than "tear down" or devalue, a student's background and experiences. Students should not have to *subtract* or deny their culture and heritage in order to achieve in schools (Valenzuela, 1999, 2002).

Culturally responsive teaching (also called "culturally relevant teaching") has been identified as a major approach to address racial inequality (Gay, 2000, 2002). For instance, Ladson-Billings (1994) argues against any suggestions that students of color are incapable of learning; rather, teachers should be trained on how to teach with expectations that all children can learn. According to Nieto (2000), culturally responsive pedagogy validates and effectively affirms the experiences and cultural backgrounds of students. Johnson and Bush (2006) describe what they view as the main components of culturally responsive teaching, learning, and schools, and add some additional aspects drawn from the literature. Culturally responsive teaching, learning, and schools do the following:

- Demand high achievement.
- Have high expectations of teachers and students.
- Provide the space for students to critique the dominant culture and power relations.
- Recognize and validate color, relationships, ways of being, and culture of bicultural students.
- Bring students closer to who they are as defined in their community, culture, and history.
- Draw heavily on and affirm the cultural knowledge, language, prior experience, frame of reference, and performance styles of diverse populations.
- Ensure that cultural relevance permeates and informs classroom management and discipline procedures, instructional strategies and methods, classroom environment, student-teacher and parent-teacher relationships, and curriculum content.
- Monitor student progress continually (Johnson & Bush, 2006, p. 275).

Culturally responsive practice requires that teachers, school administrators, and others in the educational enterprise examine their own issues, biases, and cultural differences. This process necessitates that teachers are constantly aware of their positionality—"[the] identity that is shaped by power, status, rank, and sense of privilege in a given social context" (Murrell, 2002, p. 42). Implementing culturally responsive practices is not an activity, but a shift in how students and their parents are viewed, responded to, and treated. This has large implications for data inquiries, data interpretation, and implications for practice. Transforming practices can be measured by how students are taught and the level at which they are taught, how behavior is described, and student success.

THE NEED FOR LEADERSHIP

In schools and districts there are formal and informal leaders. There is a need for leaders who will challenge our current "normal" and also be able to facilitate major changes in the culture of the school/district. Several scenarios in this book describe real leaders who challenged existing conditions. There was a superintendent, a principal, two assistant principals, a math department chair, and teachers who worked alongside them to challenge existing practices. Reread some of those scenarios and reflect on the behaviors of these leaders. It will take leaders such as them, who, through collaboration, develop leadership in others, many of whom will play major roles to improve struggling schools. We need leaders who strive to make schools good places where all children are valued and viewed as capable of learning.

> There is a need for leaders who will challenge our current "normal" and also be able to facilitate major changes in the culture of the school or district.

There is a growing recognition that even though teachers are most important in improving the achievement of children they teach, even excellent teachers cannot flourish in a school with poor leadership. We see many high-quality teachers in low-performing schools working in isolation. Edmonds (1979) and others have found that one hallmark of a successful school is the consistently high-level performance of teachers and others in the organization from grade to grade and subject to subject. Dynamic leaders usually create these conditions. There are leadership programs that are being developed across the nation in cities such as Boston, New York City, and Los Angeles, to create these types of leaders. Many of these programs have a focus on mentorship and internships so exemplary leaders can coach future leaders. We hope that these programs will make a genuine difference in the lives of students.

In struggling schools, more so than other schools, principal leadership and stability are key factors. For example, some principals work very hard and are successful at creating academic learning environments. However, just when the outcomes are improving (typically in the third year of change), they are transferred in order to "clean up" another school. The reforms in the former school have barely taken hold, and when the data is reviewed from that school several years later, their academic performance is once again on a downward spiral. Districts need to review and monitor these critical data and practices.

Leadership at the school and district levels is influential. These formal leaders have powerful roles, and they must take major responsibility for moving a system. They need to construct times for teams to meet for critical dialogue. They need to reinforce and value risk taking and advocacy for young people. Culturally responsive, knowledgeable, and skilled leaders must be able to address the inequities that are not "normal" or natural. In the end, their behaviors and job performance should be evaluated as stringently as those of the teachers they ostensibly lead. (See Lindsey, Roberts & CampbellJones, 2005; Scheurich & Skrla, 2003; and Singleton & Linton, 2006 for more on this subject.)

Although we have focused on formal school leaders such as principals, we want to emphasize that all leadership does not reside in those who have formal leadership titles. In every organization there are the informal leaders who have influence and persuasion power. Leadership needs to be developed throughout the organization and in the school community, with a focus on finding leaders who will respond and do something to expose *other data* and take meaningful actions to change the current "normal."

THE NEED FOR STUDENT ADVOCACY

There is a great need for adults in schools and communities to be advocates for students who are underserved. There are students in every school district who are invisible, marginalized, and isolated who operate in systems outside of the mainstream and out of public view until they cause high-profile problems. There are students who go to school every day, do not cause problems, and are still failing and underachieving. Who are their advocates? We go back to a recurring theme in this book that a sense of urgency and disposition to act are required to address the needs of groups of students who are underachieving in our schools. We are not looking for another round of finger pointing, but rather the identification of institutional policies and practices that affect student achievement. A climate of trust, risk taking, and openness must be nurtured. Although an external facilitator is often employed to begin the process, the school community must ultimately adopt a commitment to asking and answering equity questions. In order to engage in real, deep-level reforms, professionals must assess their underlying assumptions. We must

> We must all examine what we are willing to do on behalf of other people's children.

all examine what we are willing to do on behalf of other people's children.

WHO IS MISSING FROM THE TABLE?

We need to be sure that what appears to be promising reforms are not recreating the same systems in smaller packages with fancier ribbons. Creating lasting change, rather than isolated change, needs commitment and hard work from many. Although the focus of our work and this book is schools and districts, we recognize that many outside of the schoolhouse should be at the table as equal partners. Parents, communities, community-based organizations, religious organizations, businesses, and others in the school communities must be simultaneously tackling issues of drugs, joblessness, homelessness, and a foster system that is not working well for young people. This is not solely an urban, rural, or suburban problem. It is a national problem and a national opportunity to create change.

CONCLUSION

Increasing *equity muscle* will require continuous nurturing and attention. The muscle must be exercised on a continuous basis through constantly monitoring practices, using *other data* to look at our programs and practices, keeping current with the literature, updating skills, and conducting authentic dialogue that includes colleagues, parents, and students, along with passion for the work. This chapter discussed the need to dismantle in our minds and practices what we consider "normal" and acceptable. We are asking for a rejection of accepting patterns of underachievement for certain groups of students, namely low-income, African American, Latino, Native American, English learners, and those receiving special education services. There are places where these groups demonstrate high levels of achievement and educational attainment. We know it can be done.

In order to challenge systems that are inequitable there will be a need for those who have information to do something. At the very least, the problem should be acknowledged. Peeling off the wallpaper to expose the *other data* can be a first step. We must create systems where young people have hope. Adults need to care for, protect, speak on behalf of, and educate the adults of the future. There is nothing more rewarding than to know that we have touched and improved the lives of the young people in our midst. Our hope in writing this book is that it will provide insights, tools, information, and challenges that will help in the quest to wipe out the inequities in education.

Appendix A

Overview of Other Data

These *other data* are by no means exhaustive, but represent those data that we have used to pinpoint equity issues in our work and that of others. On-site educators will no doubt peel off wallpaper and contribute their *other data*.

Note: Topics touched upon in Chapter 1, "The Wallpaper Effect: Uncovering Inequities Using the Other Data," are discussed thoroughly in subsequent chapters.

Chapter 2: Peeling the Wallpaper: Uncovering Inequities			
Area	**Typical Data**	**Other Data**	**Supportive Literature Sources**
Student Achievement	• Aggregate and disaggregated high-stakes state test results • Performance-based assessment results • Gap data between subgroups • Grades disaggregated by grade level and subjects • College admissions tests SAT/ACT	• All data disaggregated by race/ethnicity, gender, income, and programs. • Peeling data by levels (see Tables 2.1 and 2.2). • Grades and Pass/Fail rates by courses, level, and type of class (over time and by teacher). • Identifying which teachers teach which students. • Test scores compared to grades (such as how many students are in Advanced Placement that receive As receive 3 or above on the AP exam?).	Adelman (1999) Barton & Coley (2009) College Board (2010) Education Trust (2009) Hakuta, Butler, & Witt (2000) Johnson (2002) McKinsey & Co. (2009) Noguera & Wing (2006) Singham (1998) State Departments of Education

Chapter 2: Peeling the Wallpaper: Uncovering Systemic Inequities			
Area	**Typical Data**	**Other Data**	**Supportive Literature Sources**
	• High school exit exams • Advanced Placement exam results • Planned college enrollment • Snapshot data	• Performance by quartiles and categories (proficient, etc. and movement of students from lower to higher levels or the reverse). • Alignment of curriculum, instruction, and assessment. • Measures of instructional rigor. • Pathways of English learners (EL), special education, and gifted and talented students. • Analysis of retention and achievement. • Difference between subgroup performance and desired goal (GAP). • Direction of gap increase and direction. • Longitudinal data by individuals and cohort groups. • Instructional and engaged time. • Staff compared to parent and student expectations and perceptions. • Measures of intervention impact.	

Chapter 3: The Journey Through School: Starting With the End in Mind			
Areas	**Typical**	**Other Data**	**Supportive Literature Sources**
Dropouts	• Dropout counts • Dropout counts by ethnicity/ gender	• All data disaggregated by race/ethnicity, gender, income, and programs. • Tracking where missing but "non-dropout" students go. • Relationship between dropout and retention for students receiving special education services and English learner rosters.	Allensworth & Easton (2005) Balfanz & Letgers (2004) Flores-Gonzalez (2002) Neild & Balfanz (2006)

Chapter 3: The Journey Through School: Starting With the End in Mind			
Areas	**Typical**	**Other Data**	**Supportive Literature Sources**
		• Pipeline K–12 school-based indicators of nongraduation. • Ninth-grade retention/support elements. • Transcript analyses. • Student voice.	Oakes (1985) Viadero (2006) Wakelyn (2009)
High School Graduation	• Percentage of students who graduate each year • Graduates by subgroup	• All data disaggregated by race/ethnicity, gender, income, and programs. • Cumulative promotion index (CPI) • Transcript analyses. • Tracking course completion from entry level of high school thru completion. • Comparison of grouping practices starting at elementary school and levels of attainment. • Number and percent with standard or alternative diploma. • Pipeline K-12 school-based graduation and college going indicators. • Student voice.	Editorial Projects in Education (2006, 2009) Wakelyn (2009)
College Readiness	• Number of students taking SAT/ACT • Number of student taking advanced math or science • Number of students taking college prerequisite courses • Number of students self-reporting their plans to attend university or two-year colleges	• All data disaggregated by race/ethnicity, gender, income, and programs. • Calculations of College Opportunity Ratio (COR) by subgroup. • Monitoring course rigor. • Affiliation with college-related peers, mentors or groups. • Participation in study groups. • Student voice. • Actual two- or four-year college enrollment. • Student and parent expectations and aspirations. • Pipeline K-12 school-based college going indicators.	Adelman (1999) Johnson (2002) Noguera & Wing (2006) Stanton-Salazar (2010) University of California/ACCORD

Chapter 4: Special Education and Gifted and Talented			
Areas	**Typical**	**Other Data**	**Supportive Literature Sources**
Special Education	• Achievement gap data • Student counts by program	• All data disaggregated by race/ethnicity, gender, income, and language. • Ethnic/racial/ linguistic proportionality of identified students compared to population. • Sources of referrals (when and by whom), designations by program, race/ethnicity, gender, income. • Accuracy of the service and label. • Levels of service. • Type of label by subgroup. • Percentage of time spent in general program. • Measures of expectations. • Achievement data by years in program, program type. • IEP analyses for goal attainment and levels of performance changes over time. • Secondary course enrollments. • Suspensions, expulsions, and other behavioral information. • Dropout, graduation, and college enrollment. • Type of diploma awarded (standard or alternative).	Artiles, Harry, Reschly, Chinn (2001) Artiles, Klinger, & Tate (2006) Blanchett (2006) Harry & Klinger (2006) Losen & Orfield (2002) O'Connor & DeLuca Fernandez (2006) Olson (2004)
Gifted and Talented	• Percentage of students identified GATE	• All data disaggregated by race/ethnicity, gender, income, and programs. • Percentage of students identified GATE by subgroup. • Ethnic/racial/ linguistic proportionality of identified students compared to population.	College Board (2010) Ford & Grantham (2003) National Association for Gifted Children (2008b) Renzulli & Park (2000)

Chapter 4: Special Education and Gifted and Talented			
Areas	**Typical**	**Other Data**	**Supportive Literature Sources**
		• Analysis of the long-term effect of GATE services on student achievement. • Percentage of identified GATE students, by subgroup, and placement in advanced courses or lower-level courses.	

Chapter 5: English Learners			
Areas	**Typical**	**Other Data**	**Supportive Literature Sources**
English Learners (EL)	• Number of EL students (aggregate) • Annual language proficiency assessment • State and other standardized assessments • Teacher qualifications • Number of students in each program • Achievement in primary language • Achievement in English compared to other school or district students (gap) • Reclassification percentage	• Number of years labeled EL. • Academic performance and English proficiency by years labeled EL. • Data disaggregated by language group, immigrant refugee status, education level in native country, and income. • Academic scores by courses, repeat ELD classes, representation in gifted, special education programs. • Operation definition of specific programs. • Teacher effectiveness. • Mobility and attrition rate in each program. • Achievement in English compared to the expected target for each additional year labeled EL. • Achievement in English compared to the expected target for all students. • On-track versus on-watch numbers. • Percentage of students labeled EL over five years who reclassified.	Flores, Painter, Zachary, & Pachon (2009) Gersten & Baker (2000) Hakuta, Butler, & Witt (2000)

Chapter 6: Nonacademic Indicators Associated With Achievement Outcomes			
Areas	**Typical**	**Other Data**	**Supportive Literature Sources**
Use of Time	• Scheduled time • Allotments of time for instruction • Pacing	• Actual use of time during 180-day calendar. • Teacher planned versus actual instructional and engaged time by type and levels of courses. • Percentage of instructional time diverted to other activities. • Shadows of different levels of students to observe use of time. • Out-of-class student time by student groups. • Time lost by scheduling delays. • Traveling teacher loss of time.	Silva (2007)
Extracurricular	• Data on numbers of students participating in different activities, particularly athletics	• Number, types (structured or unstructured), characteristics of activities and membership by grade, race, ethnicity, language groups, and gender. • Level of participation by students in activities. • Alternative schools and special education student participation. • Academic achievement of students in various activities. • Distribution of resources to different activities. • Student perceptions of activities—is there a feeling of openness to join different activities or are there unwritten codes about who should participate in different activities?	Eccles & Barber (1999) Feldman & Matjasko (2005)

Chapter 6: Nonacademic Indicators Associated With Achievement Outcomes			
Areas	**Typical**	**Other Data**	**Supportive Literature Sources**
		• Role adults play in steering or discouraging participations in high-profile activities such as student council, yearbook, sports, cheerleading • Grades of students in different programs. • Graduation and dropout rates. • Student voice.	
Discipline	• Suspensions and expulsions	• Disproportionality by demographic group and gender. • Referrals by teachers/student ethnicity and gender. • Observation of the impact of classroom management on referrals. • Severity of punishment by demographic group. • Loss of learning time. • Differential treatment in class and school. • Long-term impact. • Responsiveness to cultural behaviors. • Monitoring of in-school suspensions and detention. • Unintended consequences of zero-tolerance policies. • Student voice.	ACLU (2009) BASRC (2001) Children's Defense Fund (2007) Civil Rights Project and Advancement Project (2000) Collier (2007) Holzman (2006) Noguera & Wing (2006) Reyes (2006) Skiba (2000) Texas Appleseed (2007)
Transience/mobility for students and staff	• Summary statistics	• Turnover rates of principals and teachers and stability of staff. • Back and forth movement of student. • Information on homeless students. • Information on neglected and delinquent youth. • Student voice.	Search state website for school, district, and state data on neglected and delinquent youth and pregnant minors

Chapter 6: Nonacademic Indicators Associated With Achievement Outcomes			
Areas	**Typical**	**Other Data**	**Supportive Literature Sources**
Attendance: Staff and Students	• Summary statistics (ADA/teacher present, excused absences) • Tardies (unduplicated)	• Class-tardy total by student. • Subject-by-subject attendance. • Period-by-period attendance by teacher. • Types of teacher and student absences. • Categories of students and subjects that have long-term and multiple short-term substitutes. • Student voice.	Noguera & Wing (2006)

Chapter 7: Systemic Inequities: Structures, Policies, and Practices			
Areas	**Typical**	**Other Data**	**Supportive Literature Sources**
Policies	• Promotion • Retention • Number of days of instruction • School calendar • Curriculum • Discipline	• Use of time by category. • Student pathways— longitudinal to assess effects of policies on different groups. • Impact of grouping on certain groups. • Analysis of master schedule with of focus on equity. • Assessment of curriculum rigor for all subjects.	Bryk et al. (1993) Crawford & Dougherty (2000) Johnson (2002) Losen & Orfield (2002) Noguera & Wing (2006) Shade, Kelly, & Oberg (2004) Valenzuela (2002)
Practices	• Course enrollments/ placements • Informal ("the way we do things here") • Grouping and sorting • Teacher placements	• Student pathways disaggregated by course placement, test scores, grades. • Analysis of the master schedule. • Students in office—what courses are they in; what are their GPAs? • Counselor-student contact rosters. • Written placement criteria compared to student transcripts.	Adelman (1999) Barton & Coley (2009) College Board (2010) Crawford & Dougherty (2000) Gay (2000) Johnson (2002) Oakes (1985) Valenzuela (1999, 2002)

Chapter 7: Systemic Inequalities: Structures, Policies, and Practices			
Areas	**Typical**	**Other Data**	**Supportive Literature Sources**
	<ul><li>Student discipline</li><li>Grades</li><li>Courses offered</li><li>Content</li></ul>	<ul><li>Schedules of counselor visits by class.</li><li>Ethnic distribution of classes by level.</li><li>Facilities maps locating advanced and other classes in relation to information bulletins and counseling activities.</li><li>Instructional delivery.</li><li>Culturally responsive pedagogy.</li><li>Opportunity to learn.</li><li>Consistency/rigor across grades and school.</li><li>Quality of curriculum in alternative programs.</li></ul>	Irvine (1990) Johnson & Bush (2006) Ladson-Billings (1994) Lee (2006) Shade, Kelly, & Oberg (2004)
Teacher/ Counselor/ Administrator Quality	<ul><li>Credentials</li><li>Number of years</li></ul>	<ul><li>Student achievement track record with different groups and levels of students over time.</li><li>Placements of teachers and paraprofessional by student groups.</li><li>Race, ethnicity, and gender placements.</li><li>Traveling teachers.</li><li>Classes of students and subjects that have long-term and multiple short-term substitutes.</li><li>Culturally responsive indicators.</li><li>Individual and cohort achievement indicators before and after participation in a class, program, school.</li><li>Student and parent evaluations.</li><li>Attendance data.</li><li>Value-added data.</li></ul>	Cicourel & Kitsuse (1963) Darling-Hammond, Berry, & Thoreson (2001) Delpit (1988, 1995) Edmonds (1979) Lezotte (2010)

Appendix B

Sample Data-Bite Responses (Chapter 2)

DATA BITE 1: NUMBER OF STUDENTS AT EACH GRADE LEVEL TAKING EACH MATH COURSE

Findings: The number of students who progress through the math sequence drastically decreases each year. The majority of students taking math are in below-grade-level courses. A minority of students take the expected high school sequence beginning with algebra or geometry in the ninth grade. Very few students make it to calculus.

Implications: Ninth grade is a pivotal grade, with the highest dropout rate. Students who begin high school with at least algebra have an advantage over students who begin in lower-level courses. Once students are programmed into a lower math class, a domino effect occurs. Due to master schedule constraints, these students will likely spend much of their day grouped with less successful students. The lack of an academically oriented peer network, coupled with the high failure rate of lower-level classes leaves those students at the highest risk of failure. They are more likely to drop out, and, if they stay in school, will more than likely not be able to complete the college prerequisite course sequence.

Other Data **Needed:** Are there patterns (ethnic, gender, language proficiency, students with disabilities, GATE, feeder middle school) apparent for the students who begin at lower-level classes and those who begin on grade level? What explains the huge attrition rate from year to year for students advancing to the next math level? Are grades the obstacle? What are grades based on? Are grades consistent from teacher to teacher and course to course? What is the relationship between grades and test scores (state exams, common assessments, AP exams)? What types of support do students receive if they struggle in math?

Next Steps: Once *other data* are gathered, a team of interested parties should come together to uncover the story beneath the numbers in Data Bite 1. The team should consider the desired minimal goal for all students at the school by aligning to the university minimum requirements (such as two years of high school math, for instance algebra and geometry). Once the target is set, the team should study the *other data* to identify what obstacles would keep students from meeting the goal of college readiness. Plans should be created to prevent those barriers from limiting students, including preview-review companion math courses, extended-day intervention programs, tutoring, and regular data chats with students and teachers. Once plans are made, the team should develop a monitoring plan, collecting data each grade-reporting period, to assess progress and intervene as necessary.

DATA BITE 2: NUMBER OF STUDENTS AT EACH GRADE LEVEL TAKING EACH SCIENCE COURSE

Findings: The science profile is similar to the math profile in Data Bite 1. Most students are in life science, a simplified form of biology. Many juniors take general science. Both of these courses are not usually university approved. A minority of students take biology, the generally accepted entry-level science course in high school, as it is the first of the traditional science sequence accepted by universities (biology, chemistry, and physics). The numbers of students in chemistry and physics is very low.

Implications: The profile suggests that most students do not take biology, the generally desired course for college-going students. If the hope is that life science will help prepare students for biology, the numbers indicate that it is not effective, as the attrition for advanced levels of science is very high. The fact that most juniors take general science indicates that they are taking a second year of science required for high school graduation, but are not on the college-going path. The lack of the university-required science sequence eliminates most students at this school from being accepted to most colleges and universities.

Other Data **Needed:** Are there patterns (ethnic, gender, language proficiency, students with disabilities, GATE, feeder middle school) apparent for the students who begin at lower-level classes and those who begin on grade level? What explains the huge attrition rate from year to year for students advancing to the next science level? Are grades the obstacle? What are grades based on? Are grades consistent from teacher to teacher and course to course? What is the correlation between grades and test scores (state exams, common assessments, AP exams)? What types of support do students receive if they struggle in science? Are students being disqualified from taking biology because they are in below-algebra math?

Next Steps: Same as Data Bite 1.

DATA BITE 3: COMPARISON OF AFRICAN AMERICAN STUDENTS' AND PARENTS' EXPECTATIONS FOR COLLEGE/ UNIVERSITY ENROLLMENT TO PERCENTAGE OF GRADUATES ENROLLED IN COLLEGE

Findings: Overwhelmingly, students and parents reported their expectation that students would attend a four-year university and not a two-year college. By senior year, however, the largest number of students enrolled in postsecondary schooling enrolled in two-year colleges (42%). Less than 10% of seniors enrolled in a four-year university.

Implications: An absolute mismatch exists between parent and student expectations for university enrollment and actual enrollment. Somewhere before the senior year, students changed their mind, never understood the implication of below-grade course work, or realized they are otherwise not qualified to attend a university.

Other Data **Needed:** At what point did students and parents realize students would not be attending university? What specific factors prohibited students from enrolling in a university (funds, prerequisite courses, SAT/ACT scores, grades, extracurricular activities)? What is the transfer rate of graduates who enrolled in a two-year college to a four-year university? Are their particular courses that created a bottleneck for students, such as biology or algebra? What is the backstory from the perspective of students, parents, and school people? What is the expectation among teachers, counselors, and administrators that African American students go to either a two- or four-year college?

Next Steps: A team including students and parents needs to study these *other data* to completely understand the conditions. Then, the team should thoroughly discuss the findings, especially if there is a discrepancy between parent/students expectations and staff expectations for them. Set a measurable goal, such as, "All students will graduate college ready." With a clearly articulated goal, the team should initiate an informational campaign to ensure that the staff understands the student and parent intention and that the "system" is built to support that goal.

DATA BITE 4: NUMBER OF YEARS AT A MIDDLE SCHOOL THAT STUDENTS HAVE BEEN LABELED EL

Findings: Ninety-one students have been EL for five or more years and most have been labeled EL for seven or more years, without reclassifying to fluent status. Forty-eight students are relative newcomers (labeled EL less than four years).

Implications: The forty-eight newcomers might be "on track," even though they have not reached English fluency, because it generally takes longer than four years to gain enough academic English and content knowledge to meet redesignation criteria. However, the ninety-one students are definitely "on watch," because they should be candidates for redesignation after five or more years labeled EL. On-watch students' achievement tends to decline the longer they remain EL and do not reach English fluency. The on-track students must make continuous annual progress in English language development (ELD) to ensure that they reach English fluency in about five years.

Other Data **Needed:** How many EL students demonstrate reasonable annual ELD growth? How many students move up, stay the same, or go backward in ELD each year? What programs or services are students receiving by growth group mentioned in the previous question? How many students are at each level of ELD, by years labeled EL? For students at each year labeled EL, what is their ELD level and their achievement level in English and mathematics? For on-watch students, what redesignation criteria are they not meeting to qualify for redesignation? What is the instructional program in place that targets each of those areas? Why do students think they have not reached redesignation? Why do teachers think on-watch students have not reached redesignation?

Next Steps: The first priority is to study the data to better understand on-watch students' situations. Study all the *other data* to identify bottlenecks to expected progress in the areas that are part of redesignation criteria (ELD level, achievement in English and math, writing in English, and possibly primary language literacy level for some programs). Delineate the instructional program components intended to support each area. Gather data to determine the effectiveness of each program component. Make necessary adjustments to target desired outcomes. Create a quarterly monitoring plan to assess progress and make any needed modifications.

DATA BITE 5: EIGHTH-GRADE COURSE ENROLLMENT IN ALGEBRA: SAMPLE PRESENTATION OF A SCHOOL'S SUMMARIZED DATA

Findings: All subgroups increased the percentage of students taking algebra in the eighth grade from 2007–08 to 2008–09. Although enrollment for all groups increased in the second year, the gap remained the same. The Native American student group has the lowest enrollment rate and the Asian student group has the highest. African American and American Indian students had similar increases of 17% and 16%. Latino students had the greatest growth in algebra enrollment. White students had the least growth.

Implications: Since the goal is to have all eighth graders in algebra by a fixed point in time, enrollment for some groups needs to be more accelerated than for others. For example, Native American students must enroll in algebra at a greater rate of increase than White students in order for every group to reach the goal at the same time. While Asian and White groups appear to be closer to the goal; a large percent of African American, Native American, and Latino students are not taking algebra, and are probably enrolled in lower-level courses. Success in algebra in the eighth grade greatly increases the likelihood of academic success in high school, for reasons discussed in Data Bites 1 and 2. This data bite suggests that most Native American and about half of African American and Latino students will likely be programmed into lower-level or regular courses for many of their high school years. This puts them at a huge academic disadvantage.

Other Data **Needed:** By what criteria are eighth graders placed in algebra? By ethnic group, what criteria are students not meeting in order to qualify for eighth-grade algebra? Are there any patterns to the reasons why students don't qualify for algebra? Are the criteria objective, subjective (grades, teacher recommendation), or both? At what point in the students' education can the nonqualifying criteria be traced? For example, does homogeneous grouping begin in fourth grade, with students not having access to grade-level curriculum? What are the skill sets that students lack that prevent them from taking algebra in eighth grade? What do students think is their mathematical situation? What do they understand about the significance of algebra to their high school and college careers? What do elementary and middle school teachers and administrators understand about the significance of algebra to students' high school and college careers? Are there differential patterns of achievement for certain groups of students by assigned teacher?

Next Steps: As a collaborative team, analyze the *other data* to tell yourselves the "real story" behind why certain groups are enrolled in algebra in the eighth grade at such different rates. Brainstorm solutions for each of the barriers identified by the data. Create an action plan and a monitoring plan. Monitor and adjust on a frequent, regular schedule.

DATA BITE 6: SECOND-GRADE PROFICIENCY LEVELS BY GENDER

Findings: A difference exists in the proficiency level of girls and boys at the higher-level classes. More males than females score at the highest band and more females than males scored at the proficient band. Very few students are in the lowest proficiency band.

Implications: It is important to ensure that nothing in the intended instructional program is biased against any gender. Also important is to assess whether anything unintended is differentially affecting each gender.

Other Data **Needed:** Are core classes balanced for gender? Are core classes heterogeneous? Is this pattern similar each year with every new group of second graders? Does this second-grade cohort have a particular achievement profile coming in from kindergarten and first grade that is being perpetuated? What do students in the proficient and advanced bands, boys and girls, think accounts for the difference in performance by gender at their grade? What do classroom observation data reveal about teaching practices as they relate to gender? What do other measures of achievement indicate about gender performance?

Next Steps: Collect all the relevant data possible to determine whether this profile is a concern, or whether or not it is supported by *other data*. If possible, look at trend data to assess long-term implications and then decide on the appropriate next steps.

DATA BITE 7: GRADE 2 COMPARISON OF COMMON ASSESSMENT RESULTS FOR UNIT 5 AND SPRING STATE TESTING RESULTS

Findings: The results of the teacher-created common assessments given the month before state testing nearly parallel the results of the state exam. For example, about the same proportion of students scored in the proficient/advanced range on the common assessment as did on the state exam, administered the following month.

Implications: Teacher teams create frequent, common assessments to monitor progress as students move through the school year. The purpose is to collect frequent (monthly) data on student progress in order to inform instructional adjustments to support individual and group academic growth. Common assessments should measure student proficiency on high-value curricular standards. Assuming that state exams align to state and school standards, then common assessments can be designed to give teachers clues about how students would demonstrate their understanding of the standards on state assessments as well. Common assessments that do not align to state standards offer indications of how well students understand a concept or standard in the given format, but may not provide clues about the limitations students have on high-stakes standardized assessments. The ability to demonstrate knowledge in various formats, including on standardized assessments (such as highschool graduation exams, SAT/ACT) is a valuable skill required of high-achieving students.

Other Data **Needed:** How are students performing on other indicators? Do they parallel the common assessment results? What are the characteristics of students at each performance level (gender, ethnicity, language proficiency, special program, and so on). Is their any difference in the instructional program, curriculum, or grouping of students in each band? What skills are students in the below-proficient bands lacking? How did students perform on previous common assessments? Has there been steady growth or have some students remained in the same band over months?

Next Steps: Knowing that the fifth common assessment closely parallels performance on the state exam, triangulate the *other data* to see if performance on the common assessments parallels student performance on other measures, and do this for each subgroup. After answering this question, discuss a plan to help more students reach proficiency, including in-class differentiation, interventions (response to intervention), or extended-day support. Devise and implement a frequent monitoring plan.

DATA BITE 8: GRADE 3 COMPARISON OF COMMON ASSESSMENT RESULTS FOR UNIT 5 AND SPRING STATE TESTING RESULTS

Findings: In this grade, the common assessment result did not parallel the state exam results. For example, 53% of students scored proficient or advanced on the common assessment given a month before state testing, but only 29% of students scored at that range a month later on the state exam. The common assessment results demonstrate much higher achievement than do the state exam results.

Implications: There exists a lack of alignment between the state exam and the common assessment. The common assessment may have value in assessing student proficiency on the content and in the format of that assessment. However, it is not helpful in giving clues about how students are able to generalize their proficiency on the standardized exam.

Other Data **Needed:** What is the alignment between the standards on the common assessments and the state exam? What is the alignment of the format of the common assessments and the state exam? What instructional practices are used in teaching the standards? Is there less rigor? How well do the prevailing teaching strategies help students transfer their knowledge to various contexts? Why do students believe a difference exists between their performance on the common assessment and the state exam?

Next Steps: Study the *other data* to better understand the real story hidden beneath the graph. Then, provide time for the third-grade teacher team, led by a facilitator, to make necessary adjustments to the common assessment design so that results provide more complete information about which instruction can be tailored.

Appendix C

Summary of the Main Points Gathered Through Interviews (Chapter 7)

Interview Subjects	Questions	Responses
Head Counselor	What do you think explains the gap between Latino, African American, and Native American and White and Asian students in university-preparation rates?	Asian and White students are more interested in college. They are more academically oriented.
	What makes you believe that?	African American, Latino, and Native American students do not ask about college like Asian and White students do. They are not knowledgeable about what it takes to go to a university. They are mainly interested in graduating from high school.
	How does information about college get to students?	At each school, counselors go to classrooms and do presentations. We go to every English class. We are in classrooms very often.
Eleventh-Grade Counselor	What do you think explains the gap between Latino, African American, and Native American and Asian and White students in university-preparation rates?	I don't know why African American, Latino, and Native American students are not doing as well. To be honest, I don't have the same rapport with those students. I am very close to many Asian and White students on my roster, but I just don't have close relationships with many of those other students.

Interview Subjects	Questions	Responses
	How much contact do you have with your assigned students?	I see them all the time. Mostly I call them in for graduation checks or college counseling and I do presentations in classrooms.
	Is there any difference in the number of type of contacts you have with different groups of students?	No. I see all my students regularly. I do presentations in classrooms many times each quarter and I conference with my assigned students any time I need to.
AP, Honors, and Advanced Course Teachers	What do you think explains the gap between Latino, African American, and Native American and Asian and White students in university-preparation rates?	Asian and White students work very hard. Advanced courses are rigorous and they are willing to put forth the effort. Latino, African American, and Native American students do not generally challenge themselves that way.
	Do you have Latino, African American, and Native American students in your classes?	Only a few. They are AVID students. They actually do very well in my class. I meet regularly with the AVID teacher and she gives them support in their AVID elective. I know they are in tutorials and learn study skills. My AVID students actually do as well as my other students.
	Why do you have so few Latino, African American, and Native American students in your classes?	Not sure. I think they don't qualify. Maybe they don't have the grades or test scores. You have to be a very strong student to handle the advanced classes.
	How much information do your students receive about college requirements?	They get overloaded with college information. Counselors send over bulletins every week and we read and discuss them in class. Counselors also visit our classes about twice a quarter and more right before SAT, ACT, financial aid, scholarship, and college application deadlines. If students are confused by anything, they ask to see their counselor and we always allow that. Counselors set up university campus visits and have recruiters speak at the high schools. Counselors come to our classes to invite students and sign them up. They are quite assertive! We give students extra credit if they participate in any college events.

Interview Subjects	Questions	Responses
Regular "College-Prep" Teachers	What do you think explains the gap between Latino, African American, and Native American and Asian and White students in university-preparation rates?	Students who take our classes know they are not going to college. They just want to graduate.
	What is the ethnic makeup of your classes?	Mostly all are Latino, African American, and Native American.
	Why are so many Latino, African American, and Native Americans not in advanced classes?	Not sure. They probably don't qualify for advanced classes. Several years ago, our district eliminated separate graduation-track classes and made the lowest class "college-prep." But we teach the classes like we always have; they just changed the name. We get the kids that would have been assigned to the lower-level classes. Our students are good kids; they do whatever you ask of them, but they don't take the initiative do more.
	Do your students know about college-entrance requirements?	Not really. They generally want to graduate and go to community college.
	Where do they get college information?	I think there is a bulletin board outside the AP teacher's classroom where all that information is posted.
	Do counselors visit your classrooms?	Yes, once a year they come around for graduation credit checks. They explain how many credits are required and they hand students a sheet with their information.
University-Preparation Track Students	What do you think explains the gap between Latino, African American, and Native American and Asian and White students in university-preparation rates?	Typical Responses: Asian Student Response: Not sure. White Student Response: I never noticed. I can't answer why it is so. They seem nice, but we don't spend much time together. They have different classes and don't participate in the same activities.

Interview Subjects	Questions	Responses
		Summarized Latino, African American, and Native American Student Responses (AVID): It's hard. You have to take the right classes and sometimes that doesn't happen. You have to know what you need to take and then make sure you get it. Our AVID counselor helps us watch out for that. Also, the good classes don't have that many of our friends, and that's weird. Many students just avoid that. They say they don't belong. Honestly, it takes a lot of study time to do well in the advanced classes and some students have to work after school and weekends. They may not have the time to study like they would need to.
	How do you find out about college requirements?	All Students: Counselors are always coming to our classes with information. They bring applications, remind us of timelines, and push us to follow through. Our teachers are very supportive also. We get extra credit if we do what the counselors tell us and go to their events. Also, friends in class always have tips that they get from different places and we share that information also.
Graduation-Track Students	What do you think explains the gap between Latino, African American, and Native American and Asian and White students in university-preparation rates?	No response.
	What are your plans after high school?	College.
	What college? For what purpose?	Community college to be . . . teachers, lawyers, engineers, bankers, contractors, business owners, nurses.
	How much information do you have about requirements for universities, community college, transferring?	Not much.

Interview Subjects	Questions	Responses
	How often do you see your counselor and for what purpose?	Counselors came to our classes once or twice since we've been at the school. This year, some students were called to the counselor's office because they are behind in credits. They have to do summer school or go to the continuation school.
	Has anyone ever discussed university options with you?	Yes, of course. As freshmen, we went to the auditorium and they gave us a presentation about all of that. Seniors who already had plans for after high school spoke to us. We did not know any of the students going to university, but we knew the ones going to community college. They said it was college that was cheaper and closer and might take less time, too. After that presentation, counselors asked us what plans we had for after high school. We pretty much all said community college and they signed us up for the right classes.

Annotated Resources

This list is by no means exhaustive. Many websites included here have links to other organizations with similar missions, free publications, current research, and data tools. We encourage our readers to explore these other sites.

A BROADER, BOLDER APPROACH TO EDUCATION

Contact Information: See website

http://www.boldapproach.org/who.html

A Broader, Bolder Approach to Education advocates expanding the education of underserved youth beyond the walls of the school. The approach includes cocurricular afterschool programs and programs for parents and the community. They invite others to use the information gained from their reports. The authors of the reports are a diverse set of nationally recognized education policy makers and researchers. Information can be downloaded from the website.

ACHIEVE, INC.

1775 Eye St. NW, Suite 410
Washington, DC 20006
Phone: (202) 419–1540
Fax: (202) 828–0911
www.achieve.org

Achieve is a Washington, DC–based organization that was created in 1996 by the nation's governors and corporate leaders to assist educational reform at the state level to improve academic standards, graduation rates, and accountability in schools. Achieve is a leader in the area of creating K–16 strategies for high school graduation and readiness for college attendance. Publications can be downloaded from the website.

AMERICAN ASSOCIATION FOR THE ADVANCEMENT OF SCIENCE (AAAS)

1200 New York Ave. NW
Washington, DC 20005
Phone: (202) 326–6400
http://www.aaas.org/programs/education/

The American Association for the Advancement of Science promotes science literacy K–16. One of their most well-known education projects is *Project 2061,* which has a focus on science, mathematics, and technological literacy. The organization focuses on diversity and the delivery of high-quality science education for *all* students. It provides networking opportunities, career advice, and information that will guide curriculum and textbook development.

AMERICAN EDUCATIONAL RESEARCH ASSOCIATION (AERA)

1430 K St. NW
Washington, DC 20005
Phone: (202) 238–3200
Fax: (202) 238–3250
http://www.aera.net/

The American Educational Research Association is an educational professional organization that focuses on the study of education through venues of research. Professionals in the field are given the opportunity to share knowledge through conferences and publication in their professional journal. AERA serves as a source of information exchange for educators in K–12 and higher education.

THE ASSOCIATION FOR SUPERVISION AND CURRICULUM DEVELOPMENT (ASCD)

1703 N. Beauregard St.
Alexandria, VA 22311–1714
Phone: (800) 933–2723
Fax: (703) 575–5400
www.ascd.org

Founded in 1943, the Association for Supervision and Curriculum Development provides current professional information through publications, conferences, and in-depth professional development opportunities. They focus on areas of educational leadership, teaching and learning, instruction and pedagogy, and reform primarily at the K–12 level. The organization provides resources in multiple areas of education.

BILL & MELINDA GATES FOUNDATION

Main Office:
PO Box 23350
Seattle, WA 98102
Phone: (206) 709–3100:

Grant Inquiries:
Phone: (206) 709–3140
info@gatesfoundation.org
http://www.gatesfoundation.org/about/Pages/overview.aspx

The education strategy of the Bill & Melinda Gates Foundation promotes improvement in education that results in students graduating from high school prepared to either attain a college degree or a certificate that has value in the workplace. The website includes publications on issues related to effective teachers, standards, college readiness, and postsecondary success. The foundation awards grants to tax-exempt organizations.

CALIFORNIA TOMORROW

1904 Franklin St., Suite 300
Oakland, CA 94612
Phone: (510) 496–0220
Fax: (510) 496–0225
www.californiatomorrow.org

California Tomorrow engages with a group of educational stakeholders including the community, K–12 schools, policy makers, and advocates. Their focus is on working toward an "equitable and inclusive multicultural society" to help institutions transform, grow, and reform a more diverse population. They issue publications on current issues that affect diverse student populations.

Center for Applied Linguistics (CAL) and National Center for Research on Cultural Diversity and Second Language Learning (NCRCDSLL)

4646 40th St. NW
Washington, DC 20016–1859
Phone: (202) 362–0700
www.cal.org/Archive/projects/ncrcdsll.htm

Located in Washington, DC, the Center for Applied Linguistics provides a wide-ranging collection of research-based information, tools, and resources related to language and culture. The CAL website has information in the areas of bilingualism, English as a second language, literacy, and foreign language education; dialect studies; language policy; refugee orientation; and the education of linguistically and culturally diverse adults and children. The website includes links to downloadable publications.

Center for Multilingual, Multicultural Research

Rossier School of Education
University of Southern California
Waite Phillips Hall, Suite 402
Los Angeles, CA 90089–0031
Phone: (213) 740–2360
Fax: (213) 740–7101
www.usc.edu/dept/education/CMMR/cmmrhomepage.html

The Center for Multilingual, Multicultural Research is located at the Rossier School of Education, University of Southern California. The major thrusts are to support research on English as a second language, multicultural education, and foreign language instruction. Their work encompasses four areas: research, publication, training, and public service.

CENTER FOR RESEARCH ON THE EDUCATION OF STUDENTS PLACED AT RISK (CRESPAR)

Mary Maushard, Communications Director
CRESPAR/Johns Hopkins University
Phone: (410) 516–8810
Fax: (410) 516–8890
E-mail: mmaushard@csos.jhu.edu

and

Howard University (Capstone)
2900 Van Ness St. NW
Washington, DC 20008
Phone: (202) 806–8484
Fax: (202) 806–8498
http://www.csos.jhu.edu/crespar/index.htm

The Center for Research on the Education of Students Placed at Risk is a collaboration between Johns Hopkins University and Howard University. They aim to dismantle a sorting paradigm in schools using a "talent development model" that has high expectations for children at risk. The collaborating institutions conduct research and evaluation. They disseminate strategies that they deem replicable and "designed to transform schooling for students who are placed at risk due to inadequate institutional responses to such factors as poverty, ethnic minority status, and non-English-speaking home background." The website provides information on publications and programs.

CHILDREN'S DEFENSE FUND (CDF)

25 E St. NW
Washington, DC 20001
Phone: (202) 628–8787
http://www.childrensdefense.org/helping-americas-children/elementary-high-school-education/

Founded in 1973, the Children's Defense Fund has been a champion for our nation's children's well-being in areas such as health, poverty, and education. CDF offers comprehensive reports on the status of children in every state. Fact sheets show data on the status of children in every state, and on programs such as Freedom Schools, which are summer and after-school programs. Two major publications from the CDF are *The School to Prison Pipeline* (2007) and *The State of America's Children* (2008).

The Civil Rights Project (CRP)/ Proyecto Derechos Civiles

8370 Math Sciences
Box 951521
Los Angeles, CA 90095–1521
E-mail: crp@ucla.edu
Phone: (310) 267–5562
Fax: (310) 206–6293—with "ATTN: CRP/PDC"
http://www.civilrightsproject.ucla.edu/

The Civil Rights Project is a major organization that focuses on civil rights research. Their website is a rich source for information in this area. In addition to a research agenda, CRP convenes national conferences and roundtables, commissions new research and policy studies, and publishes reports and books. A recent 2010 publication is *The Dropout/Graduation Crisis Among American Indian and Alaska Native Students: Failure to Respond Places the Future of Native Peoples at Risk*. Many of their publications can be downloaded at no cost.

The College Board

45 Columbus Ave.
New York, NY 10023
Phone: (212) 713–8000
www.collegeboard.org

The College Board is a nonprofit organization that provides a variety of free online services and a variety of resources for professionals, students, and parents. Additionally, resources are available for K–12 schools and higher education institutions to assist with both schools and students for successful matriculation to graduation from college. Their primary focus is to work with schools to help prepare students for college, specifically with testing required for admissions, assistance with the college admissions process, and financing a college education. The website provides a wide range of information to multiple stakeholders in education including student, parent, and school.

The Consortium for Chicago School Research (CCSR)

1313 E. 60th St.
Chicago, IL 60637
Phone: (773) 702–3364
http://ccsr.uchicago.edu/content/index.php

The Consortium on Chicago School Research conducts research on many of Chicago's school reform efforts. Their findings have informed reform efforts in other cities and have had a far-reaching impact at the national level. They provide a variety of free online services and a variety of resources for professionals, students, and parents, as well as downloadable publications. Resources are available for K–12 schools and higher education institutions about ways to keep students on track to high school and college graduation.

Council of Great City Schools

1301 Pennsylvania Ave. NW, Suite 702
Washington, DC 20004
Phone: (202) 393–2427
Fax: (202) 393–2400
www.cgcs.org

The Council of Great City Schools is a coalition of sixty-six of the nation's largest urban public school systems. The Council promotes and supports urban education through influencing legislation, conducting research, and using other strategies to improve urban education. Some activities include conferences and collaborating with other organizations and agencies. Current publications can be downloaded from their website.

Data Quality Campaign (DQC)

One Dupont Cir. NW, Suite 340
Washington, DC 20036
Phone: (202) 251–2612
Fax: (202) 293–2223
http://www.dataqualitycampaign.org

The Data Quality Campaign promotes the availability and the use of high-quality data in schools with the ultimate of goal of improving student achievement. DQC offers tools and resources and assists states in the use of longitudinal data systems.

Decent Schools for California

Williams et al. vs. The State of California et al.

www.decentschools.org

This is a website for the *Williams* case. A coalition of advocates brought the *Williams* lawsuit (and represented the plaintiff schoolchildren in the case). The coalition included civil rights organizations, public interest law groups, and private law firms. The site provides background information on the lawsuit and settlement and updates on implementation in schools.

Diplomas Count

www.edweek.org/go/dc09

Diplomas Count is one of the publications issued by Editorial Projects in Education. The website provides current and useful information on what data to collect, analyze, and monitor on dropouts and high school completion. Strategies for increasing high school graduation rates, college readiness, and college enrollments for all students are available through links to webinars, publications, state-by-state trend data, and other useful information.

Education Trust

1725 K St. NW, Suite 200
Washington, DC 20006
Phone: (202) 293–1217
Fax: (202) 293–2605
www.edtrust.org

The Education Trust has a major focus on closing the gaps in opportunity and achievement particularly for those young people from low-income families or who are African American, Latino, or Native American. Areas of focus include high school graduation, college readiness, college retention, and degree completion. Some resources that the organization offers include a national conference, publications, and presentations that are available for downloading, and parent and community involvement programs.

Education Week and Editorial Projects in Education Inc.

6935 Arlington Rd., Suite 100
Bethesda, MD 20814–5233
Phone: (800) 346–1834
Fax: (301) 280–3100
www.edweek.org

Education Week is a weekly national education publication that provides up-to-date information about issues in education from the local to the national level PK–12. It is published by Editorial Projects in Education. The website includes a research center with current reports. For example, a 2010 report that is available for download is *Cities in Crises: Closing the Graduation Gap.*

Harlem Children's Zone (HCZ)

35 E. 125th St.
New York, NY 10035
Phone: (212) 360–3255
Fax: (212) 289–0661
E-mail: info@hcz.org
http://www.hcz.org/

The Harlem Children's Zone Project is a comprehensive approach to rebuilding a community to keep children on track from birth through college so they will successfully negotiate the job market. The website provides information on HCZ Project's comprehensive system of programs that encompasses nearly one hundred blocks of Central Harlem. HCZ's programs include in-school, afterschool, social-service, health, family, and community-building programs.

Jobs for the Future

88 Broad St.
Boston, MA 02110
Phone: (617) 728–4446
Fax: (617) 728–4857
http://www.jff.org/projects/current

Jobs for the Future develops education and workforce strategies, and works with a network of partners to assist current K–12 students, out-of-school youth, and working adults to advance learning and careers. The website provides publications for download.

Knowledge Is Power Program (KIPP)

135 Main St., Suite 1700
San Francisco, CA 94105
Phone: (415) 399–1556
Fax: (415) 348–0588

See website for contact numbers in Chicago and New York
http://www.kipp.org/

The Knowledge Is Power Program has a national network of charter schools that have been receiving attention for their focus on preparing students in underserved communities for college enrollment. The schools are free and have open enrollment and are currently in nineteen states and the District of Columbia. They enroll more than 21,000 students. The website provides links to the annual report, independent studies, and a press center that describes the achievement results of the KIPP schools.

NATIONAL ALLIANCE OF BLACK SCHOOL EDUCATORS

310 Pennsylvania Ave. SE
Washington, DC 20003
Phone: (800) 221–2654
Fax: (202) 608–6319
www.nabse.org

The National Alliance of Black School Educators is a group of child advocates with a specific focus on African American students. They provide mechanisms that enhance the exchange of ideas and strategies to improve opportunities for African American students through conferences and other forums. The website also provides information on publications.

NATIONAL ASSESSMENT OF EDUCATIONAL PROGRESS (NAEP)

1990 K St. NW
Washington, DC 20006, USA
Phone: (202) 502–7300
http://nces.ed.gov/nationsreportcard/about/

The National Assessment of Educational Progress is a nationally representative and ongoing assessment of our nation's students' knowledge in certain subject areas. Assessments are administered periodically in mathematics, reading, science, writing, the arts, civics, economics, geography, and U.S. history. There are two websites that provide information on NAEP and NAEP Report Card results. The websites also provide data tools, publications, and other resources.

National Association for Asian and Pacific American Education (NAAPAE)

PO Box 280346
Northridge, CA 91328–0346
Phone: (818) 677–6853
Fax: (818) 366–2714
www.naapae.net

The National Association for Asian and Pacific American Education's focus is on addressing and advocating for the needs of Asian and Pacific American students. They advocate for policies and programs that will meet these students' needs. They also promote the inclusion of Asian and Pacific American's history and culture in the curriculum.

National Association of Multicultural Education (NAME)

2100 M. Street, Suite 170–245
Washington, DC, 20037
Phone (202) 679–6263
Fax (214) 602–4722
www.nameorg.org

The National Association of Multicultural Education is an organization with members from preschool through higher education and representatives from business and communities. The organization produces publications on multicultural education and convenes for national and international conferences that provide forums for dialogues on equity, diversity, and multicultural education.

National Black Child Development Institute

1101 15th St. NW, Suite 900
Washington, DC 20005
Phone: (202) 833–2220
Fax: (202) 833–8222
www.nbcdi.org

The National Black Child Development Institute aims to improve and advance the quality of life for Black children and their families through advocacy and education. They offer a variety of programs, services, and resources, such as a literacy campaign and a parent empowerment program.

National Center for Educational Statistics (NCES)

1990 K St. NW
Washington, DC 20006
Phone: (202) 502–7300
www.nces.ed.gov

The National Center for Education Statistics serves as the federal government's primary resource for collecting and analyzing data related to education. Their website provides information on publications, data tools, and searches for information.

National Clearinghouse for English Language Acquisition (NCELA)

2011 Eye St. NW, Suite 300
Washington, DC 20006
Phone: (800) 321–6223, (202) 467–0867
Fax: (800) 531–9347
http://www.ncela.gwu.edu/about/contact/

The National Clearinghouse for English Language Acquisition is authorized under Title III of the No Child Left Behind Act of 2001. The purpose for the NCELA is to support the U.S. Department of Education's Office of English Language Acquisition, Language Enhancement, and Academic Achievement for Limited English Proficient Students and to address Title III educational needs. The website provides information on webinars that feature speakers in the area of language acquisition.

National Commission on Teaching and America's Future

Teachers College, Columbia University
525 W. 120th St., Box 117
New York, NY 10027
Phone: (212) 678–4153
Fax: (212) 678–4039
www.nctaf.org

The major focus of the National Commission on Teaching and America's Future is on improving the quality of our nation's teachers for all children regardless of background. They collaborate with major policy makers and educational leaders in order to move this policy agenda. Their major strategies include current research on quality teaching, conducting policy forums and issuing policy papers, and creating demonstration sites.

National Governor's Association (NGA) Center for Best Practices

Contact Information: See website

http://www.nga.org/portal/site/nga/menuitem.50aeae5ff70b817ae8ebb856a11010a0/

The National Governor's Association created the Center for Best Practices to inform governors about public policy issues. There are five divisions. The education division is a valuable resource for early childhood through postsecondary best practices. Some of the areas that are addressed include teacher quality, high school redesign, reading, preparation, and access to postsecondary education. They also have numerous publications that can be downloaded.

National Middle School Association (NMSA)

4151 Executive Pkwy., Suite 300
Westerville, OH 43081
Phone: (800) 528-NMSA
www.nmsa.org

The National Middle School Association focuses exclusively on the middle-level grades. This association provides educators with professional development, journals, books, research, and other information.

National High School Center

American Institutes for Research
1000 Thomas Jefferson St. NW
Washington, DC 20007
Phone: (800) 634–0503
Fax: (202) 403–5875
http://www.betterhighschools.org/

The National High School Center is one of five centers funded by the U.S. Department of Education and is based at the American Institutes for Research. This center provides current research, tools and products, and technical expertise on high school improvement issues. The center is a source for research-supported approaches especially for students with disabilities, English learners, and low-income students. They offer publications and webinars. The website provides a link to download a brochure about the center's services.

New Teacher Centers

Search the web for centers in your geographic region.

Office of Bilingual Education and Minority Language Affairs, U.S. Department of Education

600 Independence Ave. SW
Washington, DC 20202–6510
http://www2.ed.gov/about/offices/list/oela/index.html

The U.S. Department of Education Office of English Language Acquisition, Language Enhancement, and Academic Achievement for Limited English Proficient Students (OELA) website provides information about their services such as special programs, initiatives, activities, and grant programs. They identify major issues that affect the education of ELL students.

PRINCIPAL's Exchange

13502 Whittier Blvd., Suite H
Whittier, CA 90605
Phone: (562) 789–0729
www.principals-exchange.com

The PRINCIPAL's Exchange provides supports to schools and districts that are struggling with issues of student achievement. They provide support for a variety of services such as equity audits and strategies for improving the educational attainment of all students.

Quality Education for Minorities (QEM) Network

1818 North St. NW, Suite 350
Washington, DC 20036
Phone: (202) 659–1818
http://qemnetwork.qem.org/

The Quality Education for Minorities Network is committed to increasing the educational attainment of African Americans, Alaska Natives, American Indians, Mexican Americans, and Puerto Ricans. Their website provides valuable information on workshops and organizations that have similar missions for these populations of students.

The Schott Foundation for Public Education

678 Massachusetts Ave., Suite 301,
Cambridge, MA 02139
Phone: (617) 876–7700
Fax: (617) 876–7702
www.schottfoundation.org

Schott's focus is on ensuring that resources are provided for all students to have an equitable opportunity to learn in ways that produce high-achievement outcomes. They offer publications and reports on topics such as opportunity to learn, early education, the status of African American males, and policy and leadership.

Teachers of English to Speakers of Other Languages (TESOL)

700 S. Washington St., Suite 200
Alexandria, VA 22314
Phone: (703) 836–0774
Fax: (703) 836–7864
www.tesol.org

Teachers of English to Speakers of Other Languages is a global organization for English language teaching professionals. The organization's publications include books, e-resources on current issues, and strategies. TESOL offers a variety of professional development opportunities.

Texas Appleseed

1609 Shoal Creek Blvd., Suite 201
Austin, TX 78701
Telephone: (512) 473–2800 x107
Fax: (512) 473–2813
http://www.texasappleseed.net/content/

Texas Appleseed has a social justice focus with a mission to create social and economic justice for all Texans. Volunteer lawyers and others identify and provide practical solutions for systemic issues. Their strategies include research, advocacy, protection of legal rights, and public awareness. There are multiple publications including newsletters, e-bulletins, and research reports. One recent report is *Texas' School-to-Prison Pipeline: Dropout to Incarceration: The Impact of School Discipline and Zero Tolerance*.

TOMAS RIVERA POLICY INSTITUTE (TRPI)

University of Southern California
School of Policy, Planning, and Development
650 Childs Way, Lewis Hall
Los Angeles, CA 90089–0626
Phone: (213) 821–5615
Fax: (213) 821–1976
www.trpi.org

Located on the campus of the University of Southern California, the Tomas Rivera Policy Institute is a leading policy institute on Latino issues. They are noted for their ability to conduct survey research that provides national information on the attitudes of Latinos. One notable program is an outreach program that educates parents and students about higher education. The program also provides assistance in how to successfully negotiate the mazes of financial aid programs.

UCLA INSTITUTE FOR DEMOCRACY EDUCATION AND ACCESS (IDEA)

1041 Moore Hall, Box 951521
Los Angeles, CA 90095
Phone: (310) 206–8725
Fax: (310) 206–8770
http://idea.gseis.ucla.edu/

UCLA's Institute for Democracy, Education, and Access is an independent research institute with a focus on racial and social class inequalities in education. The institute provides support for educators, public officials, advocates, community activists, and young people in their efforts to design, conduct, and use research that provides information on how to create high-quality public schools, college readiness, and college enrollment for all students.

URBAN INSTITUTE

2100 M St. NW, Suite 500
Washington, DC 20037
Phone: (202) 833–7200
http://www.urban.org/education/index.cfm

The Urban Institute is a source for current research. The institute evaluates programs and offers technical assistance. Resources on their website include fact sheets and other publications. A major project is the Center for Analysis of Longitudinal Data in Education Research (CALDER).

References

Adelman, C. (1999). *Answers in the toolbox: Academic intensity, attendance patterns, and bachelor's degree attainment.* Washington, DC: U.S. Department of Education.

Ali, R. (2007). *Closing achievement and opportunity gaps in California: 12 steps for reform at the state and local levels.* Oakland, CA: Education Trust-West.

Allensworth, E. M., & Easton, J. Q. (2005). *The on-track indicator as a predictor of high school graduation.* Chicago: Consortium on Chicago School Research at the University of Chicago. Retrieved February 22, 2010, from http://ccsr.uchicago.edu/content/publications.php?pub_id=10.

Almeida, C., Johnson, C., & Steinberg, A. (April, 2006). *Making good on a promise: What policy makers can do to support the educational persistence of dropouts.* Boston: Jobs for the Future.

American Civil Liberties Union. (2009). *Reclaiming Michigan's throwaway kids: Students trapped in the school-to-prison pipeline.* Detroit: American Civil Liberties Union of Michigan.

American Educational Research Association. (2000). AERA position statement on high-stakes testing in pre-K–12 education. *American Educational Research Association, 35*(6). Retrieved April 27, 2010, from http://www.aera.net/?id=378.

Anderson, G. L., Herr, K., & Sigrid Nihlen, A. (2007). *Studying your own school: An educator's guide to practitioner action research.* Thousand Oaks, CA: Corwin.

Artiles, A. J., Harry, B., Reschly, D. J., & Chinn, P. C. (2001). *Over-identification of students of color in special education: A critical overview.* Chicago: Monarch Center.

Artiles, A. J., Klinger J. K. & Tate, W. (2006). Editor's introduction. *Educational Researcher, 35*(6), 3–5.

Artiles, A. J., & Trent, S. C. (2000). Representation of culturally/linguistically diverse students. In C. R. Reynolds & E. Fletcher-Jantzen (Eds.), *Encyclopedia of special education* (2nd ed., pp. 513–517). New York: John Wiley & Sons.

Association for Supervision and Curriculum Development. *Current position: Multiple measures of assessment.* Retrieved January 10, 2010, from http://www.ascd.org/news-media/ASCD-Policy-Positions/ASCD-Positions.aspx#multiplemeasures

Balfanz, R., & Legters, N. (2004). Locating the dropout crisis: Which high schools produce the nation's dropouts? In G. Orfield (Ed.), *Dropouts in America: Confronting the graduation rate crisis* (pp. 57–84). Cambridge, MA: Harvard Education Press.

Barton, P. E., & Coley, R. J. (2009). *Parsing the achievement gap: Policy information report*. Princeton, NJ: Policy and Evaluation Research Center, Educational Testing Service.

Bay Area School Reform Collaborative. (2001). *The color of discipline: Understanding racial disparity in school discipline practices*. San Francisco: Author.

Blanchett, W. J. (2006). Disproportionate representation of African American students in special education: Acknowledging the role of white privilege and racism. *Educational Researcher, 35*(6), 24–28.

Bryk, A. S., Easton, J. Q., Kerbow, D., Rollow, S. G., & Sebring, P. A. (1993). *A view from the elementary schools: The state of reform in Chicago*. Chicago: Consortium on Chicago School Research. Retrieved April 26, 2010, from http://ccsr.uchicago.edu/publications/AViewFromTheElementarySchools_TheStateOfReformInChicago.pdf.

Carter, T. (Director), & Gale, D. (Producer). (2005). *Coach Carter* [Motion picture]. United States: Paramount Pictures.

The Center for Comprehensive School Reform and Improvement. (2008, August). *Gifted and talented students at risk for underachievement*. Retrieved April 20, 2010, from http://www.centerforcsri.org/files/CenterIssueBriefAug08.pdf.

Checkley, K. (2004). A is for audacity: Lessons in leadership from Lorraine Monroe. *Educational Leadership, 61*(7), 70–72.

Children's Defense Fund. (2007). *America's cradle to prison pipeline: A children's defense fund report*. Washington, DC: The Children's Defense Fund.

Cicourel, A. V., & Kitsuse, J. I. (1963). *The educational decision-makers*. New York: Bobbs-Merrill.

The Civil Rights Project. (2010). *Action kit: Zero tolerance and school discipline*. Retrieved April 21, 2010, from http://www.civilrightsproject.ucla.edu/resources/action_kits/zero_tol2.php.

Civil Rights Project and the Advancement Project. (2000, June). *Opportunities suspended: The devastating consequences of zero tolerance and school discipline policies*. Proceedings from the national summit on zero tolerance, Washington, DC.

Coleman, J. S. (1966). *Equality of educational opportunity study*. Washington, DC: United States Department of Health, Education, and Welfare.

College Board. (1999). *Reaching the top: A report of the national task force on minority high achievement*. New York: College Board Publications. Retrieved April 22, 2010, from http://professionals.collegeboard.com/data-reports-research/cb/reaching-the-top.

College Board. (2010). *The 6th annual AP report to the nation*. New York: College Board. Retrieved April 26, 2010, from http://www.collegeboard.com/html/aprtn/theme_2_reflect_demographics.html.

Collier, D. L. (2007). *Sally can skip but Jerome can't stomp: Perception, practice, and school punishment*. Unpublished doctoral dissertation, California State University/ University of California Irvine.

Committee on Minority Representation in Special Education, Donovan, M., & Cross, C. T. (2002). *Minority students in special and gifted education*. Washington, DC: National Academy Press.

Conchas, G. Q., & Rodriquez, L. (2008). *Small schools and urban youth: Using the power of school culture to engage students*. Thousand Oaks, CA: Corwin.

Crawford, M., & Dougherty, E. (2000). *Updraft/downdraft: Class, culture and academic achievement in high school.* Unpublished manuscript prepared for the National Association of System Heads.

Darling-Hammond, L., Berry, B., & Thoreson, A. (2001). Does teacher certification matter? Evaluating the evidence. *Educational Evaluation and Policy Analysis, 23*(1), 57–77.

Data Quality Campaign. (2009). *Annual progress report on state data systems.* Retrieved May 2, 2010, from http://www.dataqualitycampaign.org/files/DQC_11-19.pdf.

Data Quality Campaign/Achieve. (2006). *Creating a longitudinal data system: Using data to improve student achievement.* Retrieved April 27, 2010, from http://www.dataqualitycampaign.org/resources/109.

Delpit, L. D. (1988). The silenced dialogue: Power and the pedagogy in educating other people's children. *Harvard Educational Review, 58,* 280–298.

Delpit, L. D. (1995). *Other people's children: Cultural conflict in the classroom.* New York: The New Press.

Dillon, S. (2009, April 29). 'No child' law is not closing a racial gap. *New York Times,* p. 1.

Eccles, J. S., & Barber, B. L. (1999). Student council, volunteering, basketball, or marching band: What kind of extracurricular involvement matters? *Journal of Adolescent Research, 14*(1), 10–43.

Editorial Projects in Education. (2006). The high school pipeline. *Education Week's Diplomas Count: An Essential Guide to Graduation Policy and Rates, 25*(41S), 16.

Editorial Projects in Education. (2009). Broader horizons: The challenge of college readiness for all students. *Education Week's Diplomas Count, 28*(34), 1–38.

Edmonds, R. (1979). Effective schools for the urban poor. *Educational Leadership, 37*(1), 15–24.

Education Trust. (2009). *Education watch: National report.* Washington, DC: The Education Trust.

Faircloth, S. C., & Tippeconnic, III, J. W. (2010). *The dropout/graduation rate crisis among American Indian and Alaska Native students: Failure to respond places the future of native peoples at risk.* Los Angeles: The Civil Rights Project/Proyecto Derechos Civiles at UCLA. Retrieved April 27, 2010, from http://www.civilrightsproject.ucla.edu/research/dropouts/faircloth-tippeconnic-native-american-dropouts-2010.pdf.

Feldman, A. F., & Matjasko, J. L. (2005). The role of school-based extracurricular activities in adolescent development: A comprehensive review of future directions. *Review of Educational Research, 75,* 159–210.

Ferguson, R. F. (2003). Teachers' perceptions and expectations and the black-white test score gap. *Urban Education, 38*(4), 460–507.

Flores, E., Painter, G., Zachary, H. N., & Pachon, H. (2009). *Que Pasa? Are English language learning students remaining in English learning classes too long? The Tomas Rivera Institute Policy Brief. 1–4.* Los Angeles: University of Southern California.

Flores-Gonzalez, N. (2002). *School kids/street kids.* New York: Teachers College Press.

Ford, D. Y., & Grantham, T. C. (2003). Providing access for culturally diverse gifted students: From deficit to dynamic thinking. *Theory Into Practice, 42*(3), 217–225.

Gay, G. (2000). *Culturally responsive teaching: Theory, research, & practice.* New York: Teachers College Press.

Gay, G. (2002). Preparing for culturally responsive teaching. *Journal of Teacher Education, 53,* 106–116.

Gersten, R., & Baker, S. (2000). What we know about effective instructional practices for English Language Learners. *Exceptional Children, 66*(44), 454–470.

Gewertz, C. (2009a). NCLB rules back common rate. *Education Week's Diplomas Count, 28,* 19, 22.

Gewertz, C. (2009b). Beyond a focus on graduation: Postsecondary work seen as key to success. *Education Week's Diplomas Count, 28*(34), 6–9.

Gibb, A. C., & Skiba, R. (2008). Using data to address equity issues in special education. *Center for Evaluation & Education Policy Education Policy Brief, 6*(3), 1–8.

Goldenberg, C., & Coleman, R. (in press). *Promoting academic achievement among English language learners: A guide to the research.* Thousand Oaks, CA: Corwin.

Haberman, M. (1991). The pedagogy of poverty versus good teaching. *Phi Delta Kappan, 73*(4), 290–294.

Hakuta, K. (2001). A critical period for second language acquisition? In D. B. Bailey, J. T. Bruer, F. J. Symons, & J. W. Lichtman (Eds.), *Critical thinking about critical periods* (pp. 193–205). Baltimore: Paul Brookes.

Hakuta, K., Butler, Y. G. & Witt, W. (2000). *How long does it take English learner to attain proficiency? The University of California Linguistic Minority Research Institute policy report 2000-1.* Santa Barbara: University of California.

Hale, J. E. (2001). Culturally appropriate pedagogy. In W. H. Watkins, J. H. Lewis, & V. Chou (Eds.), *Race and education: The roles of history and society in educating African American students* (pp. 173–189). Needham Heights, MA: Allyn & Bacon.

Hall, D. (August, 2007). *Graduation matters: Improving accountability for high school graduation.* Washington, DC: The Education Trust.

Haney, W., Madaus, G., Abrams, L., Wheelock, A., Miao, J., & Gruia, I. (2004). *The education pipeline in the United States, 1970–2000.* Chestnut Hill, MA: Lynch School of Education, Boston College.

Harry, B., & Klingner, J. (2006). *Why are so many minority students in special education?* Understanding race and disability in schools. New York: Teachers College Press.

Harry, B., Klingner, J. K., Sturges, K. M., & Moore, R. F. (2002). Of rocks and soft places: Using qualitative methods to investigate disproportionality. In D. J. Losen & G. Orfield (Eds.), *Racial inequity in special education* (pp. 71–92). Cambridge, MA: Harvard Education Press.

Haycock, K. (1998). Good teaching matters a lot. *Thinking K–16, 3*(2), 4–13.

Haycock, K. (2006). *Promise abandoned: How policy choices and institutional practices restrict college opportunities.* Washington, DC: Education Trust. Retrieved November 3, 2009, from http://www.edtrust.org/sites/edtrust.org/files/publications/files/PromiseAbandonedHigherEd.pdf.

Heppen, J. B., & Therriault, S. B. (2008). *Developing early warning systems to identify potential high school dropouts.* Washington, DC: National High School Center.

Hilliard, III, A. (1991). Do we have the will to educate all children? *Educational Leadership, 49* (1), 31-66.

Hoff, D. J.(2008). Rules mandate uniform graduation rates: Spellings issues NCLB regulations with pieces from legislative agenda. *Education Week.* Retrieved July 7, 2010, from http://www.edweek.org/ew/articles/2008/10/28/11nclb.h28.html?qs=NClb+Rules_mandate_uniform_graduation_rates

Holzman, M. (2006). *Public education and black male students: The 2006 state report card.* Cambridge, MA: The Schott Foundation for Public Education.

Irvine, J. J. (1990). *Black students and school failure: Policies, practices, and prescriptions.* New York: Greenwood Press.

Jerald, C. (2006). *Identifying potential dropouts: Key lessons for building an early warning data system. A dual agenda of high standards and high graduation rates.* Retrieved May 2, 2010, from http://www.achieve.org/files/FINAL-dropouts_0.pdf.

Johnson, R. S. (2002). *Using data to close the achievement gap: How to measure equity in our schools.* Thousand Oaks, CA: Corwin.

Johnson, R. S., & Bush V. L. (2006). Leading the culturally responsive school. In F. English (Ed.), *Sage Handbook of Educational Leadership* (pp. 121–148). Thousand Oaks, CA: Sage.

Jordan, H., Mendro, R., & Weerasinghe, D. (1997, July). *Teacher effects on longitudinal student achievement.* Paper presented at the CREATE annual meeting, Indianapolis, IN.

Kain, J. F., & Singleton, K. (1996, May/June). Equality of educational opportunity revisited. *New England Economic Review, 87–114.*

Ladson-Billings, G. (1994). *The dreamkeepers: Successful teachers of African American children.* San Francisco: Jossey-Bass.

Ladson-Billings, G. (2001). The power of pedagogy: Does teaching matter? In W. H. Watkins, J. H. Lewis, & V. Chou (Eds.), *Race and education: The roles of history and society in educating African American students* (pp. 73–88). Boston: Allyn & Bacon.

Laitsch, D. (July 2005). *A policymaker's primer on testing and assessment, Association of Supervision and Curriculum Development.* Info brief 42. Alexandria, VA: Association for Supervision and Curriculum Development. Retrieved April 27, 2010, from http://www.ascd.org/publications/newsletters/infobrief/jul05/num42/toc.aspx.

Lee, C. (2006). 'Every good-bye ain't gone': Analyzing the cultural underpinnings of classroom talk. *International Journal of Qualitative Studies in Education, 119*(3), 305–327.

Lezotte, L. (2010). *Effective schools: Past, present, and future.* Retrieved February 7, 2010, from http://www.effectiveschools.com/images/stories/brockpaper.pdf.

Lindsey, R. B., Roberts, L. M., & CampbellJones, F. (2005). *The culturally proficient school: An implementation guide for school leaders.* Thousand Oaks, CA: Corwin.

Losen, D. L. (2006). Cost of not graduating tallied by researchers. *Education Week's Diplomas Count, 25*(4), 7.

Losen, D. J., & Orfield, G. (Eds.). (2002). *Racial inequity in special education.* Cambridge, MA: Harvard Education Press.

Love, N., Stiles, K. E., Mundry, S., & Diranna, K. (2008). *The data coach's guide to improving learning for all students.* Thousand Oaks, CA: Corwin.

McKinsey & Company. (2009). *The economic impact of the achievement gap in America's schools.* McKinsey & Company Social Sector Office, pp. 1–24. Retrieved April 19, 2010, from http://www.mckinsey.com/clientservice/Social_Sector/our_practices/Education/Knowledge_Highlights/Economic_impact.aspx.

Mathews, J. (1988). *Escalante: The best teacher in America.* New York: Henry Holt and Company.

Murrell, P. (2002). *African-centered pedagogy: Developing schools of achievement for African American children.* Albany: State University of New York Press.

National Alliance of Black School Educators (NABSE) & ILIAD Project. (2002). *Addressing over-representation of African American students in special education: The prereferral interventions process—An administrator's guide.* Arlington, VA: Council for Exceptional Children, and Washington, DC: National Alliance of Black School Educators.

National Association for Gifted Children (2008/2009). *State of the states.* Retrieved January 5, 2010, from http://www.nagc.org/uploadedFiles/Information_and_Resources/State_of_the_States_2008–2009/2008–09%20State%200f%20the%20Nation%20Overview.pdf.

National Association of Gifted Children. (2008a). *Frequently asked questions.* Retrieved April 20, 2010, from http://www.nagc.org/index2.aspx?id=548.

National Association of Gifted Children. (2008b). *Ensuring that diverse learners participate in gifted education programs and services.* Retrieved April 24, 2010, from http://www.nagc.org/index.aspx?id=4658&terms=english+learners.

National Psychological Association of School Psychologists. (2003). *Position statement on student grade retention and social promotion.* Retrieved January 8, 2010, from http://www.nasponline.org/about_nasp/pospaper_graderetent.aspx

Neal, L. I., McCray, A. D., Webb-Johnson, G. C., & Bridgest, S. T. (2003). Effects of African American movement styles on teachers' perceptions and reactions. *The Journal of Special Education, 37*(1), 49–57.

Neild, R., & Balfanz, R. (2006). An extreme degree of difficulty: The educational demographics of the urban neighborhood high school. *Journal of Education for Students Placed at Risk, 11*(2), 123–141.

New York Association of Community Organizations for Reform. (1996). *Secret apartheid.* New York: New York Association of Community Organizations for Reform.

Nichols, S. L., & Berliner, D. C. (2007). *Collateral damage: How high-stakes testing corrupts America's schools.* Cambridge, MA: Harvard Education Publishing Group.

Nieto, S. (2000). *Affirming diversity: The sociopolitical context of multicultural education.* New York: Longman.

No Child Left Behind (NCLB) Act of 2001, Pub. L. No. 107-110, § 115, Stat. 1425 (2002).

Noguera, P., & Wing, J. Y. (Eds.). (2006). *Unfinished business: Closing the racial achievement gap in our schools.* San Francisco: Jossey-Bass.

O'Connor, C., & DeLuca Fernandez, S. (2006). Race, class, and disproportionally: Reevaluating the relationship between poverty and special education placement. *Educational Researcher, 35,* 6–11.

Oakes, J. (1985). *Keeping track: How schools structure inequality.* New Haven, CT: Yale University Press.

Obama, B. (2010, January 27). State of the Union address. Washington, DC.

Olson, L. (2004). Enveloping expectations: Federal law demands that schools teach the same content to children they wrote off a quarter-century ago. *Education Week's Special Education in an Era of Standards: Count Me, In Quality, 23*(17), 8–20.

Olson, L. (2006a). The down staircase. *Education Week's Diplomas Count, 25*(041). Washington, DC: Editorial Projects in Education, p. 5–7, 10-11. Retrieved April 27, 2010, from http://www.edweek.org/ew/articles/2006/06/22/41s_overview.h25.html.

Olson, L. (2006b). Opening doors: Keeping close track of students' progress would help more teenagers leave high school with diplomas. *Education Week's*

Diplomas Count, 25(41S), 23–24, 28–30. Retrieved April 27, 2010, from http://www.edweek.org/ew/articles/2006/06/22/41s_solve.h25.html.

Orfield, G. (2004). *Dropouts in America: Confronting the graduation rate crisis.* Cambridge, MA: Harvard Education Press.

Payan, R. M., & Nettles, M. T. (2008). Current state of English-language learners in the U.S. K-12 student population. 2008 English Language Learner Symposium, Princeton, NJ. Retrieved February, 2009, from http://www.ets.org/Media/Conferences_and_Events/pdf/ELLsympsium/ELL_factsheet.pdf.

Reeves, D. (2003). *High performance in high poverty schools: 90/90/90 and beyond.* Retrieved May 2, 2010, from http://www.sabine.k12.la.us/online/leadership academy/high%20performance%2090%2090%2090%20and%20beyond.pdf.

Reid, D. K., & Knight, M. G. (2006). Disability justifies exclusion of minority students: A critical history grounded in disability studies. *Educational Researcher, 35*(6), 18–23.

Renzulli, J. S., & Park, S. (2000). Gifted dropouts: The who and the why. *Gifted Child Quarterly, 44*(4), 261–271.

Reyes, A. J. (2006). *Discipline, achievement, race: Is zero tolerance the answer?* Lanham, MD: Rowman & Littlefield Education.

Ross, P. (1993). *National excellence: A case for developing America's talent.* Washington, DC: U.S. Department of Education, Office of Education Research and Improvement.

Ross, R. (1999). How class-size reduction harms kids in poor neighborhoods. *Education Week, 26.* Retrieved March 8, 2008, from http://www.edweek.org/ew/articles/1999/05/26/37ross.h18.html?r=2120571402.

Rumberger, S., & Scarcella, R. (2000). Academic English. *Linguistic Minority Research Institute Newsletter* (pp. 1–2). Santa Barbara: University of California.

Russo, C. J., Harris, J. J., & Ford, D. Y. (1996). Gifted education and law: A right, privilege, or superfluous? *Roeper Review, 18*(3), 179–182.

Saavedra, E. (1996). Teacher study groups: Contexts for transformative learning and action. *Theory Into Practice, 35,* 271–277.

Sanders, W. L., & Rivers, J. C. (1998). Good teaching matters a lot. *Thinking K–16, 3*(2), 4–13.

Scheurich, J. J., & Skrla, L. (2003). *Leadership for equity and excellence: Creating high-achievement classrooms, schools, and districts.* Thousand Oaks, CA: Corwin.

Shade, B. J., Kelly, C., &, Oberg, M. (2004). *Creating culturally responsive classrooms.* Washington, DC: American Psychological Association.

Skiba, R. J. (2000, August). *Zero tolerance, zero evidence: An analysis of school disciplinary practice. The Indiana Education Policy Center policy research report* (No. SRS2). Retrieved May 2, 2010, from http://www.indiana.edu/~safeschl/ztze.pdf.

Skiba, R., Michael, R., Nardo, A., & Peterson, R. L. (2002, December). The color of discipline: Sources of racial and gender disproportionality in school punishment. *The Urban Review, 34*(4), 317–342.

Silva, E. (2007). On the clock: Rethinking the way schools use time. *Education Sector Reports,* p. 1–14.

Singham, M. (1998). The canary in the mine: The achievement gap between black and white students. *Phi Delta Kappan, 80*(1), 8-15.

Singleton, G. E., & Linton, C. (2006). *Conversations about race: A field guide for achieving equity in our schools.* Thousand Oaks, CA: Corwin.

Singleton, G. E., & Linton, C. (2007). *Courageous conversations about race: A field guide for achieving equity in schools: Facilitator's guide.* Thousand Oaks, CA: Corwin.

Smith, L. T. (2004). *Decolonizing methodologies: Research and indigenous peoples* (7th ed.). London: Zed Books.

Stanton-Salazar, R. D. (2010). *A social capital framework for the study of institutional agents and their role in the empowerment of low-status students and youth.* Manuscript submitted for publication.

Swanson, C. B. (2004). Sketching a portrait of public high school graduation: Who graduates? Who doesn't? In G. Orfield (Ed.), *Dropout in America: Confronting the graduation rate crisis* (pp. 13–40). Cambridge, MA: Harvard Education Press.

Swanson, C. B. (2007). Preparing students for college, careers, and life after high school. *Education Week's Diplomas Count, 26*(40). Retrieved April 27, 2010, from http://www.edweek.org/chat/transcript_06_14_2007.html.

Swanson, C. B. (2008). *Special education in America: The state of students with disabilities in the nation's high schools.* Bethesda, MD: Editorial Projects in Education.

Swanson, C. B. (2009). Gauging graduation, pinpointing progress: Districts with higher rates offer bright spots. *Education Week's Diplomas Count, 28*(34), 24–31.

Texas Appleseed. (2007). *Texas's school-to-prison pipeline: Dropout to incarceration: The impact of school discipline and zero tolerance.* Retrieved May 2, 2010, from http://www.texasappleseed.net/pdf/Pipeline%20Report.pdf.

UC/ACCORD. (2010). *College Opportunity Ratio (COR) for District 44.* Retrieved May 2, 2010, from http://ucaccord.gseis.ucla.edu/indicators/assembly/maps/ad44.html.

U.S. Department of Education, National Center for Educational Statistics. (2007). *The condition of education 2007* (NCES 2007–064). Washington, DC: U.S. Government Printing Office.

U.S. Department of Education. (1994). *What do student grades mean? Differences across schools.* Washington, DC: Author.

U.S. Department of Health, Education, and Welfare. (1971). *Education of the gifted and talented: Report to the Congress of the United States by the U.S. Commissioner of Education.* Washington, DC: Author.

Valenzuela, A. (1999). *Subtractive schooling: U.S. Mexican youth and the politics of caring.* Albany: State University of New York Press.

Valenzuela, A. (2002). Reflections on the subtractive underpinnings of education research and policy. *Journal of Teacher Education 53*(3), 235–241.

Viadero, D. (2004). Disparately disabled. *Education Week's Quality Counts, 23*(17), 22–25.

Viadero, D. (2006). Signs of early exit for dropouts abound. *Education Week's Diplomas Count, 25*(33), 20–22.

Wakelyn, D. (2009). *Raising rigor, getting results: Lessons learned from AP expansion.* Washington DC: National Governors Association Center for Best Practices.

Weinberg, L. (2007). *The systematic mistreatment of children in the foster care system: Through the cracks.* New York: The Haworth Press.

Winfield, L. F., Johnson, R. S., & Manning, J. B. (1996). Managing instructional diversity. In P. B. Forsyth & M. Tollerico (Eds.), *City schools: Leading the way.* (pp. 97–130). Thousand Oaks, CA: Corwin.

Williams et al. v. State of California et al. (S.P. San Francisco County, 2000).

Williams, T., Hakuta, K., Haertel, E., et al. (2005). *Similar students, different results: Why do some schools do better? A large-scale survey of California elementary schools serving low-income students.* Mountain View, CA: EdSource.

Williams, T., Perry, M., Oregon, I., et al. (2007). *Similar English learner students, different results: Why do some schools do better?* Mountain View, CA: EdSource.

Index